Introducing Psychoanaly

Introducing Psychoanalysis brings together leading analysts to explain what psycho-analysis is and how it has developed, setting its ideas in their appropriate social and intellectual context.

Based on lectures given at the British Psychoanalytical Society, the only body which trains psychoanalysts in the UK, the contributions capture the diversity of opinion among analysts to provide a clear and dynamic presentation of concepts such as:

- Sexual perversions.
- Trauma and the possibility of recovery.
- Phantasy and reality.
- Interpreting and transference.
- Two views of the Oedipus complex.
- Projective identification.
- The paranoid-schizoid and depressive positions.
- Symbolism and dreams.

Frequently misunderstood subjects are demystified, and the contributors' wealth of clinical and supervisory experience ensures that central concepts are explained with refreshing clarity. Clinical examples are included throughout and provide a valuable insight into the application of psychoanalytic ideas.

This overview of the wide variety of psychoanalytic ideas that are current in Britain today will appeal to all those training and practising in psychoanalysis and psycho-analytic psychotherapy, as well as those wishing to broaden their knowledge of this field.

Susan Budd and **Richard Rusbridger** are both full members of the British Psycho-analytical Society.

Contributors: Kate Barrows; Dana Birksted-Breen; Susan Budd; Don Campbell; Giovanna Rita Di Ceglie; Michael Feldman; Catia Galatariotou; Caroline Garland; Jennifer Johns; Betty Joseph; Gregorio Kohon; M. Eglé Laufer; David Riley; Priscilla Roth; Richard Rusbridger; Margret Tonnesmann.

Introducing Psychoanalysis

Essential themes and topics

Edited by Susan Budd and
Richard Rusbridger

Routledge
Taylor & Francis Group

LONDON AND NEW YORK

First published 2005
by Routledge
27 Church Road, Hove, East Sussex BN3 2FA

Simultaneously published in the USA and Canada
by Routledge
711 Third Avenue, New York NY 10017 (8th Floor)

Routledge is an imprint of the Taylor & Francis Group

Copyright © 2005 Editorial matter, Susan Budd and
Richard Rusbridger; individual chapters, the contributors

Typeset in Times by RefineCatch Limited, Bungay, Suffolk

Paperback cover design by Hybert Design

British Library Cataloguing in Publication Data
A catalogue record for this book is available from the British Library

Library of Congress Cataloging-in-Publication Data
Introducing psychoanalysis/edited by Susan Budd and
Richard Rusbridger.–1st ed.
    p. cm.
Includes bibliographical references and index.
ISBN 1-58391-887-6 (hbk)–ISBN 1-58391-888-4 (pbk)
1. Psychoanalysis. I. Budd, Susan, 1941– II. Rusbridger, Richard.

RC504.156 2005
616.89'17–dc22
                                        2004009053

ISBN 978-1-58391-887-6 (hbk)
ISBN 978-1-58391-888-3 (pbk)

For Alan and Gill

Contents

Contributors

Kate Barrows is a training analyst of the British Psychoanalytical Society and a child psychotherapist trained at the Tavistock Clinic. She writes and lectures on a variety of clinical and literary topics and lives and works in Bristol.

Dana Birksted-Breen is a training analyst of the British Psychoanalytical Society. She is currently the General Editor of the New Library of Psychoanalysis. Her main publications include *The Birth of a First Child: Towards an Understanding of Femininity* (Tavistock, 1975); *Talking with Mothers* (Jill Norman, 1981 and Free Association Books, 1989); *The Gender Conundrum: Contemporary Psychoanalytic Perspectives on Femininity and Masculinity* (Routledge, New Library of Psychoanalysis, 1993). She won an international prize for her paper 'Phallus, penis and mental space' in 1995 (*International Journal of Psychoanalysis*, 1996: 77, Part 4). She has given lectures and taught internationally. She maintains a full-time private practice in London.

Susan Budd is a member of the British Psychoanalytical Society and is in private practice in London and Oxford. She is a member of the editorial boards of the *International Journal of Psychoanalysis* and the *British Journal of Psychotherapy*, and of the management committee of the Freud Museum. She has been external assessor to the TCPP training course in Birmingham for many years. She was formerly a sociologist and historian.

Don Campbell is a training analyst for children, adolescents and adults at the British Psychoanalytical Society and a past President. He is a former chairman of the Portman Clinic. He has written on violence, suicide, child sexual abuse, fetishism and adolescence. He is currently Secretary General of the International Psychoanalytical Association.

Giovanna Rita Di Ceglie is a psychoanalyst and a psychiatrist. She is a member of the British Psychoanalytical Society and is in full-time private practice in south London.

Michael Feldman qualified in psychology and medicine in London, and completed his postgraduate training in psychiatry at the Institute of Psychiatry and the Maudsley Hospital where he was a consultant in the psychotherapy unit. Since 1998 he has been in full-time psychoanalytic practice. He is a training and supervising analyst of the British Psychoanalytical Society, and is also involved in clinical teaching in Europe. He has edited the collected papers of Betty Joseph, with Elizabeth Bott Spillius, and has published a number of papers on psychoanalytic technique.

Catia Galatariotou is an associate member of the British Psychoanalytical Society. A former barrister-at-law, she holds a degree in the history of art and English literature, and a PhD in the cultural history of Byzantium. She is currently an historian and a psychoanalyst in private practice in London.

Caroline Garland read English at Cambridge before going on to study psychology, and eventually to train as a psychoanalyst. She now works in private practice, as well as in the Adult Department of the Tavistock Clinic, where she is a teacher, trainer, clinician and writer.

Jennifer Johns worked as a family doctor prior to becoming a psychoanalyst, and has always had a particular interest in body–mind problems as well as in psychic development. Her work was supervised briefly by Donald Winnicott during her psychoanalytic training, the experience being interrupted by his death. She works mainly in private analytic practice, and teaches psychotherapy both privately and at University College Hospital in London. She is currently Chairman of the Winnicott Trust, the body responsible for the publication of Winnicott's papers, and together with Ray Shepherd and Helen Taylor Robinson has co-edited *Thinking About Children* (Karnac Books 1996), the final volume of his previously unpublished papers.

Betty Joseph is an honorary member and training analyst of the British Psychoanalytical Society, working in private practice in London with adults and children. A collection of her papers entitled *Psychic Equilibrium and Psychic Change* was published in 1989 (Routledge). She received a Mary S. Sigourney Award in New York in 1995.

Gregorio Kohon is a training analyst of the British Psychoanalytical Society. In 1988 he co-founded, with Valli Shaio Kohon, the Brisbane Centre for Psychoanalytic Studies, which he directed until 1994. He is the editor of *The British School of Psychoanalysis – The Independent Tradition* (1986) and of *The Dead Mother – The Work of André Green* (1999). His book *No Lost Certainties to be Recovered* was published by Karnac (1999). He has also published three books of poems in Spanish; his novel *Papagayo Rojo, Pata de Palo* (Libros del Zorzal, 2003) was finalist in the Fernando Lara Prize for fiction in 2001.

M. Eglé Laufer is a member and training analyst of the British Psycho-analytical Society, consultant psychoanalyst and founder member of the Brent Adolescent Centre, and co-author together with Moses Laufer of *Adolescent Development and Developmental Breakdown* and co-editor, also with Moses Laufer, of *Developmental Breakdown and Psychoanalytic Treatment in Adolescence*.

David Riley is a member of the British Psychoanalytical Society and a gradu-ate of the Tavistock Clinic Course in Adult Psychotherapy. He works as a psychoanalyst in private practice in London. Formerly he worked as a clinical psychologist and then part-time as a psychotherapist in the Health Service, and was an honorary consultant psychologist to the directorate of the London Clinic of Psychoanalysis.

Priscilla Roth is a training and supervising analyst of the British Psycho-analytical Society. Until 2002 she was a principal child and adolescent psychotherapist at the Tavistock Clinic. She has taught extensively in Britain and abroad and has published a variety of papers on psycho-analysis. She now works in private practice as a psychoanalyst in London.

Richard Rusbridger is a training analyst and child analyst of the British Psychoanalytical Society in full-time psychoanalytic practice in London. He trained as a child psychotherapist at the Tavistock Clinic. He is a member of the Education Section of the *International Journal of Psycho-analysis*, and of the advisory board of the New Library of Psychoanalysis.

Margret Tonnesmann is an associate member of the British Psychoanalytical Society and a fellow of the British Association of Psychotherapists. She has taught and supervised psychoanalysts and psychotherapists for many years. She is the author of papers on various subjects, in particular aspects of British Independent psychoanalysis, and she edited *About Children and Children No Longer*.

Acknowledgements

We would like to thank all our contributors for redrafting their lectures to the Introductory Lectures series at the Institute of Psychoanalysis. We would also like to thank all the conveners and seminar leaders who have done so much for this series over the years; Ann Glynn, who has so capably and pleasantly acted as its secretary; but perhaps above all, all the students who have taken part, who have showed us by their questions what we need to make clear about psychoanalysis, and by their enthusiasm, have emboldened us to make this written record.

We are indebted to the anonymous publisher's readers for their detailed and helpful comments, and to Kate Hawes and Helen Pritt, our capable Routledge editors.

We are indebted to the History Workshop Journal, Oxford University Press and Brunner-Routledge for permission to use Susan Budd's *Recent Developments in the Psychoanalytic Theory of Dreams*, and to DACS and to the Prinzhorn Collection of Heidelberg University for permission to reproduce the illustrations to Chapter 7. An earlier version of Giovanna Di Ceglie's chapter was published in the *British Journal of Psychotherapy* 17, 3, spring 2001, under the title: 'The inner world and symbol formation: some developmental aspects'. Some of the clinical material in the chapter by Caroline Garland also appears in the second edition of *Understanding Trauma*, edited by Garland, reprinted by Karnac Books, London, 2002. The extract used in Chapter 11 is from *No Lost Certainties to be Recovered* by Gregorio Kohon, published by Karnac Books, London, 1999.

All quotations from Freud's work are from the *Standard Edition of the Complete Psychological Works of Sigmund Freud*, translated by James Strachey and others, published by the Hogarth Press and the Institute of Psychoanalysis. It is referred to in the text as *Standard Edition*. The data given is that of the first German publication.

General introduction

Susan Budd and Richard Rusbridger

Each year since 1986, a series of 20 weekly lectures and seminars for the general public have been held at the Institute of Psychoanalysis in London. These occasions are an opportunity for psychoanalysts try to explain what psychoanalysis is, what its concepts mean, and how we put them into practice in the consulting room. One of the challenges of being a seminar leader on this series is that the reactions of the audience are so varied, and their motives for attending the seminars are so mixed. Many, perhaps most, of them are fellow practitioners – trainees, psychotherapists and counsellors, who have come along to see what psychoanalysts have to say for themselves. So, whilst they can be sharply critical of psychoanalysis in particular, it comes as no surprise to them that there is an unconscious that it affects our beliefs and actions, and that people in trouble can be helped by various versions of the talking cure. Others are far more sceptical of the whole enterprise, but still want to see why we think what we do.

On the whole, people have enjoyed the series and over the years we have been asked for a permanent record of those lectures which have struck their hearers as being particularly good. So, as former seminar leaders, we have asked all those who have given lectures recently for permission to include them, and have selected those which cover the main areas of the subject. We are grateful to our colleagues for their cooperative response, and for redrafting their lectures for publication. Whilst we cannot promise that your favourite lecture will be here, we have included a wide selection of the lectures which have been given in recent years, with suggestions for further reading if you would like to follow up any of the topics. In one case, that of the Oedipus complex, we include two lectures on the topic, because we think that they are both excellent and show the variations in thinking about this problematic concept.

There are two common prejudices about analysts: that they disagree about everything, and that they are absolutely monolithic and unyielding, and hold to their beliefs as if they were religious dogmas. These prejudices often come into play when the status of psychoanalysis is being discussed If you have never been to the lecture series, you should find here a sense of what English psychoanalysts think about some of the key areas of their subject, and how they go about applying their theory in practice. You may be surprised, as the seminar groups often are, at how much variation there is between different analysts, and how many different viewpoints are discussed here: Is psycho-analysis a science? And if it isn't, does that mean it is a religion? We would like to comment on the nature of psychoanalytic knowledge itself, and how it is transmitted.

Psychoanalysis and science

Freud originally hoped that psychoanalysis would be accepted as a science. Many of the terms and analogies that he used suggest that he had in mind a science like physics or chemistry. He hoped that developments in neuro-anatomy would confirm or replace his model of the mind. But at the same time, he was aware that something very different was involved when we con-sider what the nature of psychoanalysis is in practice: two people talking in a room, one trying to understand the other. He could see that questions of subjectivity were involved: of the use of language, of the social relativity and hegemony of terms such as 'mature', 'masculine', 'feminine', and so on, and of one person's passionate response to another. Indeed, he could see that ultimately case histories are understood as exemplary kinds of narrative. In other words, support can be found in Freud's writings for almost any approach – positivist, relativist, phenomenological, structuralist, monist, etc. Freud's admirers and critics are less pluralistic.

A common ploy is to define only one form of knowledge as legitimate, and claim that psychoanalysis either does or does not conform. For some philosophers of science, in order to be valid psychoanalysis would need to be like a 'hard' science. For structuralists, it would need to be centrally con-cerned with language, and the way that language is used. For doctors, it would need to approximate to the medical model of diagnosis, treatment and cure, based on theories of the aetiology of disease, and backed up by double-blind investigations of treatment. It is interesting that if psychoanalysis fails to meet the desired criteria, then it is generally dismissed as 'a religion'. Religion in our time has become a kind of wastepaper basket for the secular intellectual's collection of undesirable knowledge. Like its founder, most psychoanalysts are not religious; but we are conscious that we deal with the unknown and the irrational, the left out, the bits that do not add up and, above all, the parts of ourselves that we have lost because we don't want to know about them. There is a plurality of viewpoints inside psychoanalysis. One of our difficulties is how we can simultaneously accommodate them, and yet maintain that there are important criteria in clinical work which mean that we can get it right or not; that the possibility of error remains; that there is demonstrably such a thing as a specifically psychoanalytic perspec-tive, and that there are others which are not. For an excellent discussion of these questions, and a defence of pluralism against complete relativism, see Hamilton (1996: Chapter 2).

How can a profession articulate itself in such circumstances? A fruitful approach, as in the history of science, is to ask not whether what a psychoanalyst does measures up to a set of criteria that someone has called 'scientific', but rather how does someone who calls himself a scientist learn to do science? How does he learn what are appropriate questions to ask of himself, and ways of finding out the answers? (Ravetz 1971). In the chapters of this book you can read about how some British psychoanalysts go about answering this question in various contexts: how they look at clinical evidence, and return to various significant ancestors in trying to interpret it; how they are conscious that the concepts we are taught, and through which we structure clinical observation, may buckle and twist under the strain.

Behind this process lies a period of apprenticeship, as is equally true of other disciplines. Once nearly all knowledge was transmitted in this way, through the long and close association of the neophyte with an acknowledged master. Now it is much rarer, although studies which have been made of American medical students also show how the student comes to downplay theoretical knowledge under the urgency of learning how to do it, and how the influence of individual doctors on students enables them to endure traumatic experiences and identify themselves as members of the profession. Consequently, psychoanalysts find that it is difficult to convey to those who have never had an analysis or taken clinical responsibility the particular nature of the experience, and the way in which it underpins psychoanalytic theory for us.

The interpretation of case material is complex and uncertain. Initially, Freud conceived of it as the search for historical truth; the intrusion of the past into the patient's present via the welling up of unconscious fantasy: 'Hysterics suffer mainly from reminiscences' (Freud 1893). But he soon realized that memory is more complex, and that the telling of the tale lends its own logic; that the tale varies, acquires a narrative smoothing, is a construction rather than a reconstruction. (Freud was to make this explicit in a fascinating late paper, 'Constructions in Analysis', 1937a.) In other words, memory is not and cannot be objectively true. This fact was more and more clearly realized throughout the twentieth century; a century which we can now see to have been the century of relativism, of the realization that each person brings his own meaning-world to every encounter, and consequently that there is no single 'true' account. Donald Spence (1982) considered the problems that this creates in trying to call psychoanalysis a science. In doing so, he is implicitly addressing Grünbaum's critique of psychoanalysis (1984) for failing to measure up to the correspondence theory of truth; i.e. to show that its theories correspond to facts that are independent of our subjective experience.

There are two kinds of answer to this challenge. One is to point out that we all have motes, if not beams, in our eyes; that scientists and philosophers are also guided by their passions and assumptions; that we all have to think in language, and in culturally created constructs (Forrester 1997). The other is to assert a hermeneutic position: psychoanalysis is a theory of personal meanings and is therapeutic because patient and analyst construct together a satisfactory and meaningful account of why the patient feels as he does. Or, more subtly, because the patient comes to feel that he can think about himself, construct his own meanings; that he is in possession of his own mind. This can explain why we must concede that psychoanalysts, and indeed other therapists, with whom we disagree theoretically can nonetheless help their patients. Yet however much we attribute the effect of psychoanalysis to the personal relationship between two people, and there is much evidence for this, it is still necessary to think about theory and be clear about terms, and to think about external reality. Indeed, many of us feel that at times patients need to be believed, and know that we believe them, in order to speak. They do not need a repetition of the situation in which no one was able to hear or acknowledge the truth of what they had to tell.

The twenty-first century seems to be bringing postmodernity back to earth with a bump. There is an increased focus on the genetic aspect of mental states such as autism, homosexuality or addiction. The search for a genetic explanation can be carried to extraordinary lengths; to take a recent example, in order to account for the suicide of a man whose mother had also killed herself, his action was explained by a postulated inherited gene for suicide. The possibility of legal intervention in psychotherapy (lawyers do assume that there is one true story) in various ways, for example, over the question of remembered childhood sexual abuse/false memory syndrome, and the pressure from insurance and other health agencies to identify clear treatment goals and progress toward them, are compelling the psychotherapy profession to clarify its claims.

Since the work of psychoanalysts and psychotherapists takes place behind closed doors, it is difficult to demonstrate what we do and the effect that it has. The requirement of clinical confidentiality means that we can only reveal what happens in sessions in very limited, circumscribed ways. (See, for example, the papers in the *British Journal of Psychotherapy* Dec. 2003 dealing with confidentiality and the law, data sharing and the establishment of a profession. For a discussion of issues around the presentation of case material, see Ward 1997.) Some advocate that we should never discuss patients' material without asking their permission; others believe that this is traumatic for them and will limit what can be discussed, to the detriment of the discipline. Since we cannot be present at a session, we only have the reports of the two people involved. Under such circumstances, total objectivity is unlikely and great weight has to be placed on the moral qualities of the psychoanalyst; on their honesty, discretion, self-criticism without undue masochism, trust, and a capacity to rely on and be taught by the more experienced.

These practical realities can make outsiders feel as if we are indeed true believers, faithfully attached to a quasi-religion. Many psychoanalysts, perhaps particularly Otto Kernberg (1986, 1989, 1996), have criticized our trainings for promoting conformity and having a stultifying effect on creative originality. The fact that psychoanalysis is a second career, and increasingly has tended to be embarked upon in middle age, only increases the tendency to conservatism. So does taking responsibility for the lives of distressed and vulnerable people, who come to us because they hope that the profession has some kind of accumulated wisdom which can help them.

With these thoughts in mind, we can see that how the practitioner reads psychoanalytic writing differs from how the interested enquirer approaches it. The latter may be surprised to see how many of the essays here move straight from an exposition of basic psychoanalytic concepts to their use in clinical discussion. The close interweaving of theory and clinical practice is seen as the hallmark of British, above all Kleinian, psychoanalytic writings. It has many virtues: it is a vivid reminder of why we are here, doing what we do; it helps practitioners to think about their clinical work, and it reminds us of the complexity, subtlety and uncertainty about what we are trying to do. There are two flaws in such an approach: a lack of theoretical sophistication, so that we have tended to regard insightful clinical description as evidence of the correctness of the theoretical assumptions of the analyst; and a tendency to reject new theoretical ideas if they are not associated with a highly regarded clinical practice. For these reasons, English analysts have been slow to assimilate Lacan's ideas since we do not accept his views on technique (Roudinesco 1990; Nobus 2000). If we now increasingly refer to them (see Chapter 9 by Birksted-Breen and Chapter 11 by Kohon) it is because they are part of a wider intellectual interest in structuralism and linguistics, which is leading to their assimilation by the profession.

Right from the beginning there were theoretical divisions between analysts that led to the development of different bodies of thought; Jung and Adler were among the first of Freud's followers to leave and form their own schools. The psychoanalytic movement in Britain has tried to allow for theoretical differences without dividing into separate organizations. Until the Second World War, divisions in theory were largely coterminous with divisions between analytic societies in different countries. For example, there were considerable differences in the approach to the analysis of children between Freud's daughter, Anna, working in Vienna, and Melanie Klein, working in Berlin and, from 1926 onwards, in London. Their disagreements extended further than their very different views on the appropriate technique to use with children, since their diverse clinical approaches involved crucial questions of the timing of mental and sexual development. When Klein moved to London in 1926, she did so because some English analysts were already thinking in similar ways, but her differences with the Viennese analysts became more salient once Freud and his daughter had come to London in 1938 to escape the Nazis. Disagreements about child analysis, the nature of unconscious phantasy, and the nature of male and especially female sexuality intensified, and three different strands of psychoanalysis began to separate out within the British Psychoanalytical Society.

Some analysts aligned themselves with Melanie Klein and her ideas; another group, arriving from Vienna, identified themselves as followers of Freud and his daughter Anna; and a third group tried to remain eclectic, unaligned and politically neutral. They became known as the Independents or Middle Group, with a plurality of ancestors and allegiances. Donald Winnicott, for example, although influenced by Klein's thinking, had rather different views from her about the mother–baby relationship and the existence of the death instinct. John Bowlby also diverged from Kleinian thinking and was to make important connections between psychoanalysis and biology as one of the founders of the study of attachment behaviour.

As in other disciplines, theoretical differences are more easily tolerated in some contexts than others. To control what students are taught is to define the future of a profession. Debate as to which theories should be taught came to a head during the war, and the British Society held a series of formal debates on the bases of psychoanalytic theory and technique, which came to be known as the 'Controversial Discussions'. (These have been published, together with a useful commentary and background material by King and Steiner 1991.) The result was the informal, mostly unwritten, agreement that there should be three groups in the society, whose theories should be taught equally and who should be represented equally on committees. These groups persist to the present day, although there is increasing doubt as to their usefulness. Disagreements about theory and technique persist, but there is much common ground and mutual influence between the groups; in fact many North American analysts see all English analysts as simply Kleinian.

This perception arises partly because nowadays almost all English psychoanalysts would describe themselves as being within the object-relations tradition. ('Object' is a confusing term: Freud used it to mean other people as seen by us. We cannot know them directly; they are the *objects* of our desires, beliefs, etc.) Freud thought that we unconsciously relate to other people and the world in terms of our instinctual *drives*, which cause us to use other people as objects. It is this aspect of analysis, which brings it closer to human biology, that is now less fashionable in Britain. Daniel Stern and others working in this field have shown us that the human baby, thought by Freud to be capable of only instinctual responses for some months, relates to and discriminates between people from birth (Stern 1985).

Melanie Klein is an interesting halfway case. Although she is classified as an object-relations thinker because she saw the baby as relating to others from birth, she also saw the baby as reacting with instinctive aggression to the inevitable frustrations of existence. Other psychoanalysts have argued that we do relate to others in terms of a drive, but it is a drive for attachment; the desire to feel safe through the real or symbolic proximity of a protective object. How much difference the reality of the infant's relation with its mother makes to its psychic experience is constantly debated. However, perhaps the antithesis between English object relations and North American drive psychology is too sharp. Our instincts are mediated by and expressed through other people, but nor are we completely plastic. Our unconscious is formed not only as a result of the demands of our instincts/drives, but also as a consequence of our infantile powerlessness (much greater in humans than animals) and dependence on other people. Freud argued that since it is intolerable for babies not to be able to command the world, they hallucinate what they wish as a defence against painful perceptions and knowledge. This is the bedrock, so to speak, from which grows unconscious fantasy. Whether we lay stress on the drives or on the other people represented in our minds as creating and moulding that fantasy, we can no more separate them than we can the mind and the brain; they are different aspects of the same phenomenon.

Conclusion

We hope that you will enjoy this diversity of essays on psychoanalysis. They do not cover the whole field and nor do we attempt to cover all the ways in which psychoanalysis has been taken up and used by writers, literary scholars and artists. However, the essays do give a good sense of the wide variety of psychoanalytic ideas which are current in Britain at the moment. They include the perennial return to questions of the origin and evidence for our ideas and, above all, to the complex and fascinating question of the difference between the real and the imagined; of the ceaseless transactions between the external shared world and the inner world of each one of us, which is the only medium through which we can comprehend external reality.

References

British Journal of Psychotherapy (2003) 20: 129–90. Papers given by Coline Covington, Rob Hale, Pip Garvey, Alexander Layton, Christopher Bollas, and David Tuckett to a conference on 'A Question of Confidence – Privacy under Pressure'.

Forrester, J. (1997) *Dispatches from the Freud Wars: Psychoanalysis and its Passions*, Cambridge, MA: Harvard University Press.

Freud, S. (1895) *Studies on Hysteria, Standard Edition*, vol. 2, London: Hogarth Press.

—— (1937a) 'Constructions in analysis', *Standard Edition*, vol. 23, pp. 255–70, London: Hogarth Press.

Grünbaum, A. (1985) *The Foundations of Psychoanalysis*, Berkeley: University of California Press.

Hamilton, V. (1996) *The Analyst's Preconscious*, New Jersey: Analytic Press.

Kernberg, O. (1986) 'Institutional problems of psychoanalytic education', *Journal of the American Psychoanalytic Association* 34: 799–834.

—— (1989) 'The temptations of conventionality', *International Review of Psychoanalysis* 16: 191–2.

—— (1996) 'Thirty methods to destroy the creativity of candidates', *International Journal of Psychoanalysis* 77: 1031–40.

King, P. and Steiner, R. (1991) *The Freud–Klein Controversies, 1941–45*, London: Routledge.

Nobus, D. (2000) *The Freudian Practice of Psychoanalysis*, London: Routledge.

Ravetz, J.R. (1971) *Scientific Knowledge and Its Social Problems*, Oxford: Oxford University Press.

Roudinesco, E. (1990) *Jacques Lacan & Co.: A History of Psychoanalysis in France, 1925–1985*, London: Free Association Books.

Spence, D. (1982) *Narrative Truth and Historical Truth: Meaning and Interpretation in Psychoanalysis*, New York: Norton.

Stern, D. (1985) *The Interpersonal World of the Infant*. New York: Basic Books.

Ward, I. (ed.) (1997) *The Presentation of Case Material in Clinical Discourse*, London: Freud Museum Publications.

Part I

Basic concepts and psychic pain

Freud's model of the mind is a dynamic one – that is, it envisages the mind as being in a constant state of flux and conflict between impulses arising in one part of the mind and defences against these impulses. His first model of the mind had been based on repression. What we cannot stand to think or remember, we learn to repress from consciousness. The unconscious – usually metaphorically conceived of as a *deeper* layer of the mind – exerts constant pressure to bring this material back to light. It comes up again in dreams, jokes, forgettings, 'Freudian slips', associations of ideas. Ideas are smuggled across the repression barrier in various forms, and in various ways we continue to forget and deny. This simple model, of repression, and the return of the repressed, is still a perfectly adequate way of describing many mental manoeuvres. Much psychic pain can be relieved by enabling people to remember what happened in a context where they feel safe. One of its virtues is to remind us that if we have to repress a lot, we lose a great deal of mental energy in the process. Psychoanalysis should enable us to accept ourselves more and thus release some of the instinctual energy which makes experience more vivid and life more enjoyable.

Quite soon, Freud came to realize that it was not just a question of getting people to remember. So many of his female patients 'remembered' sexual advances from their fathers that he came to believe that in at least some cases the memory was an unconscious fantasy, prompted by the universal and intolerable wish that we could have a sexual relationship with both our parents. It was this development of the theory which was to make Freud, and psychoanalysis, notorious. The idea that babies and children had sexual desires, even if they were expressed via oral and anal images and ideas, was unbearable. Persistent attempts were made to get him to redefine the sexual basis of our interest in each other as love; and some argue that attachment theories come close to doing the same thing. Freud was adamant. He wanted to keep the link between psychoanalysis and the body, and the promptings of the body, although he also wanted to maintain that unconscious fantasy about the body was distinct from physiological reality. Conversely, he has frequently been accused of avoiding the fact that some adults really do act on their sexual impulses towards children; that this is not the patient's childish fantasy but memory. It is clear that he always knew that sexual abuse of children by adults was possible, but here too there is continuing indignation at the idea that children might have spontaneous sexual and aggressive fantasies as well as being subject to those of adults. The object-relations tradition has laid more emphasis on their aggressive fantasies.

Freud then began to visualize the mind less as composed of layers – as in his favourite archaeological metaphor – than as being made up of agencies or structures; the ego, the super-ego and the id. The id is the reservoir of instinctual impulses; the superego the fiercely irrational, unreasonable half-instinctual force which suppresses them; and the ego the rational part of the mind which is in touch with the external world, and which tries to mediate between our desires and reality so that we can stop insisting on what is impossible, and settle for what is. From the beginning, these terms were problematic. The German terms are simply the 'I', the 'above-I', and the 'it'. Freud's translators, Alix and James Strachey, wanted to keep these ordinary words; so did John Rickman; but Ernest Jones wanted a more abstract and formal terminology (Meisel and Kendrick 1985). In consequence, the terms have too often been reified; they have come to be seen not as metaphors for mental processes but as real entities.

Perhaps because the terms seemed so barren and far from experience, the next step was to reconceive of these processes less in terms of the structural model than of object relations. (The most systematic attempt by a British analyst to rewrite Freud's metapsychology is probably still that by Ronald Fairbairn 1952.) The unconscious mind contains the history of how each one of us has been influenced by and conceives of the people who are important to us; how we have taken our versions of them into ourselves, where they support us, attack us, quarrel with other bits of us, and so on. Patients can often express this quite concretely: as in the man who described a little man sitting on his shoulder, talking in his father's voice, telling him what to do and not to do; or the woman who felt that her mother took up the whole of her insides, so that she was just a thin skin on the outside. English psychoanalysis became less concerned with models of the mind than with the ghosts within the mind.

In Chapter 1, Catia Galatariotou gives a lucid description of the idea of mental defences, showing how Freud conceived of them as defending the equilibrium of the mind against disturbance from both internal and external factors. As Freud did, she gives a central place to repression, but goes on to describe the further work done by Freud's daughter Anna, and by Klein on defences, in which they linked them up to inner objects. She makes it clear that, although she is describing the defences separately for the purposes of explication, in real life we use many simultaneously. It is easy in psycho-analytic writing to reify concepts, use concrete thinking, forget that our ideas are just models by which we hope to describe psychic internal reality, and have no actual existence.

The terms that Galatariotou describes and defines – amongst them regression, repression, disavowal, identification with the aggressor, projection, introjection, false self, etc. – constitute most of the basic vocabulary of psychoanalysis. Very often these terms are used without awareness that they belong to a theoretical framework, that of the analysis of the defences. The chapter shows how, from ideas which are conceptually quite simple, a subtle and powerful way of understanding mental processes can be built up. The basic approach, 'defence analysis', is often seen as more characteristic of North American ego psychology, but in fact it underpins the Kleinian and object-relations approaches as well. It describes the mechanisms which the mind uses to maintain its equilibrium and avoid psychic pain, rather than the specific unconscious phantasies which may result.

The next two chapters, by Betty Joseph and Priscilla Roth, show how the idea of a defence against psychic pain was developed by Melanie Klein into the concept of a position, something between a habitual set of defences which are the basis of unconscious phantasy ('fantasy' is spelt 'phantasy' to denote that it is unconscious, i.e. not a daydream) and a developmental stage. The idea of two positions, between which we all oscillate, moves us away from Freud's more developmental linear theory, with its forward and regressive movements, to the idea of a perpetual alternation between two states of mind. Joseph has developed a technical approach (1989; Hargreaves and Varchevker 2004) which depends on the close observation of the movements of analyst's and patient's minds during the session, and here she describes the paranoid-schizoid position: normal and ubiquitous, indeed healthy, in babies.

Klein had developed the view, taken up by Freud in a late paper, that the ego not only suppresses what is unacceptable: it may split if it feels intolerably anxious (Klein 1946; Freud 1940). There are similarities between the young child's defences, adult psychosis, and what happens to us all under conditions of great pain, anxiety or fear (a theme taken up by Caroline Garland's in Chapter 16). At the psychotic extreme, this can result in deeply divided personalities, Jekylls and Hydes; in everyday experience, we all know people who seem to be triggered by certain situations to show a different side to their personalities. Jungians speak of 'the shadow side'. Again, splitting is only a metaphor for a particular kind of mental manoeuvre which differs from repression in that the personality itself seems more divided, and gets rid of painful aspects of itself by attributing them, 'projecting' them, onto others.

In Chapter 2, Joseph focuses on a particular kind of splitting known as projective identification, and the way in which it can be used as a defence against various intolerable feelings. Sometimes analytic patients cope with painful feelings about their analysts by a fantasy of incorporating them; they unconsciously adopt their voices, opinions, ways of behaving, and so on. Joseph pays careful attention to how we get rid of painful thoughts and feelings, including those created in analysis, as our psychic defences begin to shift, and the way in which, having got rid of them by attributing them to someone else, we then experience ourselves as rather empty and hollow.

In Chapter 3, on the next stage of development, the 'depressive position', Priscilla Roth describes the stage of mental development that evolves from that of the paranoid-schizoid position. Klein described this as a particular set of anxieties, and defences against these anxieties, which begin when a child is about four months old as a result of neurological maturation of the brain. In her view, the baby becomes able to develop a complex, three-dimensional view of his object which supersedes the earlier feeling that it is either ideally good or wholly bad. The consequences of this development are profound: dread lest his hate for his object should have been too strong for his love for it, and guilt at having damaged it, which can lead to a realistic appraisal of the object, respect for its separateness and an urge to repair it. This represents the arrival of a moral universe and the basis of creativity. Roth shows how painful and precarious this development is, and how difficult it is for anyone to bear for very long. We all use defences – typically, manic defences that devalue the object, or regression to more primitive states of dividing our objects into perfect and wholly bad ones – against this pain. The two 'positions' oscillate in our minds throughout life. The normal paranoid-schizoid position is essential for maintaining healthy discrimination between good and bad, and for what could be life-saving responses of fight and flight in the face of danger. It gives clarity, intensity and vividness to experience.

Klein may have been the first psychoanalyst to discuss envy, but as Kate Barrows reminds us in Chapter 4, it is hardly something new in human life. Envy as a conscious emotion is painful, but it is part of our capacity for admiration to try to do better. It can represent both hatred and, in a less destructive form, 'emulatory envy', in which we can admire and learn from others. It is when it is destructive, and above all unconscious, that it is truly damaging. It is the most intractable obstacle to successful relationships, including those with analysts and therapists. Freud first described it as the negative therapeutic reaction, or the process by which a patient is compelled to undo and deny any good which he feels he has been done. He saw it more narrowly, in the context of penis envy, but in a late, great paper, 'Analysis terminable and interminable' (Freud 1937), he broadened the concept to something resembling the Lacanian concept of lack, and confessed to feeling defeated by the intractability of envy. Barrows argues that the concept is often used too restrictively; more broadly, envy represents a hatred and intolerance of difference.

Klein described one defence against the operations of envy as a kind of projective identification; a process whereby we get rid of our unwanted feelings by attributing them to other people, or being critical of them, in order to conceal our shameful envy. She showed vividly how the attack on goodness and creativity in the other leads to its destruction within the self, and to a terrible sense of hopelessness and worthlessness. She saw human beings as oscillating between a split up, fearful and suspicious state in which bad things happening are somebody else's fault, and a state in which we can acknowledge that part of it is our fault, bear our guilt, and do what we can to make things better.

Another defence may take the form of attacking ourselves, trying to avoid showing our real or imagined superiority to others, in order not to attract their envy, since we unconsciously feel its malign power. Barrows discusses this as a peculiarly English trait; such envy is restrictive and damaging, but can also be the basis of 'fair play'. The impact of envy on other people has always been felt as inexplicable, almost demonic. In the many societies which practise witchcraft, the impact of such projective identification is seen as being due to spirit possession.

There is a major difference in emphasis in clinical psychoanalysis in Britain at this point: do we lay more stress on innate guilt and destructiveness, or on the tragedy that has led someone to feel so depleted because of the painful and difficult circumstances of their upbringing, which have left them without much sense of inner or outer goodness? Stephen Mitchell (1993) points out that the division between those who think that aggression is innate in man and those who see it as reactive and defensive has been perennial throughout the history of psychoanalysis, but it is hardly surprising that we have been unable to resolve it: the problem has long been familiar to moral philosophers and psychologists. Just as in England the Kleinians and Independents tend to vary on this issue (see Riley, Chapter 14), in the United States classical Freudians disagree with Kohutians and self-psychologists.

References

Fairbairn, W.R.D. (1952) *Psychoanalytic Studies of the Personality*, London: Tavistock.

Freud, S. (1937) 'Analysis terminable and interminable', *Standard Edition*, vol. 23, pp. 209–54, London: Hogarth Press.

—— (1940) 'The splitting of the ego for the purposes of defence', *Standard Edition*, vol. 23, pp. 271–8, London: Hogarth Press.

Hargreaves, E. and Varchevker, A. (eds) (2004) *In Pursuit of Psychic Change: The Betty Joseph Workshop*, London: Brunner-Routledge.

Joseph, B. (1989) *Psychic Equilibrium and Psychic Change: Selected Papers of Betty Joseph*, M. Feldman and E. Bott Spillius eds, London: Routledge.

Klein, M. (1946) 'Notes on some schizoid mechanisms', *International Journal of Psychoanalysis*, 27: 99–110. Revised version in M. Klein, P. Heimann, S. Isaacs and J. Rivière, *Developments in Psycho-Analysis*, London: Hogarth Press, 1952, pp. 292–320. Reprinted in *The Writings of Melanie Klein*, vol. 3, pp. 1–24, London: Hogarth Press, 1975, Virago 1997.

Meisel, P. and Kendrick, W. (eds) (1985) *Bloomsbury/Freud: The Letters of James and Alix Strachey*, New York: Basic Books.

Mitchell, S. (1993) 'Aggression and the endangered self', *Psychoanalytic Quarterly* 62: 351–82.

Chapter 1

The defences

Catia Galatariotou

In its everyday meaning, the word 'defence' is familiar to us all. It conjures up an interaction between two parties: one attacking or threatening to attack, the other protecting themselves against aggression. Similarly in medicine, the dictionary tells us, 'defence mechanism' denotes 'the body's reaction against attack from disease organisms'. The psychoanalytic concept of defence is essentially the same. It differs in that its particular focus is the mind.

Freud was the first to discover and explore the vast territory of the defences. His findings remain essentially valid and crucially important after more than a century of psychoanalytic research, and are the basis of subsequent psychoanalytic thinking on the defences. I shall begin with an account of Freud's ideas, then give an account of some of the most influential post-Freudian theoretical contributions, and close with a brief discussion of the technique of defence analysis.

Freud on defences

In discussing Sigmund Freud's work I shall be referring to his structural model of the mind. In this, the mind is made up of three agencies, the id, the ego and the superego, with the external world amounting almost to a fourth agency. The id is an entirely unconscious part of the mind, from which all our basic instinctual impulses emanate. It is dominated by the 'pleasure principle' – the tendency to seek the pleasure that comes from the gratification of instinctual impulses. The id is a 'seething cauldron', Freud thought, which knows nothing about time, place, external reality, shame, disgust, morality. It has no conscience. All the id knows is that it wishes, and it wants its wishes gratified, now. The stronger the wish, the more it clamours for expression and satisfaction, building up pressure, pushing towards consciousness in order to obtain expression and satisfaction. For example, when the pressure of hunger becomes sufficiently strong, the infant cries and so demands to be fed; the warm milk that flows from the breast gratifies its instinctual demand and extinguishes the unpleasantness of hunger – for a while at least, until the cycle begins again. In the adult, the parallel can be a sexual wish, and its gratification.

However, almost from the moment of birth we begin to learn that the road between wish and gratification is not straightforward. The infant learns soon enough that a full breast will not materialize necessarily the moment it wants it. This is frustrating, and the experience of frustration sets in motion the long process of adaptation to the environment. And it is not long before the impact of shame, disgust and morality begins to be felt. The 'dams' of civilization, as Freud (1905: 178) called them, the dams, that is, of 'disgust, shame and morality', attempt to limit, control and canalize desire. We gradually learn that wishes and needs not only have to wait, and may not be gratified, but further that some of them are downright forbidden. Conflict between what we want and what we learn is unacceptable to want is built into the structure of psychological development almost from birth. The biggest lesson we learn is that gratification may come at a price, and sometimes the price is too high: to gratify some desires would be so unacceptable or costly to the rest of our self, that it would produce more unpleasure than pleasure. A decision has to be made, whether a particular wish is acceptable, or whether it is so unacceptable or unfeasible that it must be fought against and resisted.

This is the job of the ego. The ego has to decide whether to allow the gratification of an instinctual wish or whether, having judged it to be unacceptable or impossible, to try and block the troops of desire on their way from the id towards consciousness and gratification. It does this by mobilizing a counter-force – a defence – to pit against the forces of desire. Thus the troops of the defensive forces are stationed, as it were, in the ego; and they are ready to go into action as soon as unacceptable or unbearable ideas or affects threaten to invade and overwhelm the ego.

These defensive forces have reason to expect to be called to action very often indeed, for threats to the mind's equilibrium do not only come from the id. They also come from the superego (the agency that prohibits and threatens punishment in the shape of a bad conscience for unacceptable thoughts and feelings) and from the external world, which presents the mind with stimuli that may also lead to tempting but forbidden ideas and feelings. Where there is conflict between the agencies of the mind, the ego has to perform the difficult task of keeping the peace – the peace of the mind, its equilibrium – as best it can. How does the ego know how to mobilize its defences? Freud came to think that anxiety was the signal that sets the defences in motion. (This is the 'second theory of anxiety', 1926, in which repression is a response to anxiety. Freud had previously thought that anxiety was due to repression.) Anxiety warns the ego that there is an approaching danger, namely the danger of a possible future trauma which would overwhelm it. As Freud's biographer Peter Gay (1998: 488) put it: 'Anxiety is the sentinel on the tower sounding the alarm [and] the defences are the troops mobilized to check the invader.'

The ego is the conscious part of our mind – but it is also, in its deeper layers, unconscious. This is important to remember because defences are unconscious processes. They are like troops working under cover of darkness. Consciously, we do not normally know of their existence and operations, but the tell-tale signs of their existence become more obvious in pathology.

To begin with, defences need to be formed to allow us to adapt to our environment, and as such they are universal to all human beings. They are indispensable, especially in the developing infant and child, in helping us to negotiate the difficult process of adaptation to reality, and to enable us to function appropriately as social beings. It is impossible to do so without defences. So they come into being as our allies. However, when they overgrow, when they are overused, when they cause us to deny reality as too painful, when, in short, they go wrong, then they turn into enemies: from servants of adaptation they turn into obstacles to adaptation, and inhibit rather than enhance our potential. This is what happens in the neuroses.

Neurotics do not have a monopoly on defences. As I implied earlier, the defences operating in pathology are only an exaggeration, a caricature of what happens in relatively healthy people, but there we do not see any obvious evidence of the operation of the defences, precisely because they are unconscious. When they are successful in their operations against the threatening invaders, the result is that all the elements involved in the conflict are completely excluded from consciousness, and so no evidence of their existence appears on the surface. By contrast, when a defence fails the ego is left insufficiently protected from overwhelming anxieties, and so it loses its balance, its equilibrium. What has happened is that the original impulse has proved too strong for the defence – or the defence has proved too weak for the impulse. The difficulty now is that the threatening idea or feeling continues to be unbearable or unacceptable to consciousness, yet since the defence is too weak it threatens to break through the defensive barrier and into consciousness. A compromise has to be hastily reached, between the instinctual impulse and the struggling and failing defence. The compromise solution is that the offensive idea or feeling will finally surface and thus be at least partially gratified. It will surface not in its original form, but disguised and sufficiently removed from the original to make it consciously acceptable. This compromise solution is what appears as a neurotic symptom: a phobia, or an inhibition, or a psychosomatic complaint, and so on. Thus what we can actually observe of defence mechanisms comes when the failed defences manifest themselves on the surface, in the inhibiting, tormenting shape of symptoms. These symptoms are the tell-tale signs that below the surface there is conflict and a malfunctioning or failed defence mechanism. It can be said therefore that neurosis is due to the failure of defence.

It was the study of neurosis that first brought the defences to Freud's attention. Specifically, he noticed a piece of paradoxical yet ubiquitous behaviour in analytic patients – namely, that even the most committed analysand proves less than a fully willing participant in the work of psychoanalysis. Having come freely into analysis, he or she begins to resist the analytic work. For instance, her free associations dry up, she dismisses or ignores the analyst's interpretations out of hand, she misses sessions, she forgets dreams, she – most ironic of all – becomes a 'good patient' who hides under the cloak of compliance her true thoughts and feelings. Freud understood this apparent paradox as the manifestation of a struggle between the wish to know, understand, change; and the wish not to. The resistances that the patient employs are defences in action – the surface manifestations of defences operating in the unconscious.

Presented as they were in the consulting room, Freud could begin to understand and work with them. He came to describe the defences in many ways: as 'measures the ego takes', 'techniques', 'modes' or 'types of operation', 'manoeuvres', or (the term his daughter Anna later thought should be exclusively used) as 'mechanisms'. Freud used the term 'mechanism' to emphasize that many psychical phenomena, including the defences, are organized in such a way that we can scientifically observe and analyse them. The term 'mechanism of defence' denotes the way in which a particular defence works; it looks at it rather as if it were a piece of machinery, and tries to understand what it is made of, how it is constructed, how it works. Freud also used the term to denote the whole of a defensive process which comes to characterize a specific neurosis (e.g. projection in paranoia).

Specific defences

I have so far discussed the defences in general, as a group of mental processes aimed at the avoidance of painful or unbearable ideas and affects. Now I would like to discuss some of them individually. I will try to look at three different expressions which each defence can take: in the individual in pathology; in the individual in normality; and as a group process in society. I want to do this not just because I think it is interesting but also because it reflects Freud's own vision: he saw everyone as linked by 'an unbroken chain' which ultimately connects the most balanced and normal psychic manifestation to the most extreme and perverse. He thought that about the defences, just as much as he thought it about sexuality, or aggression. He also saw individual and social psychology as inseparable. Just as the individual does, so society as a whole also wants change and resists change. It too struggles to strike a balance between wanting, needing to allow the gratification of desire, and fearing such gratification – and thus wanting to control, harness, regulate and at times even stifle desire altogether.

Repression

Repression is the doyen of the defences and the earliest to be systematically explored by Freud. From his earliest treatments of hysterics, one of the clinical phenomena that impressed him was that in the course of treatment his patients were able to recover many lost memories, which were vivid and extremely important. He wrote: 'It was a question of things the patient wished to forget, and therefore repressed from his conscious thought' (Breuer and Freud 1895). So Freud already, in *Studies on Hysteria*, had a basic concept of repression as exclusion from consciousness. Twenty years later, he would define repression more elaborately, as 'turning something away, and keeping it at a distance, from the conscious' (Freud 1915b: 147). He had discovered in the meanwhile that the most persistent human wishes were infantile in origin, but had been made impermissible by socialization. They had been repressed out of consciousness, and most had remained unconscious, concealed, inaccessible to conscious scrutiny. This was and remains a central theme in psychoanalysis.

The unconscious contains all our basic instinctual impulses from the start, but it also comes to contain everything that is repressed, particularly in the course of development but also later in life. It thus comes to contain the historical records and the templates, as it were, of all of the individual's repressed wishes and psychical experiences from birth onwards. This is so in all cases, normal and pathological. This universal process is what lies at the root of the differentiation of the unconscious from the rest of the mind, what constitutes it as a separate agent. Repression is the foundation of the unconscious, and since the exploration of the unconscious is the central characteristic of psychoanalysis, Freud held that "the theory of repression is the cornerstone on which the whole structure of psychoanalysis rests" (Freud 1914: 16).

For some 30 years Freud all but dropped the term 'defence' and used 'repression' instead, as though this was the only defensive process. In 1926 he reconceptualized repression as simply one amongst the defences, but a particularly important one which is also a component part of the mechanism of other defensive processes.

The mechanism of repression that Freud described is a complex one. If the wish, emanating from the id, is judged to be unacceptable or unbearable, the ego will try to turn it away from consciousness. To the pressure from the id wish, the ego will exert a counter-pressure. The wish's way to surface expression is blocked: it is simply not allowed to enter or remain in consciousness. This is the first stage of repression, the 'turning something away [. . .] from the conscious'. However, repressed wishes do not die. As Freud put it: 'Unconscious wishes are always active'; they are 'indestructible. In the unconscious nothing can be brought to an end, nothing is past or forgotten' (Freud 1900: 577). In their imprisoned state, they remain nonetheless under the sway of the pleasure principle and continue to exert pressure for expression and gratification. Further, the repressed wish acts as a magnet, attracting elements which are connected to it whether because they derive from it or because they have become connected with it through association. They add to the pressure towards expression, and are also likely to be judged by the ego as threatening and necessitating repression, in case admitting one may by association bring others to the surface too. Therefore, the ego now has to exert further pressure, a counter-pressure against the increased pressure from the unconscious repressed. So we have a push and pull, an attraction and a repulsion. This is the second phase of repression, the so-called 'repression-proper' or 'after-pressure'. This is what Freud meant when he spoke not only of a 'turning something away' but also of 'keeping it at a distance from the conscious'. Repression is thus not a static but a dynamic ongoing process. Where the defence mechanism fails, the process of repression enters a third phase, the 'return of the repressed': the repressed, or a part of it, finally manages to break through to the surface, albeit disguised, in the form of symptoms, dreams, parapraxes (slips of the tongue, forgetfulness, etc.) and so on.

A clinical example

Ms A, a woman in her early thirties, came to analysis to relieve herself from symptoms which included panic attacks and the inability to form a good and stable relationship with a man. She consciously loved and was extremely attached to her parents, both of whom were alive. One day she brought a dream to the analysis. She dreamt that two of her front teeth were missing. There was a gap, an emptiness where they used to be. On her gums, where the teeth used to be, she could see a smooth flat hard shiny white surface, like a slab. The roots of the teeth were buried underneath this slab. She put her tongue in and out of this gap, and this was pleasant, it was fun.

Ms A's associations led us to understand that the two teeth represented her parents, dead. The white slab was their tombstone. The dream expressed her repressed wish that they should die; and her unconscious phantasy that once they were dead and buried she would be free at last to find sexual pleasure with a man. Ms A was completely unaware that she had been harbouring a death wish towards her parents. That while loving them she also hated them enough to wish them dead was consciously unbearable. She had therefore repressed the death wish, and its accompanying phantasy that she would then be free to have a relationship with a man. The disguised form in which it emerged in her dream is an example of 'the return of the repressed'.

The effects of repression are perhaps most spectacularly seen in cases of 'conversion hysteria' (hysteria with psychosomatic symptoms). For example, one of the symptoms of Freud's famous patient 'Dora' (Freud 1905), was a persistent cough. Analysis revealed that her symptom was the disguised expression of her repressed sexual phantasy in which her father and his mistress were having oral sex.

In normality, as much as in pathology, repressed material is the very stuff our dreams are made of. And think of those 'dams' of civilization: shame, disgust, morality, and the drastic extent to which they suppress our infantile urges. Think too of the Oedipus complex, and how its resolution entails the massive repression of the passions of ambivalence (exclusive love and murderous hatred combined) towards both parents.

In social life, repression – of manifestations of both the sexual and the death or aggressive instincts – is universal in all cultures at all times. Where they differ is in the extent and shape of the repressive measures each society takes.

Reaction-formation

The 'return of the repressed' is one possible outcome of a repressed wish; another is the defence Freud called reaction-formation. This refers to an attitude which is diametrically opposed to a repressed wish. For example, bashfulness may be a reaction-formation against a repressed wish to be exhibitionistic; cleanliness and orderliness may be a reaction-formation against a repressed wish to be dirty and messy.

The tell-tale signs of a pathological reaction-formation appear, as you might expect, in the form of symptoms: we suspect the presence of a pathological reaction-formation when someone's conscious attitude towards, say, cleanliness, is overemphasized, very rigid, or even compulsive. Sometimes the reaction-formation fails altogether in its purpose and, ironically, someone who is supposedly single mindedly pursuing one aim ends up doing the complete opposite of what he or she consciously intended – and so unwittingly reveals the repressed wish: for example, the compulsively cleaning housewife who is continuously, obsessively thinking about dirt and mess is in effect living with dirt and mess constantly present, in her head.

In pathological states, reaction-formation is especially characteristic of 'anal characters': it is a very important defence in hysteria and in obsessional neurosis. It can be localized, manifested in specific behaviour and confined to a particular relationship; so that for example, 'a hysterical woman [. . .] may be specially affectionate with her own children whom at bottom she hates; but she will not on that account be more loving in general than other women or even more affectionate to other children' (Freud 1926: 158). In other instances the reaction-formation may be more spread out and appear as a character trait. The specificity of the ideas and phantasies involved in the conflict are then concealed: for instance, a person who harbours intense unconscious aggression against specific others may, through a reaction-formation, develop the general character trait of being pitiful and compassionate towards people in general.

But of course not everybody who is bashful or clean and tidy is manifesting a pathological reaction-formation. Freud (1905) also drew attention to the non-pathological and indeed crucially important role of reaction-formation in normal development: human character and virtues are constructed in part as reaction-formations against the potentially polymorphously perverse sexual licentiousness of early childhood. Socialization usually turns much sexual activity from a pleasure to an unpleasure, and thus leads to its repression. Reaction-formation may then ensure that the very opposite attitude becomes a permanent attitude in a person. These are instances of 'successful defence' in that the elements involved in the conflict (the sexual or aggressive idea and its prohibition) are excluded from consciousness. What we have instead is a normally clean, tidy, conscientious, caring, etc. person who is unconflictedly so.

Freud thought that non-pathological reaction-formation also occurs at the collective level. In his writings on The Great War, he noted that the primitive aggression whose destructiveness we see in war can in peace be converted into its opposite by reaction-formation. Then, it can use the same enormous amount of energy to serve civilization rather than to destroy it.

Sublimation

In society then, as in the individual, Freud thought that reaction-formation was part of the story of the origins and development of human creativity, character and virtue. The other part was another defensive process, which Freud called sublimation, and of which reaction-formation was merely a 'sub-species' (Freud 1905: 238).

The term 'sublimation' is borrowed from chemistry, where it means 'purification', the way in which a body can pass from a solid to a gaseous state. In psychoanalysis, sublimation means the 'purification' of the energy of the repressed sexual wish until it has ceased to have a sexual aim and has acquired a socially acceptable expression. For example, the energy of repressed exhibitionistic wishes may enable someone, through sublimation, to become an accomplished public performer – an actor, a public speaker, a politician; he or she remains an exhibitionist of sorts, but a socially acceptable and valued one. Sublimation, Freud thought, accounts for all sorts of human activities which appear to have no connection with sexuality yet are in fact powered by the energy of the sexual instinct, having displaced its aim without diminishing its intensity. Artistic creation and intellectual inquiry were the two main activities Freud described as sublimated. He thought that sublimated sexual instincts, especially if perverse or unintegrated, are the powerhouse for all creative cultural activity.

It is difficult to see how sublimation can be a pathological process. Its great advantage over other defensive processes is that it bypasses repression's pathogenic potential: instead of keeping sexual energy repressed it purifies and channels it into creative use. Freud emphasized that civilization as we know it is inconceivable without sublimation. He also thought that the capacity for sublimation is no more evenly distributed between individuals than it is among societies: different societies across time manifest widely different capacities for sublimation. Take the two most powerful societies in classical Greece, for instance. Fifth-century Athens, with its unparalleled flowering of civilization, must surely represent a triumph of the human capacity to sublimate. Yet in its backyard there was Sparta, with its totalitarian militaristic society, a lack of anything other than the most rudimentary and repetitive expressions of artistic creativity (themselves near-exclusively militarist) and a deep contempt for the Athenian cultural enterprise.

Regression

Of all the defences, regression is the one that most clearly reveals Freud's intense sense of the importance of the historical past. 'To regress' means literally to walk back, to retrace one's steps. Psychoanalytically, the theory of regression is based on the understanding that human development follows a preordained path which takes us through specific psychosexual stages. Freud described these as oral, anal, phallic and genital sexuality. And there are other ways of describing stages of development, for example, as types of identification, or of object relationships (from the more primitive and narcissistic to ones less so). Each developmental phase is negotiated and in normality superseded, but it is never completely obliterated: passing through it leaves an imprint, an inscription on the mind. In later life, the ego may defend itself by regressing to an earlier phase of development.

Certain strikingly pathological cases make it easy for us to think of regression in a literal sense: the catatonic is said to return to a foetal stage; the obsessional, with his controlling needs, is said to have regressed to the anal stage. In the course of analysis, the patient may regress in the transference, for example, when he or she develops a dependence on the analyst which resembles that which a child or even an infant normally has to its mother.

We are all familiar with regression in its non-pathological form: when we fall bodily ill, for instance, we tend to regress to an earlier stage of development, longing to be attended to, to be taken care of, rather like a small child.

When Freud emphasized that the past remains forever with us, he was referring not only to the individual but also to society: for in both 'the primitive stages can always be re-established; the primitive mind is, in the fullest meaning of the word, imperishable' (Freud 1915d: 286). Collective regression is especially apparent in war, when whatever stage of civilization has been reached suddenly gives way and regresses to a much earlier, savage, primitive stage.

More primitive defences

The defence mechanisms I have described – repression, reaction-formation, sublimation, regression – are sophisticated, not least because they presuppose a mind in which the differentiation between ego and id, conscious and unconscious, has already been established. By contrast, other defences are more primitive in origin: they can and do appear in earliest infancy, during that prehistoric era which precedes language and the differentiation of the mind into separate agencies. Once the mind has become more structured, such primitive defences can achieve more sophisticated expression, but their origins bequeath them a distinctive character.

Projection

Projection is one such primitive defence. Projection is a way of dealing with wishes, thoughts, feelings, qualities – anything which the individual refuses to recognize as belonging to him or rejects about himself. Instead, he expels it from himself and attaches it to another person or thing. He recognizes in others what he refuses to acknowledge in himself. And since he has projected something precisely because he found it intolerable in himself, when that same thing is perceived as belonging to another person it will again be experienced as intolerable. If, as often happens, the intolerable feeling is experienced as belonging to someone else but also now as aimed at the person who denied that feeling in the first place, something he has rejected in himself now seems to come at him from the outside, like a psychic boomerang. It is then inevitably experienced as a personal threat, a reproach or a persecution. The external object is perceived as the feared threat to be avoided, when in fact the threat is and remains an internal one. For example, a woman who finds her own feelings of envy intolerable in herself may deny them in herself, project them onto another person and accuse the other of envy; further, and more tormentingly, she may experience the other as being envious of her.

Pathological projection is especially characteristic of paranoia. Freud describes how the paranoiac judge Schreber felt persecuted by his doctor whom he believed to have homosexual feelings towards him. The intense homosexual longings were in fact Schreber's own, but were intolerable to him; so he tried to get rid of them by projecting them onto his doctor, only to then experience them as an external persecution.

Projection is not always pathological. Indeed, non-pathological projection is a major part of normal psychic life. For instance, would we be able to feel empathy or pity without an element of normal, non-hostile projection? Surely this is one of the ways in which we step into the shoes of a fellow human being – even of one who is a complete stranger to us. Further, we habitually seek the causes of our internal mental processes in the outside world. Societally, Freud saw projection as central to human belief in the supernatural, in mythology, in superstition: mythological creatures, gods, demons and ghosts are in part projections of human qualities and passions, and embodiments of unacceptable, repressed human desires.

Introjection

Projection begins to operate at the very start of life, and so does another primitive defence: introjection. Like projection, introjection also involves a change of locus, a relocation, but this time in a direction opposite to that of projection. In introjection something that is outside is taken inside: an external object is incorporated, wholesale as it were, within one's own self. It is easy to think of these two mechanisms in bodily, oral terms: for projection, think of throwing up, spitting out, evacuating; for introjection think of eating up whole, of swallowing up. Indeed that is how Freud articulated them: 'Expressed in the language of the oldest – the oral – instinctual impulses, the judgment is: "I should like to eat this" or "I should like to spit it out" ' (Freud 1925: 237).

The newborn infant can not distinguish between himself and the external world. The capacity to distinguish between the self and the external object, between 'me' and 'not me', is acquired through the mechanisms of projection and introjection. The infant introjects whatever object is presented to it which is pleasurable, therefore 'good', and projects whatever within itself causes unpleasure, experienced as 'bad'. In this primitive, intensely narcissistic way of functioning, in which you are everything good, and everything bad is not you, the rudiments of a differentiation between what is 'me' and what is 'not me' are laid down. Later in development, the infant learns that things are not so clear-cut; that there are bad things inside us, and good things outside the self. Later still, when the superego – the agency of our conscience – is formed by the introjection of parental figures, these introjects will be, in normal development, whole, composite figures, a mixture of good and bad.

Introjection as a normal developmental process helps us to become autonomous: it is used, as a normal defence, against overwhelming separation anxiety, which it diminishes by carrying the introjected object within the self.

Freud discussed the pathological form of introjection in 'Mourning and melancholia' (1917). He described how, in a pathological reaction, the bereaved person introjects the dead person (towards whom he unconsciously holds ambivalent feelings) into the ego, replacing the relationship with an object 'out there' by one with an imagined object within the self. The result is the inability to mourn; instead, mourning gives way to melancholia (depression).

Identification

Other defences related to introjection can begin to operate once the differentiation between the self and external objects is established. In identification the person takes on some of the characteristics of the object, and is transformed, wholly or partially, into it. In its simplest observable form this is what happens when a little girl puts on her mum's lipstick and high heels. Identification is an extremely important part of the process of structuring of the personality, which is effected essentially through a series of identifications.

Internalization

Internalization is yet another way of taking the external world into the mind. For example, the young child at first follows parental rules and injunctions when he is in the actual presence of parental figures, and then begins to comply out of love for his parents and the fear of loss of their love, and of punishment. Through internalization, the need for the physical presence of the external authority figure dwindles; compliance now rests on their internalized presence. Strictly speaking, introjection in the non-infant is proceeded by internalization. It should be noted here that internalization and introjection are very closely related, and the two terms are sometimes used synonymously.

This brings me to an important point which needs to be made about all defences.[1] I have described the defences as if there were clear-cut definitions and distinctions between them, but what psychoanalytic theory describes are model defences. In reality defences often overlap, they are interdependent, they appear in clusters, and in different degrees, they can have different characteristics at different ages, and they can all be used in health or illness. Attempts to classify them run into problems. For years, analysts at what is now the Anna Freud Centre tried to classify defences by differentiating between 'defence mechanisms' and 'defensive measures', which included any behaviour that has a defensive purpose. The list for the latter grew longer and longer and the project remains unfinished. Following this to its logical conclusion, the North American psychoanalyst Charles Brenner proposed that there are no separate defence mechanisms at all: only ego functions which can sometimes serve defensive purposes (Cooper 1989).

Post-Freudian contributions

Following Freud's work there have been many and extremely important developments in the psychoanalytic understanding of the defences and of their role in the constitution and functioning of our internal world. I will give a brief presentation of a few of the most influential post-Freudian ideas on defence, which I hope will hint at the variety, richness and importance of post-Freudian psychoanalytic thinking on the subject.

Anna Freud

Following Freud's 'Inhibitions, symptoms and anxiety' (1926), the study of defence mechanisms became a major theme in psychoanalytic research. Anna Freud, Sigmund's daughter and a psychoanalytic pioneer in the psycho-analysis of children, maintained a lifelong interest in the defences. *The Ego and the Mechanisms of Defence* (1936) established her reputation as a psycho-analytic thinker in her own right and became a classic in the field.[2] She brought together, described in detail and clarified the mechanisms that Sigmund Freud had uncovered, which had remained scattered throughout his writings. In considering what it is that is being defended against, while main-taining her father's emphasis on defence against drive pressures, Anna Freud elaborated the view that defences also arise against affects; as well as (follow-ing intimations in his late writings) against any situation in the external world which gives rise to overwhelming anxiety. She proposed a systematic classification of defences against internal and external dangers, anxiety and unpleasure. Her descriptions of the complex interplay between the external and internal worlds effectively made the defences part of a drives-based object relations theory. Within this context, Anna Freud described a devel-opmental line, a sequence showing the gradual shift from primitive to more mature forms of defence during development. Finally, she identified and described several new defence mechanisms, such as 'identification with the aggressor', 'altruism' and 'denial' in phantasy, word and act.

Identification with the aggressor

Identification with the aggressor is probably the best known of these new defences. It describes how the attempt to master the anxiety generated in the victim by a perceived or real aggression can take the form of identifying with the aggressor. In a simple example, this is what a child does when follow-ing hospitalization she 'becomes', in play, a doctor performing an operation on her doll. Similarly, a school bully is often a child identifying with a bullying sibling or adult at home, whose victim he already is. In more complex instances the use of this defence mechanism becomes enmeshed in superego development, where identification with the aggressor may well be supplemented by feelings of guilt – as when, for instance, the child becomes aggressive in an attempt to forestall the criticism or punishment he expects to receive from adults. Anna Freud exemplified this when she presented the case of a child who became excessively aggressive in play. She understood this to be linked to masturbation: the boy expected to be punished by adults for it, but had also identified with his parental figures and metabolized their prohib-ition into internal superego feelings of guilt; and so he treated his objects in the punitive way he expected himself to be treated by the grownups he had identified with.

In the course of my psychoanalytic work, Anna Freud's concept of identification with the aggressor came to my mind while treating Ms B. A young woman of studiedly 'butch' appearance and a self-declared 'man-hating lesbian', Ms B was physically and emotionally violent towards her long-term female partner. Ms B's parents had been locked in a miserable, sado-masochistic relationship during their married life, which lasted throughout Ms B's childhood and early adolescence. At the conscious level Ms B was filled with hatred, rage, contempt and helpless fear towards her father, who had been emotionally and physically abusive towards her mother and eventually also towards his daughter. However, it became apparent in analysis that Ms B also had a powerful unconscious identification with this father-aggressor. Thus she both rejected her father – and by extension all men – and had also 'become' him, as far as possible, in external appearance, erotic object choice and behaviour, and in subjecting her lover to the emotional and physical abuse that she and her mother had once been subjected to. The limits of Ms B's identification with the aggressor were marked by her feelings of guilt and remorse about her violence towards her lover (feelings which her father appeared never to have had towards his wife and daughter); it was these feelings which led her to seek analysis.

At the societal level, identification with the aggressor helps us understand apparently paradoxical phenomena – how it happens, for instance, that members of an oppressed or even actively persecuted group can admire, wish to be and in phantasy 'become' members of the group persecuting them. How, for instance, some Jews during and after the Second World War came to harbour a sneaking admiration for the Nazis.

Klein and post-Kleinians

Melanie Klein focused on the earliest period of human life. While rooted in Freud she effectively developed a new theory, consisting of two psychological 'positions': the 'paranoid-schizoid' and the 'depressive'. Each exhibits a characteristic constellation of defences, anxieties and object relations. Each occurs during the first few months of life, the 'depressive' position succeeding the 'paranoid-schizoid'. But both recur, in individually varying intensities and frequency, throughout life. Within this context Klein described what she considered to be very primitive defences, developing in her own way the concept of particular defences already found in Freud's and W.R.D. Fairbairn's work, and also introducing and elaborating on new defences and defensive organizations, most notably 'introjection', 'projection', 'reintrojection', 'idealization', 'splitting' (of the object and of the ego), and 'projective identification'. Klein saw primitive defences employed most potently and clearly by the undifferentiated mind of the infant and by the primary-process-dominated mind of the psychotic. The most influential and studied defence in post-Kleinian literature has been that of *projective identification* (see Roth, Chapter 3 this volume).

Klein's definition of projective identification remained almost casual, but it is clear that she thought that it involves 'putting part of oneself into the other person' so that the ensuing 'identification is based on attributing to the other person some of one's own qualities'. A distinction between normal and pathological projective identification is discernible in Klein (though its clear articulation and elaboration came with Bion, in his theory of containment). In its normal form, projective identification of a 'friendly nature' is the basis of empathic understanding for, as Klein put it, 'by attributing part of our feelings to the other person, we understand their feelings, needs and satisfactions; in other words, we are putting ourselves into the other person's shoes'. However, if the projecting person is psychically persecuted, his projections will be hostile and his ability for real empathy and understanding of others will be correspondingly impaired. Further, people who employ projective identification excessively may 'lose themselves entirely in others and become incapable of objective judgment'; while the correspondingly excessive introjection of the other into the projecting person 'endangers the strength of the ego because it becomes completely dominated by the introjected object' (Klein 1975: 252–3). In these pathological states violent psychic relocations of phantasies (and consequently of emotions, thoughts and attributes) take place, blurring the boundaries between the projecting person and the recipient. At the extreme, in psychosis, projective identification provides the means of entering into and assuming another's identity.

Projections do not always emotionally affect their recipient. Post-Kleinian authors discuss whether the term 'projective identification' should be used irrespective of whether or not the recipient is emotionally affected, or whether it should be restricted to instances where he or she is affected. Those who argue for the more restricted use of the term point out that if the recipient is not affected then 'projective identification' becomes very difficult – if not impossible – to distinguish from simple 'projection'. Those who argue in favour of using the term in its unrestricted sense (as Klein herself did) point out that to restrict it is to impoverish its usefulness. Indeed, in the Kleinian understanding, projective identification is a concept of very wide application, employed for a variety of defensive reasons: to control the object, to acquire its attributes, to evacuate a bad quality, to protect a good quality, or to eliminate separation anxiety. Wanting to preserve the term but also to curb its vague and over-generalized use, some post-Kleinian authors have identified specific subtypes of projective identification. For instance, Elizabeth Spillius (1988: 83) has proposed the term 'evocatory' to describe cases where the recipient is emotionally affected by the projected phantasies. Ron Britton (1998) has proposed distinguishing between two subtypes: 'acquisitive projective identification' occurs when another person's identity or attributes are claimed for the projector ("I am you"); whilst 'attributive projective identification' describes the attribution of an aspect of the projector's self to another person ("You are me"). In the latter case, *pace* Spillius, the projection can be 'evocatory' or 'non-evocatory'. Britton gives as an example of 'acquisitive projective identification' a psychotic patient's belief that he was the Emperor Hadrian (whereas in a less omnipotent patient the same phantasy might have surfaced in the form of a dream); and as an example of 'attributive projective identification' the poet Rilke's fear that to love and be loved would cause him to lose his identity.

Here are a couple of clinical examples of projective identification. Mrs G sought psychoanalysis in her late thirties, following the onset of severe anxiety attacks. In the course of her analysis Mrs G's mother emerged as a narcissistic woman who lived through her daughter. For instance, during Mrs G's late adolescence the mother would phone 'chat-up lines' and flirt with unknown men, assuming her daughter's name, age, appearance, university studies – assuming, in short, her daughter's identity. It seemed probable that the mother was not simply pretending, but that in phantasy she 'became' her daughter in these and many other quieter instances. If so, this would be an example of a gross surface manifestation of projective identification. Specifically, following Britton's classification, it would be projective identification of the 'acquisitive' subtype: 'I (the mother) am you (the daughter)'. Another example of projective identification came as Mrs G begun to be able to analyse a paradoxical psychic manifestation: whilst she appreciated and was fond of her husband, she also felt angry towards him and found herself compelled to constantly attack, denigrate and, in her phantasy, castrate him. Mrs G came to understand that her attacks on her husband were psychically identical to her mother's attacks on her husband, Mrs G's father. She felt that her rage and castrating intent were not authentically hers, but had originally belonged to her mother and had relocated, as it were, within her. Mrs G felt that her mother's phantasies had penetrated her, become embedded within her and were now operating through her. Mrs G's hostile relating to her husband was the end result of projective identification of the 'attributive' subtype: 'You (the daughter) are me (the mother)'. And this was also an 'evocatory' projective identification since the daughter-recipient of the projections was emotionally affected by and indeed acted them out.

The psychic violence of hostile projective identification, and its consequences, acquired a surface expression in Mrs G's hostile relating to her husband. At a deeper level, they were most clearly and eloquently expressed in a cluster of powerful feelings. These feelings had, we discovered, an ancient and permanent presence in Mrs G's unconscious mind, but prior to her entering analysis they had only made themselves known during her anxiety attacks, when she described feeling that she did not own her body, that she was empty, she was losing herself, she floated in terrifying nothingness. Such words described how Mrs G unconsciously experienced her mother as having enviously invaded her mind and body, scooped out its contents and taken up residence inside her. A part of the daughter thus had become possessed by a projected envious, hostile part of the mother. Mrs G felt that her mind had come to be so extensively occupied by her mother's insinuating psychic presence that she had been left feeling empty, had lost her own self, and existed in terrifying nothingness.

D. W. Winnicott

A sense of 'nothingness' is also evoked by D. W. Winnicott's description of *the false self* (1965) – his main and most influential contribution to the theory of defence. Winnicott saw the self as divided between a 'true self' (corresponding to Freud's descriptions of a central, instinctually powered core) and a 'false self' – 'a part that is turned outwards and is related to the world'. For Winnicott, the origins of the false self are found in the early infant–mother relationship. At the start of life outside the womb the infant cannot differentiate between its own self and the external environment, and thus has no way of differentiating what comes from within – its own id demands – from what comes from the external world. The mother plays a crucial role in building up the ego strength it needs to make this distinction. Through the way in which the mother emotionally 'holds' her baby, she will facilitate or hinder her infant's progress (see Johns, Chapter 5 this volume).

In the course of ordinary maternal devotion to her infant, a facilitating mother will be able to celebrate and nurture her infant's spontaneous expressions of its needs, its id-demands, rather than impose her own needs and satisfactions as the only valid emotional currency in the interaction between her and her infant. Thus, the infant will be allowed to start life by existing and not just by reacting, gradually becoming able to recognize its id-needs and satisfactions as rightfully and acceptably its own, and utilizing them to strengthen its ego or true self. Such a mother is, in Winnicott's phrase, 'ordinarily good-enough'.

By contrast, a 'not-good-enough' mother repeatedly fails to meet her infant's spontaneous gestures, its first primitive expressions of a potential true self. Instead, she substitutes her own gesture. The infant's id-excitements become traumatic rather than ego enhancing because between them and satisfaction lies an emotional minefield. As the 'not-good-enough' mother sabotages her infant's true self potential, the infant senses that to expose the self to its mother is to risk its annihilation. It therefore takes defensive measures to protect its existence: it begins to set up a false self, to hide and so protect and preserve the true self from the impingements of the intrusive and exploitative mother. Early and extensive compliance in a baby indicates the beginnings of the formation of a false self.

In normality, a healthy false self is proof that we have foregone our infantile omnipotence, and are able to function appropriately as social beings. The ability to comply to some extent, and not to be exposed, to compromise between our desires and the environment, is an achievement. The adult who has a healthy false self is ordinarily polite and well mannered, does not constantly wear his heart on his sleeve, overexposing his true feelings and thoughts, but remains in touch with and allows the expression and satisfaction of his true desires and needs. The capacity to symbolize and be spontaneous and creative resides in the true self and is protected by the false self. In normality the false, caretaking self is a necessary and healthy defence, an ally of good and flexible adaptation.

In pathology, however, as in all defences, the false self changes from being an ally of adaptation to its enemy; from being a protector of the true self to its jailer and even, in extreme cases, as when it leads to suicide, its executioner. Winnicott (1965) described four decreasingly rigid and pathological organizations of the false self.

At the pathological extreme, the false self has set up as real: the observer meets only a truly split-off, compliant false self. When the split is so severe a chasm is created between the omnipresent false self and the lost, cut-off true self. The person may not be able to put into words the severity of her condition, but her feelings and way of relating speak of it: she has a profound dread of emptiness and 'nothingness'. Such a person may superficially appear to be doing well in life but in fact is dissociated, with poor capacity for symbolization and with marked restlessness, forever searching for impingements from external reality so that her life can be filled by reactions to these impingements. Being out of reach of a true self and therefore of creativity, she fails whenever relationships require a deeper, more meaningful bond. Whenever she is expected to be a whole person, the false self will be found wanting in some essential way.

In a less deeply split-off and pathological expression of false self organization, the true self is not entirely lost; it is acknowledged as a potential but is confined to a secret life, hidden from the rest of the world. Though the link between the true and the false self is allowed to exist, the link between the true self and the outside world is not: the true self remains hermetically sealed, secret, unrealized; the person remains deeply mistrustful, terrified that to allow outsiders to know his true self will lead to its annihilation.

In a third, less pathological organization, the true self is acknowledged and the caretaker false self looks for conditions which will allow the true self to come into its own. Though healthier than the two organizations above, it still carries the risk of suicide. If the true self seems threatened with destruction, the caretaker false self will organize a suicide, destroying the whole self in an ultimate act of defence against the betrayal and annihilation of the true self.

Finally, in the fourth and least pathological organization Winnicott described, the true self is acknowledged, but severely compromised through too great a degree of compliance. Such persons exhibit an extensive false self built on compliant identifications; they are embarrassed by and denigrate past or present expressions of their true self.

The defences and psychoanalytic technique

The clinical issue of how to deal with a patient's defensive structures has been heatedly debated amongst psychoanalysts. This is partly because of the diversity of theoretical views on defence, but it is above all because it concerns what matters most in psychoanalysis: not the theory but its clinical application within the encounter between analyst and analysand. The debate was begun by those two formidable ladies of post-Freudian psychoanalysis and pioneers of child psychoanalysis, Anna Freud and Melanie Klein.

Anna Freud developed a specific approach to defence analysis. She differentiated the defences as separate entities and argued that it was as important to explore the patient's defences as her id impulses. She was opposed to interpreting early on in an analysis, and for a number of years advocated an 'introductory phase' to nurture the development of the child's trust in the analyst before 'real analysis' could begin. Although she later abandoned this view, she always maintained that transference manifestations do not occur at the beginning of an analysis and that the negative transference in particular should not be interpreted early on. She was not convinced that children can develop a full transference, or that transference analysis is always appropriate. For example, she thought that some internal conflicts which the child was restaging as external battles with the analyst should not be interpreted within the transference, but should be explained to the child as coming from within itself. She also believed that analysis should follow the classical Freudian developmental sequence (pre-Oedipal elements should be analysed first) and so was sceptical about the analysis of very young children.

Melanie Klein thought differently. She believed that defences were not separate entities but part components of psychic constellations, so that anxieties and defences must be interpreted together. She saw no objection in analysing very young children since she believed that the transference situation is active from the very beginning of the analysis, that transference is all-enveloping and that transference interpretation is the main agent of therapeutic change. And since transference includes defences (indeed, for the post-Kleinians transference is based on projective identification), anxieties and defences, including the negative, hostile transference, must be interpreted early on in the analysis. This, Klein thought, relieved the patient and helped the analytic work, because it showed him that the analyst understood his deepest anxieties and was not afraid to take the patient where he had been afraid to go alone.

Klein's critics argued that there is something hostile in the early interpretation of defence: that it might unsettle the patient unduly, maybe even traumatize him by dismantling too abruptly the defensive structures which had helped him maintain a psychic equilibrium. Or, less dramatically, that early interpretation may cause a strengthening rather than a loosening up of defensive structures, either because the patient may feel attacked or because the interpretation may be so outside the patient's grasp that he will register it as a bee in the analyst's bonnet. Klein however thought that it was bad practice not to interpret deep anxieties and defences early on (although, as is evident in her accounts of her work, not before a number of pieces of evidence had emerged); and that to wait is to prolong the patient's suffering unnecessarily and to harm the potential of the rest of the analysis, as the patient will feel alone, anxious and not understood.[3]

There have been many developments since the initial confrontations and debates over defence analysis. Winnicott (1965) selectively criticized and adopted aspects of both approaches. In his discussion of the false self he argued that for a time it is necessary not to challenge but to work with the defensive structure of the false self – for it is the false self which has brought the patient to the analysis. But he also warned that this must be merely an initial period, during which the analyst must never forget that the function of working with a false self is to enable subsequent work with the true self. Eventually, as Winnicott put it, the caretaker or nurse who brought the patient to analysis will have to go out of the room and leave its charge and the analyst alone. Voicing one of the criticisms of Anna Freud's approach, Winnicott warned that if the analyst dwelt for too long on elements closer to the ego surface he might neglect the deeper layers of the self altogether. Too much of a 'softly-softly' approach may lull the analyst into a permanent collusion with the patient's false self. The analysis will then be itself false from start to finish; or may become interminable because the true self is absent from it.

The diversity of views regarding defence analysis today is exemplified by the plurality of opinion amongst North American psychoanalysts. At first they published extensively on defence in the context of Ego Psychology, the branch of psychoanalysis inspired by Anna Freud's focus on the study of the ego.[4] At that time, they insisted that defence analysis should be carried out in the way Anna Freud had indicated. But the subsequent winds of change in North American psychoanalytic thinking also influenced defence analysis, as shown for instance by the contrasting views of Heinz Kohut (1971) and Otto Kernberg (1974). In Kohutian Self Psychology, it is crucially important for the progress of the patient that her analyst should tolerate and leave well alone some of her narcissistic defences, especially – and most controversially – her idealization of the analyst. For Kohut, narcissistic defences are not resistances to be overcome and do not need to be interpreted. They will dissolve, he thought, without interpretation. In sharp contrast, Kernberg, inspired by – albeit also diluting – Klein, thinks that Kohut's suggestion is a recipe for bad practice. He insists that especially with borderline, narcissistic patients, it is essential to confront the patient's defences directly, and that they should be interpreted early on.

So what, you may ask, is really going on in the consulting room today? I have no hard evidence on which to base an answer, but I have formed an impression regarding clinical practice in Britain, mostly from listening to psychoanalytic colleagues' informal clinical presentations (often a better indicator of currently employed technique than published clinical work).

Many psychoanalysts continue to follow strictly a particular school's original technical orientation. For the rest, however, the old rigid differentiations between the techniques of different schools have softened very considerably. The different schools have had their own internal developments of ideas on technique; each has been variously influenced by the ideas and critique of other schools; there has been a general shift, in Britain and internationally, toward emphasizing the importance of transference interpretation and the close monitoring of the countertransference. All of these developments have had a big impact on defence analysis. Increasingly, many analysts are less inclined to adhere to one inherited clinical approach, and more inclined towards greater flexibility, integration of different approaches, and allowing themselves to be guided by the unique atmosphere which is created in the course of each analysis through the vicissitudes of transference and countertransference. This implies acknowledging that the full picture of the complexities of the human mind is far from known to psychoanalysts collectively, let alone to any single thinker or school; that no patient is the same as another; and that any analyst able to listen openly and responsively will inevitably be from slightly to considerably different with each one of her patients. An approach which is appropriate for one patient (or for one stage of an analysis) may be inappropriate for another. Differences between analytic schools have certainly not disappeared, but my impression is that this more flexible, more integrative approach is now more common. It is a more difficult approach in practice, but it is also, I believe, more true to the inquiring and open spirit of psychoanalysis, and ultimately more rewarding for patient and analyst than rigid adherence to a closely specified set of rules.

Notes

1 Freud identified and discussed four more defences in addition to the ones presented in this chapter. *Isolation* refers to the isolation of thoughts or behaviour so that their links with other thoughts or the rest of the person's life are broken. This is a defence especially characteristic of obsessional neurosis. The same neurosis also characteristically employs another defence, known as *undoing*. This is the attempt to make past thoughts, words or actions to have not occurred, by using thoughts or behaviour having the opposite meaning – a type of 'magical' thinking much more radical in its implications than denial. Finally, Freud described the defences *of turning against the self* (a mechanism which leaves the aim of the instinct unaffected but changes the object, as for example when sadism is turned round upon the person's own ego and becomes masochism); and of *reversal* – the reversal, that is, of an instinct into its opposite: this involves a change from activity to passivity (from sadism to masochism or from scopophilia to exhibitionism) or a change of content, as when love is transformed into hate.

2 Anna Freud's work was particularly influential in North America where its local offshoot, Ego Psychology, dominated North American psychoanalysis for decades, producing an extensive body of work on defence. Because of their preoccupation with ego functions, the ego psychologists were less interested in the primitive and focused on the more sophisticated defences. The interested reader may want to find out more about their contributions by following up references in the Further Reading list.
3 On both these points see Melanie Klein 'Symposium on child analysis', in *Love, Guilt and Reparation and Other Works, 1921–1945: The Writings of Melanie Klein*, vol. I (London: Hogarth Press, 1975), pp. 139–169, esp. pp. 144–5, 147. See also Klein's clinical descriptions of sessions, e.g. in 'The psychoanalytic play technique. Its history and significance' (1955) in *Envy and Gratitude and Other Works, 1946–1963: The Writings of Melanie Klein*, vol. III (London: Hogarth Press, 1987), pp. 122–40, esp. p. 124 (Rita), p. 125 (a 7-year-old girl), and p. 130 (Peter).
4   See note 3.

References

Breuer, J. and Freud, S. (1893–95) *Studies on Hysteria, Standard Edition*, vol 2, London: Hogarth Press.

Britton, R. (1998) *Belief and Imagination. Explorations in Psychoanalysis*, London: Routledge.

Bronstein, C. (ed.) (2001) *Kleinian Theory. A Contemporary Perspective*, London: Whurr.

Cooper, S.H. (1989) 'Recent contributions to the theory of defence mechanisms. A comparative view', *Journal of American Psychoanalytic Association*, 37, 4: 865–91.

Fenichel, O. (1945) *The Psychoanalytic Theory of the Neuroses*, New York: Norton.

Freud, A. (1936) *The Ego and the Mechanisms of Defence*, London: Hogarth Press.

Freud, S. (1900) *The Interpretation of Dreams, Standard Edition*, vols 4–5, pp. ix–630, London: Hogarth Press.

—— (1905) 'Fragment of an analysis of a case of hysteria', *Standard Edition*, vol. 7, pp. 3–123, London: Hogarth Press.

—— (1905) 'Three essays on the theory of sexuality', *Standard Edition*, vol. 7, pp. 124–248, London: Hogarth Press.

—— (1914) 'On the history of the psychoanalytic movement', *Standard Edition*, vol. 14, pp. 3–66, London: Hogarth Press.

—— (1915a) 'Instincts and their vicissitudes', *Standard Edition*, vol. 14, pp. 109–40, London: Hogarth Press.

—— (1915b) 'Repression', *Standard Edition*, vol. 14, pp. 141–58, London: Hogarth Press.

—— (1915c) 'The unconscious', *Standard Edition*, vol. 14, pp. 159–216, London: Hogarth Press.

—— (1915d) 'Thoughts for the times on war and death', vol. 14, pp. 273–302, London: Hogarth Press.

—— (1917) 'Mourning and melancholia', *Standard Edition*, vol. 14, pp. 237–60, London: Hogarth Press.

—— (1925) 'Negation', *Standard Edition*, vol. 19, pp. 235–42, London: Hogarth Press.

—— (1926) 'Inhibitions, symptoms and anxiety', *Standard Edition*, vol. 20, pp. 75–175, London: Hogarth Press.

—— (1940) 'Splitting of the ego in the process of defence', *Standard Edition*, vol. 23, pp. 271–8, London: Hogarth Press.

—— (1940) 'An outline of psychoanalysis', *Standard Edition*, vol. 23, pp. 141–207, London: Hogarth Press.

Gay, P. (1998) *Freud. A Life for Our Times*, New York: Norton.

Hartmann, H. (1939) *Ego Psychology and the Problem of Adaptation*, London: Imago, 1958.

Hinshelwood, R. (1989) *A Dictionary of Kleinian Thought*, London: Free Association Books.

Kernberg, O. (1974) 'Further contributions to the treatment of narcissistic personalities', *International Journal Psychoanalysis* 55: 215–40.

Klein, M. (1975) *Our Adult World and its Roots in Infancy, The Writings of Melanie Klein*, vol. 3, London: Hogarth Press, pp. 247–63.

Kohut, H. (1971) *The Analysis of the Self*, New York: International Universities Press.

Sandler, J. and Freud, A. (1985) *The Analysis of Defence: The Ego and the Mechanisms of Defence Revisited*, New York: International Universities Press.

Spillius, E. (ed.) (1988) *Melanie Klein Today*, vol. 1, London: Routledge.

—— (1994) 'Developments in Kleinian thought: overview and personal view', *Psychoanalytic Enquiry* 14, 3: 324–64.

Steiner, J. (1993) *Psychic Retreats. Pathological Organizations in Psychotic, Neurotic and Borderline Patients*, London: Routledge.

Winnicott, D.W. (1965) 'Ego distortion in terms of true and false self', *The maturational process and the facilitating environment*, London: Hogarth Press.

Suggestions for further reading

The most concentrated discussions of defence in Freud's writings are to be found in 'Leonardo de Vinci and a memory of his childhood', *Standard Edition*, vol 11, pp. 59–138 (on sublimation); his 1915 papers 'Instincts and their vicissitudes', 'Repression', and 'The unconscious', *Standard Edition*, vol. 14, pp. 109–216 (on repression, reversal, turning against the self, sublimation and reaction formation); 'Inhibitions, symptoms and anxiety' (1926 [1925]), *Standard Edition*, vol. 20, pp. 75–175 (on repression, isolation, undoing, and the 'second theory of anxiety'); 'Splitting of the ego in the process of defence' (1940 [1938]) *Standard Edition*, vol. 23, pp. 271–8; 'An outline of psychoanalysis' (1940 [1938]), *Standard Edition*, vol. 23, pp. 141–207, especially chapters VI–VIII.

For post-Freudian thinkers in the Anna Freud tradition, see Anna Freud, *The Ego and the Mechanisms of Defence* (London: Hogarth Press, 1936) especially Chapters 4–9; for Ego Psychology see H. Hartmann, *Ego Psychology and the Problem of Adaptation*, which inaugurated Ego Psychology in North America (London: Imago, 1958); O. Fenichel, *The Psychoanalytic Theory of the Neuroses* (New York: Norton, 1945), especially Chapters VIII, IX; S. H. Cooper (1989) 'Recent contributions to the theory of defence mechanisms. A comparative view', *Journal American Psychoanalytic Association* 37, 4, pp. 865–91 (a good if now somewhat dated introduction to the main North American contributions). In the Independent tradition an essential paper is D. W. Winnicott, (1960), 'Ego distortion in terms of true and false self', in *The Maturational Process and the Facilitating Environment* (London: Hogarth Press,

1965). For an excellent introduction to Melanie Klein's work and post-Kleinian developments see E. Bott Spillius (1996) 'Developments in Kleinian thought: overview and personal view', *Psychoanalytic Inquiry* 14, 3: 324–64; also R. Hinshelwood *A Dictionary of Kleinian Thought* (London: Free Association Books, 1989), especially Chapter 9; on specific defences in the Kleinian tradition see D. Bell, 'Projective identification', in C. Bronstein (ed.) *Kleinian Theory. A Contemporary Perspective* (London: Whurr, 2001), Chapter 9, pp. 125–47; R. Britton, *Belief and Imagination. Explorations in Psychoanalysis* (London: Routledge, 1998), especially the Introduction (includes discussion of projective identification); J. Steiner, *Psychic Retreats. Pathological Organizations in Psychotic, Neurotic and Borderline patients* (London: Routledge, 1993), an important contribution to the study of pathological organizations – a specific system of defence.

Chapter 2

The paranoid-schizoid position

Betty Joseph

In this chapter I want to consider the paranoid-schizoid position, how we understand it and how we see it in operation. Immediately the question arises: Why the word 'position'? As I hope to illustrate later, Melanie Klein used the word position to indicate something different from the notion of 'stages'; she used it to show the interrelating of impulses, phantasies, anxieties and defences against them in such a way as to form particular ways of relating to people, to the self and to the external world.

How then does one visualize 'positions'? I think, allowing for oversimplification one could think of broadly two types of people and their characters, familiar to all of us. One is touchy, easily taking offence, easily hurt, tending to complain and to find reasons to complain about others and finding it very difficult to accept faults or guilt in him or herself, rather self-centred, often a bit self-righteous and grand about it. The other is, a person who seems more in touch with him or herself, with his anger or misery, pleasure or appreciation, who can take some criticism and blame, even feel concern and attempt to put things right that have gone wrong and he feels are his responsibility. Being more aware of his own impulses he is able to make reasonable judgements about others and about the external world. All of us have got something of both types in us but some people gravitate more to the one type, some to the other. In this chapter I want to concentrate on the first group, those more in the paranoid-schizoid position, and look at how this position gets built up. The second, the depressive position, belongs to a separate chapter.

In her seminal paper 'Notes on some schizoid mechanisms' (1946), Klein said that she was putting forward hypotheses relating to very early stages of development which are derived from inferences from material gained in the analysis of adults and children. We have to ask ourselves: Do these hypotheses help us to understand other people and ourselves better? I put it this way because to me the idea of the two positions and their interaction has the ring of simplicity and almost obviousness that makes one feel as if one almost ought to have discovered it oneself.

If one starts in infancy one can see how the baby is born into an unknown world with all his impulses untamed, his life and death instincts. He is born with needs, such as hunger, with powerful emotions and anxieties, and he has to deal with them. How he deals with the world of reality and his inner world of feelings and fears is going to be what we call character or personality. There must therefore be a part of the infant, present at birth, that starts to deal with this chaos, a part that we would call a very primitive ego. One can almost see this ego functioning; to take as an example the infant who is hungry. The baby will cry and then may start to suck his thumb, then he may become quiet and peaceful for a time until the hunger breaks through. This is what Freud described as hallucinatory wish fulfilment and I think it is basic to our understanding of certain early mental processes. When the infant is sucking his thumb he is no longer aware of hunger, the hunger is thus split off, discomfort, pain and anxiety are got rid of and for the moment hunger can be denied. The thing he has in his mouth, the thumb, is totally good and satisfying. More than this, the infant himself is in phantasy split, he is a totally contented self and the hungry, angry self has gone, he is no longer aware of it. This works magically, omnipotently. This may seem somewhat simplistic but I think it is basic to our understanding of the whole process of splitting and its value to the personality. It gives a moment of comfort to the infant and saves him from anxiety and if the mother with breast or bottle comes in the place of the thumb, the mother and breast will be felt as all good, as ideal, loved and giving security. Here one can see the value to the infant of the very early splitting defences, but if such profound splitting continues unmitigated into later life, then one is considering serious disturbance, neurosis or psychosis.

Klein, differing here from Freud, was suggesting that the infant from the beginning of life makes an emotional relationship to its objects, not just a relationship supplying instinctual needs. Here, as throughout most of analytic literature, the word 'object' is used to denote the people to whom the individual relates, but Klein suggests that the very early relationships will not be to whole objects, the mother or father seen and experienced as a whole person, but to the part of the person the baby is in touch with, their arms, breast, voice, etc. It is only slowly over the early weeks and months that he starts to recognize his mother as a whole person. Further, we cannot assume that the infant relates to the breast or bottle as it really is: the mother may be happy and eager to feed the baby, but if the baby for whatever reason is angry and frustrated, the anger will colour what he feels about the breast or bottle. In other words the anger will be projected into the breast and the breast will then be felt as frightening and hostile. If for example he is in an angry biting mood, the breast will be felt not only as hostile but biting towards him, which will increase his anxieties and difficulties in feeding and stir up more hostility. The opposite is also true. If the infant is in a happy contented mood, the breast or bottle will be felt as good and the milk and experience will be taken in, introjected, into the infant's inner world, and help to build up a confident, warm ego.

I am discussing here how the infant, faced with an unknown world and inevitable frustration and his own impulses, builds defences to protect himself from pain and anxiety. These defences are largely based on profound splitting, splitting off and projecting out into his objects painful and disturbing parts of his self and inner world. Thus his world becomes a persecuting place which in itself arouses further defences and hostility. If the infant and young child's anxiety and disturbance are very great, the splitting may be more profound until he feels that he is falling apart or fragmenting into bits. It is of course because of the nature of these mechanisms and their preponderance in the early part of life that Klein used the term paranoid-schizoid position. When the infant or young child is largely using these mechanisms he does not recognize what are his impulses and motives. He cannot therefore be concerned about what he does to his objects. All he can do is to try to save himself, protect himself from anxiety or panic, sometimes even to the point of attempting to annihilate his mind, or his self, fragmenting himself as one can see later in life in psychotic patients.

I want now to give an example of a young child who was very much stuck in the paranoid-schizoid position, using the kind of mechanisms we are discussing here. G was a wild, very disturbed, probably borderline, boy who came into analysis aged 3. He was constantly anxious, had difficulty sleeping, was very faddy about food and hard to control at home. In the analysis he was very wild, would grab and clutch at me, kick and attack me, becoming very quickly disturbed and anxious. There was a long period when he developed a terror of a small bush growing just outside the playroom window. He thought it would come into the playroom and grab, bite and attack him or sometimes me. When I tried in some way to link his fears of the bush with his own biting, clutching behaviour with me, it was of no avail. His fears were so concrete that the interpretations apparently meant nothing. His actual way of communicating had also this very concrete nature. At times when he was extremely anxious he would go to his drawer where his play equipment was kept and pull it out violently, scattering all the contents over the floor. This behaviour looked like aggression, but I think that it was more a communication of his state of mind, how he felt that he was falling to pieces, confused, scattered and fragmenting.

There were moments when one could see a move towards less splitting and projection and towards more integration, and even some awareness of responsibility for damage. For example, in one session he broke the leg of the playroom table, and immediately took his sellotape and wrapped it round the leg, saying 'now it is mended'. In this example he took responsibility for having done the damage. Previously he would probably have turned on me saying that I, the analyst, did it, so he would have thus projected the guilt into me. He now tried to repair it, but in a way that was magic and omnipotent, because of course the table leg would not hold. He could not yet tolerate the guilt or the difficulty in repairing, and retreated in part to omnipotence and denial. However in this boy when aged about 4 or 5 one could see shifts between moments of almost total disintegration and panic states and moments of greater integration; moments when more loving feelings would come through and soften the more violent and fearful aspects.

So far I have discussed mainly aspects of projection, but alongside this is the mechanism of introjection. These are the normal, essential mechanisms of our life. Indeed one could say that just as feeding and evacuating are essential aspects of physical life, so are introjection and projection to mental life and the building of the inner world and its internal objects. And it is these internal objects that we bring unconsciously into our daily living and our expectations of life. Some individuals assume that the people they meet are likely to be friendly and understanding. Broadly speaking these individuals are ones who have introjected and built up over their early years benign, warm internal objects, giving them a sense of security. Something of this will be projected into their relationships and colour their expectations and help to bring out warmth and assurance in their response. And the opposite is also true, that people who have not been able to internalize solid good relationships are more likely to expect and probably find or provoke unsatisfactory relationships with others.

I have described the way in which such internal objects are constructed in part from what the individual projects into his relationships, but of course one cannot underestimate the importance of their actual experiences. Good experiences, comfortably stable and solid parents, a mother who is adequately in touch with her infant's needs and can respond emotionally, a breast that is reasonably available, such experiences will tend to bring out and foster good and loving feelings in the infant and enable him to introject good, warm objects. Nevertheless good parenting and good experiences will call out different responses in different children and infants. Some will respond, as I suggested, with pleasure and warmth; in others it may stir up primitive anger or envy of what the mother or father can do that the infant or child, by the nature of things, cannot. All these different aspects are going to influence the child's feelings and the nature of what he introjects, and therefore the nature of his internal world and in the long term the nature of his personality as an adult.

I have discussed how these mechanisms of projection and introjection are not only aspects of normal relating but that they are constantly used defensively, to keep the individual's equilibrium. For example, one uses projection in order to get rid of parts of the self that cause the self disturbance, but, Klein suggests, the individual does not just split an aspect off and project it out of the self but projects it into another person. Then the other person is felt to contain that part and thus to be identified with aspects of the person who split it off; this process Klein termed projective identification. A very simple and familiar kind of example is when anyone has a minor car crash. The fault is very rarely felt by either of the drivers to be his or hers; it is almost invariably projected into the other driver who becomes the guilty person, guilt I suspect being one of the hardest emotions to bear. In other words the guilt is not only projected out, but is located in another person.

There are of course many different reasons for using projective identification. It enables the individual to get rid of anxiety, pain or guilt as in the example just quoted. Parts of the self and impulses can be projected to avoid specific feelings such as inferiority or envy. We are probably all familiar with individuals who seem to be always in a rather superior role, admired and in some way always envied by others. A patient would describe how frequently it seemed to happen that when she visited a professional person, doctor, etc. they became attracted to her, or some special relationship with them was established. It was never clear to me how much this was actually so or how much it was largely in the patient's phantasy; I suspect probably both. In the analysis it could be seen that she never really admired other people's achievements, including those of her analyst, but had to feel herself to be the special and admired figure. In this way she avoided the problems of ordinary inferiority and envy. Of course the strong projection of envy in such a way creates new problems, since the individual then feels gratified by her own superiority but fearful of the hostility and envy of people around her.

In this example and in many others, projective identification is also aimed at controlling the object. Sometimes when a patient talks in a very gloomy and hopeless way about himself and the treatment, we may find that it is not just an expression of his sense of depression and desolation, but that it is also unconsciously intended to project into the analyst a sense of hopelessness, since not just to get rid of it but to get it into the analyst makes him hopeless and prevents him or her from working constructively. Another very important example of a different use of projective identification is that of the patient who in phantasy projects part of his mind into the analyst's mind and takes it over, then starting to speak or even write about ideas which have clearly been picked up from the analyst, the patient remaining unconscious of this. Or similarly we find the patient who will bring dreams but seems only to bring associations which are possible interpretations, suggesting that he has become so much identified with the analyst that his patient self cannot for the moment be found.

A further important motive for using projective identification is that of communicating something that the patient is unable to express other than concretely. I described an example of this in the child who pulled out his drawer scattering the contents in chaos, and discussed how this gave the analyst a powerful indication of the state of his mind and his inner world.

If we turn to the receiving end of the process, we find that sometimes the analyst is affected by the projective identification and perhaps only knows about it because he is affected; at other times he may remain quite unaffected. To return to the kind of example I suggested earlier, the patient who talks in a very hopeless and gloomy way about the treatment and his future, this may so much get into the analyst that he too feels hopeless, finds himself thinking it may not be worth going on for long, perhaps the patient is right he might as well give up. Or if we think of a slightly manic patient who is quietly humorous or a bit clever with words, this may in fact invade the analyst who may find himself being slightly funny or clever in response. He may only recognize what is going on in the patient and the nature of the projective process when he becomes aware of his own emotions. All this has of course very important bearings on the whole question of countertransference, which is taken up in Chapter 12.

Often we find that projective identification does not touch the analyst but exists only in the patient's phantasy, as for example when the patient starts by saying that the analyst seems tired or bored today and the patient wonders why. The analyst may have absolutely no feeling of being bored or tired but feels ordinarily alert, and one can only assume that the patient has projected these feelings into the analyst and they have no basis in reality. This however raises an important issue; the patient may indeed have observed something in the appearance or behaviour of the analyst which indicates boredom or tiredness, and it is most important not to interpret as if something that the patient might actually have observed was just a projection. If the individual uses a great deal of projective identification as a way of keeping his equilibrium, it must have some effect on his personality and relationships. To return to an earlier example, the patient who cannot tolerate feelings of rivalry and envy may unconsciously project them into his objects and then behave in a quiet and apparently uncompetitive way, but this is likely to lead to anxieties about the rivalry, envy and hostility of others towards him which he may try to ward off by becoming placatory or by not allowing people to know about any success he has, or even by avoiding being successful. A further effect of the powerful use of projective identification is its leading to what Klein called 'a compulsive tie' to the people involved. This can be seen in individuals who are involved in a relationship, such as a sadomasochistic one, which seems to cause pain and distress but which despite constant complaints they cannot give up. If they do succeed in doing so we are likely to find that the next partner they choose is very similar.

When a patient constantly projects parts of the self or inner world into their objects, one result must be that he or she loses touch with those parts. They no longer seem to be part of him and he may appear passive, rather flat or what is sometimes described as an empty personality. The probability is that he is constantly emptying himself into others. I want to illustrate this by bringing material from a patient who left analysis some time ago but who remains rather vividly in mind. This was a woman in her middle twenties who seemed very much stuck in the paranoid-schizoid position. She had difficulty being close to people so that her relationships were very limited. She seemed highly intelligent but was holding a simple, almost unskilled job. In the analysis her material seemed repetitive and strangely superficial. When I made an interpretation she would pause, but the pause did not seem thoughtful rather as if the words and meaning were falling apart, or she might agree but would rarely take things further, or she would just go on to another topic so that I rarely felt that what I had said was of much use.

I shall focus on a dream that she brought in about the fourth year of the analysis. The patient was in a large place, something was going wrong, she was on one side of the place, the analyst on the other. I, the analyst took it on myself to phone for help, my patient felt resigned and sad. She thought, would the phone call be helpful or make more trouble since the police might just burst in. In this dream I think that one can see various elements of the patient's attitude and behaviour in her life which are reflected in the analysis, particularly her hope and yet her suspicion, doubt, sense of persecution. There is an awareness that something is going wrong, that she needs help, but the analyst is kept at a great distance, the other side of the place as we could see in the session with the long pauses and constant withdrawal of contact. The various figures carry split-off aspects of the patient and the analyst. She splits off her need for help and the active part that could seek help into me, I do the phoning and she remains passive and resigned. But I am also the police, the person whom she feels might help, but who is also experienced as dangerous as they might just burst in. This is interesting since in fact I am so frequently put into the position of either waiting and getting almost nowhere in the pauses and shifts, or feeling the need to break in and disturb the apparent passivity and resignation. The lack of proper communication in the sessions is also expressed in the dream with my patient knowing help is needed but not herself picking up the phone. The bursting in I think also refers to her fear of the actual analytic process, of my thoughts and ideas breaking into her mind, even that I expect her to change is a process to be defended against. In this material there is no indication of the patient herself attempting to take any active responsibility for getting help or putting things right. She can only attempt to protect herself from danger largely located in the analyst/police. From this brief material one can get an idea of how the use of splitting and projective identification in this patient leads to a kind of passivity and to an apparently empty personality.

In this chapter I have tried to discuss how various defences such as splitting, idealization, denial and projective identification are normal mechanisms in early infancy when the infant is largely unintegrated and necessarily attempts to ward off anxiety and pain at all costs, even to the cost of breaking up and fragmenting his own mind. In this state he can only try to protect himself, he cannot be concerned about what he is doing in fact or in phantasy to his objects. A sense of responsibility and concern for his objects can only come later as, if all goes reasonably well, he becomes increasingly integrated and moves towards the depressive position. However we have to recognize that we all continue at times to use these early paranoid-schizoid mechanisms defensively throughout our lives if the emotional strains become more than unconsciously we feel that we can manage.

Reference

Klein, M. (1946) 'Notes on some schizoid mechanisms', *International Journal of Psychoanalysis*, 27: 99–110. Revised version in M. Klein, P. Heimann, S. Isaacs and J. Rivière, *Developments in Psycho-Analysis*, London: Hogarth Press, 1952, pp. 292–320. Reprinted in *The Writings of Melanie Klein*, vol. 3, pp. 1–24, London: Hogarth Press, 1975, Virago, 1997.

Suggestions for further reading

The fundamental paper here is Klein's (1946) 'Notes on some schizoid mechanisms', reprinted in *Envy and Gratitude and Other Works, 1946–1963* (London: Hogarth Press, 1975). From then on the notion of the paranoid-schizoid position and its relation to the depressive position permeates her writing. It is elaborated and more fully developed in 'Some theoretical conclusions regarding the emotional life of the infant' (1952) also reprinted in *Envy and Gratitude*. Klein felt that her understanding of the mechanisms of the paranoid-schizoid position must throw light not only on normal development but also on the development and possible treatment of psychotic states. This certainly turned out to be so as can be seen in the writing of three of her junior colleagues: Wilfred R. Bion, *Second Thoughts* (London: Heinemann, 1967); Herbert Rosenfeld, *Psychotic States: A Psychoanalytical Approach* (London: Hogarth Press, 1965); and Hanna Segal, 'Schizophrenia and schizoid mechanisms', in *The Work of Hanna Segal: A Kleinian Approach to Clinical Practice* (New York: Jacob Aronson, 1981; reprinted London: Free Association Books and the Maresfield Library, 1986).

Chapter 3

The depressive position

Priscilla Roth

'Grief is the price we pay for love,' said the Queen, at a memorial service for the British victims of the September 11 attacks in New York and Washington. I was struck by her words because they seemed true and moving, and because they seemed to be a very concise description of Klein's concept of the depressive position. Grief is the price we pay for love.

I want to begin my discussion of the depressive position by describing a period in the analysis of a patient which took place in the autumn of 2001. At that time Mrs A, a married woman, was in her mid-thirties and had a two-and-a-half-year-old daughter. She had been in analysis with me for about five years and she had gradually begun to value her analysis, which she frequently felt helped by. However, in September, 2001, she returned from the summer holiday saying she was feeling 'high'; she said she had felt good all summer, and now did not feel she needed to be in analysis any more. We spoke about this in various ways, as various problems and issues came up, and over the weeks she came to feel, again, how important her analysis was to her, especially, she said, because it helped her not to 'disconnect' from herself, her husband and daughter, and her thoughts and feelings about her mother who had died the previous year.

The part of her analysis I want to describe comes from the week just before the half-term break in October 2001. (It will be clear in a moment why I am emphasizing the date.) I had told Mrs A early in September that I would be taking an unusually long break at half term: I would be away for a Friday and then the following week. On the Monday of the week before the break, the patient missed her session. She phoned to say the babysitter had not arrived to look after her little girl. So the following sessions took place on the Tuesday, Wednesday and Thursday of this last week before the break, in early October.

Mrs A began the Tuesday session by confirming the dates for the break. She then told me that she had not slept at all over the weekend. Her sleeplessness began on Friday night when she was up literally all night. She could not sleep; she kept thinking she heard a child crying, although in fact her daughter wasn't crying, she was fast asleep. She had felt unsettled and anxious all weekend. After a moment, she said maybe it had something to do with the fact that it was her own birthday on Sunday; but then she remembered that she had started feeling awful on the Friday night. Friday evening she had gone to a party at work and she had heard a couple talking about the bombing of Afghanistan which had just begun, and she had become furious. She said, 'I thought those stupid Americans! This is America doing exactly what Americans always do – throwing its weight around, behaving like it owns the world. They think they rule the world! The whole thing is all America's fault in any case. September 11th was really just what they deserved – although obviously they cannot admit that. Horrible Bush,' she added. 'He is bent on retaliation.'

There was a tremendous amount of cold vicious hatred in her voice. Although I had been hearing from other patients about their concern about all the events which began with 9/11, this felt different. I felt stunned at the degree of powerful and what felt like personal hatred. Of course I understood that the patient, like any patient, had an absolute right to her own political opinion. But I felt quite sure that these explosive remarks contained something more than the expression of political feelings.

After a few minutes I spoke to her about what I thought was going on. I said that she and I both know that it is a fact of her life that she has an analyst who is American. She nodded. I continued, saying that I did not think she could say what she had said in the way she had said it without it having something to do with me. She nodded again. I then spoke to her about what I thought were her feelings on the Friday night and the weekend: I spoke about her birthday, which I hadn't known about, which I thought got mixed up in her mind with her mother who wasn't there on her birthday. I spoke about the break coming up, which was obviously very much on her mind (remember she had checked the dates with me at the beginning of the session), and about the weekend break we had just had – all of which I thought left her feeling unhappy and lonely and angry. But most importantly I spoke to her about her recognition the week before of my importance to her. I said that when she is aware of how important the analysis is, and then is faced with the weekend, and the coming break, and my not having her birthday in mind – and how it links with her mother, not there for her birthday – she feels I am part of a powerful American force (perhaps a couple?) who bombs her and attacks her by making her feel jealous and left out and lonely – like a small child crying in the night – which I thought was the child she kept hearing. I said I thought it had felt like a horrible attack to be made to feel so left out and alone, and I thought today she was really attacking me back: really 'bent on retaliation'.

She responded by saying, 'I see what you mean about the attack on you. I can see that. But . . . I cannot believe that at heart you don't agree with me about the American position. I'm sure you do. I have no doubt you do.' In other words, she could *partly* see what I meant, but she could not really feel it, could not really take it on board.

On the following day she reported that she was still not sleeping well, but then went on to complain bitterly about her daughter, who had a cold and was 'grotty'. She said she hates it when the little girl gets like this. She wants her to go back to how she was before she had the cold, and she feels completely hopeless about it. She thinks she will be like this forever, somehow ruined and not as good as she used to be. The daughter was up with a stuffy nose, and kept my patient up a lot. She was furious with her. She said, 'I cannot tolerate it, cannot stand it. I hate her when she's like this . . . everything I try to do for her is no good, everything fails. I don't know what's wrong with her – she is sick, cold and uncomfortable – I do everything and she keeps crying and it makes me hate her. I feel she is getting at me, accusing me, blaming me for not making her feel better. This is not the daughter I wanted to have!' Then, very much as an afterthought, she added that she had left the little girl at a new nursery on that day.

Finally, in the early morning, right before she had had to get up to come to this session, she had fallen asleep for an hour, and during that time she had had a dream. In the dream she was in a house with Mrs Kelly, a friend of her mother's. She was talking to Mrs Kelly and suddenly she started to sing an Irish song, very loudly. She could see that her singing was waking up her little girl, but she could not stop, she just sang louder and louder and louder. It was a horrible dream, she said.

She told me that Mrs Kelly was a 'good Catholic' woman who lived next door to the mother's house in Ireland. Mrs Kelly used to give the patient instructions about how she had to marry a Catholic boy, in the church, and to raise her children as Catholics. Mum used to use Mrs Kelly as back-up: instead of asking the patient, 'Do you still go to Mass?' she would say, 'Mrs Kelly was asking whether you still go to Mass . . .'

To summarize up to this point: There was the weekend, with her birthday, and the anticipation of the half-term break at the end of the coming week. Then came the first session back, the Tuesday, when she attacked me with full force. I think it was an attack on my connections with things that she thinks matter to me: my homeland, my history, my background – my good objects. In that session I tried to help her understand that she had attacked me, and why, but I did not feel I could get through to her – she understood the words, but not the real meaning of what I was saying.

But she had gone home after that session and (as she reported the next day in the session I have just described) had felt persecuted by her child. She felt that her daughter was attacking her by blaming her, by not getting better, by not being the daughter she wanted her to be. She felt completely unforgiving. She maintained that she had no idea what was wrong with her daughter, although she let me know that she had left her at a new nursery that afternoon. So: there is a bad hateful little girl, attacking her mother, who does not love her because she is so attacking and complaining. Or, put the other way, there is a bad mother who hates her child for attacking her, and cannot love her, and wishes she were a better child. Then comes the dream, in which my patient is madly, wildly trying to please Mrs Kelly, by singing Irish songs louder and louder.

I think that after the attack on me on Tuesday, my patient was unable, even with my help, to take on board how hateful she felt and how attacking she had been. I think she literally could not imagine that I could both understand the ferocity of her attack, and forgive her and go on caring about her. So when she went home she became horribly persecuted by her little girl's complaints. Instead of being able to know, deep down inside, how awful she had been to me, she became a hating mother herself – absolutely hating the little girl who made her life so difficult that evening. I think her inability to love and feel compassion for and patience towards her little girl was a mirror of what she unconsciously feared would be my feelings towards her: utterly unforgiving. This is important. It is an example of how the picture of one's object is changed by the ferocity of one's own feelings: she attacks me with hatred, she is then convinced that I hate her, and that I don't want a daughter/patient like her.

This is, of course, a terrible state to be in: hating your object and feeling completely hated by your object. She had attacked her object; her object then is felt to hate and persecute her. So she has a dream, and in the dream she is trying desperately to please her object: in this case Mrs Kelly who is linked with her mother and, via the national loyalty (Irish songs), linked with the American me she attacked on Tuesday. In the dream she is trying with all her might to sing loud enough to make things better. She is singing louder and louder, I think, to silence the awful feelings of guilt she might otherwise have to be aware of, a guilt which she thinks she cannot bear. But she lets me know that there is a tiny little bit of worry about what she has done – a precursor maybe to feelings of guilt and responsibility floating just in the periphery of her vision, as it were. She lets me know she left her child at a new nursery yesterday, and that she is worried that she will start to feel guilty about this.

I conveyed all these thoughts to her over the session, and we worked very hard to try to understand the links between feeling attacked by my absence over the weekend, attacking me, feeling horribly persecuted and hated, and a desperate manic attempt to make things better. When she left at the end of the session I felt she was more in touch with what had been going on. This seemed confirmed in the next session, the Thursday, the last day before the half-term break. She told me she had slept well for the first time all week on Wednesday night. She said she feels better today. She knows she dreamed a lot during the night, but she could only remember one funny dream. It was just the name of a character in her dream: Leonard Lewis. That was all she remembered. She said she did not know anyone with that name, it was a puzzle to her. The only Lewis she can think of is Lennox Lewis, the fighter. She does not like boxing; she thinks it is awful. And the only Leonard she can think of is Leonard Cohen, the folk singer. She does not really know anything about either of them, she said, except that she really, really likes Leonard Cohen.

After some discussion I said to her that I thought Leonard Lewis was a bringing together of two versions of me in her mind: someone she fights with, and who she does not like; and also someone she *really* likes, and I thought that being able to bring these two aspects of me together had come about through the work we had done during the week. She was silent for awhile, and then said she felt sad that the session was now coming to an end, and that the week was ending – and why could I not have helped her to feel better sooner? But then, after a moment, she added sadly that of course she had not come on Monday, and had been late on the Tuesday, and that must have also slowed things down. As she left the session, she turned around and, *very unusually* smiled at me and said, 'Thank you. I hope you have a good break. I'll see you a week from Monday.' That's the end of the clinical material – but I will come back to it.

In Klein's (1935) paper 'A contribution to the psychogenesis of manic-depressive states', she includes right at the beginning the idea that the infant is at something she refers to as the height of sadism in his first months (Klein 1998: 262). This seems like a very disturbing idea, but it was an important one. In this paper Klein introduces the depressive position – a concept which gives psychoanalytic meaning and structure to such human emotions as pity, grief, remorse, longing and love. In order to talk about these, the most precious feelings we have, she had to talk about infantile sadism, even to describe it in very specific detail, because she had come to feel that our capacity to experience the precious ones (pity, grief, love, and so on) is intimately, causally related to the ways we have of coping with the others. That is, that our capacity to experience love is related to the ways we have of dealing with our hatred.

Beginning with this paper and continuing through the rest of her life, Klein explored what she described as two different positions: the paranoid-schizoid position and the depressive position. As has often been described, these positions have their origin in early childhood, but remain throughout life the two elemental structures of emotional life: they are two different modes of psychic functioning. Each of the two positions is characterized by its own type of relationships. Each has its own anxieties and its own defence mechanisms.

Briefly, the paranoid-schizoid position is the infant's first way of structuring his experiences. He does this by splitting and projection. In order to keep his good feelings and good objects safe in his mind – far away from his hatred and pain – he divides his perception of his world into two, and his feelings about each of the two are absolute. He is the owner of all that is good; all that is bad is not-him. Love of himself and his object, which are felt to be one, is perfect. When it exists there is only love, and self and object are the same. Hatred, when it comes, is all-powerful and totally menacing – nothing good remains in mind because there is no awareness of past or of future. *In the paranoid-schizoid position, all experiences are absolute.* As adults, we can retreat to a paranoid-schizoid state of mind when we are threatened by too much anxiety, or by illness, or by traumatic events.

Now, somewhere towards the end of the first half of the baby's first year – at around four to six months old – the gradual physical maturation of his mental capacities means that the infant is able to perceive the world more accurately and begins to hold things in mind, and to remember past experiences. This is a developmental step of enormous proportions, because the infant's developing capacity to perceive his world more accurately confronts him with a new reality: that he has only one mother, and that she is the source of the goodness in his world; it is her milk that feeds him, her arms that enclose him and her eyes that hold him. And as he realizes that she *is*, and is *expectable* and *rememberable*, he is filled with love for her. Loving her, when he takes in her milk and the attention in her eyes and the comfort of her arms, he feels he has her in himself, he feels loved and loving inside himself. These are powerful and wonderful feelings. They are the feelings we search for and, if we are fortunate, find again later in adult form: a belief that we are loving and that we are loved.

For infants, as later for adults, the possibility of losing these feelings is terrifying. The infant, now capable of more realistic perceptions, is faced with the fact that this good mother, whom he loves, is the exact same person as the bad mother whom he hates. There is only one mother, and she combines the attributes of what he thought were two polar opposite 'mothers'. And, equally as difficult, this one mother, whom he sometimes loves and sometimes hates, who is sometimes experienced as good and sometimes bad, *is a different person from him*; not part of his very self, but a whole person, with different qualities and utterly separate from him. These new and very disturbing realizations usher in the depressive position.

Faced with one complete and separate loved object, the infant is confronted with a whole new set of anxieties. Whereas in the paranoid-schizoid position, his anxiety was about threats to himself – the danger of falling to pieces, or being consumed himself by rage – in the depressive position he has to worry about his good object. When he could split his object into two – good and bad – he did not have to worry about his good object. When it was good it was completely good and he only loved it. Now, however, he feels that this very loved person, who he needs so much and values so much, is in constant danger: she can choose to go away from him and disappear, she can look angry with him or tired, and then he feels he has lost her love of him. Most dangerous of all, when he is angry with her he can tear her apart in his mind, attack her with all his rage and fury. Because he loves her, he worries about her and worries about losing her love of him and his of her – because he is afraid that his hatred of her will be stronger than his love, and will wipe out his love for her and hers for him.

This is what happened with Mrs A. I said a moment ago that the baby feels held not just physically but psychologically by his mother's arms and by her attention. If her arms and her attention are taken away, he can survive for a while, but if he is left for too long, or if the circumstances are too difficult for him to bear, he begins to feel not-held-together – he begins to fall apart. And he may experience the falling to pieces as an explosion: what might, to an adult, feel like a bombing of his very self. Once Mrs A began to really value her analysis, the birthday weekend, with its painful reminder of her mother's permanent absence, and the anticipation of the longer than usual half-term break, resulted in feeling of tremendous, uncontainable anger with me (and, of course, behind that, with her mother for not being there any more). At that point her hatred overcame her love; she exploded in a vicious attack, and she was then convinced that I would hate her in return – retaliate by withdrawing my love from her. This was the persecution – she is surrounded by hate inside and out. Daughters hate mothers; mothers hate daughters.

What had happened could be described as a retreat from the depressive position – in which she can value me and the analysis, and also be loving and patient with her daughter – back into the paranoid-schizoid position where she is Good and Righteous, and both the daughter and I are bad and persecuting. Why does this happen? I think it happens because the pain of that particular weekend was too much for her to bear. It was psychologically easier for her to attack me, make me bad and horrible in her mind, retaliate against me, than for her to be aware that the analyst she was hating was also the analyst she values and loves. She could not, at the weekend, or early in the following week, bring these two sets of feelings about me together. (It is probably important to emphasize that behind these feelings about me were much more longstanding feelings about her mother, whom she loved very much, but also now passionately hated for having died and left her. This was very, very hard for her to know about.)

Guilt about how much we can hate and attack our most loved objects *is* hard to know about. The drama of the depressive position – for the infant facing it for the first time, or for the adult facing it for the umpteenth time in later life – is the recognition of one's dependency on a much loved object, separate and distinguishable from oneself, whom one also sometimes powerfully hates and attacks. Now you might ask, 'Why would we hate people we love?' And I would answer, 'For a number of reasons. We hate them because they inevitably frustrate us. But we also hate because we have hateful feelings inside which are part of our very nature, which we frequently direct towards the most important people in our lives. And we hate them because we need them so much. And because we envy them the very qualities we need from them. But at some basic level we also hate our most loved objects because we have to recognize that fundamentally they don't belong to us: they are their own separate, individual, unique selves, with their own thoughts and points

of view. They are not, however much we try to make them so, our possessions.'
In the paranoid-schizoid position, our relationship with our loved objects
is 'narcissistic' – we manage to convince ourselves that our loved ones are
actually parts of ourselves – an extension of or a possession of ME (*my*
husband, *my* best friend). In this way we eradicate difference and the experience of dependency – if he/she is MINE, he or she belongs to me – her
desirable qualities are actually part of the Larger Me.

Patients in analysis often for a long time think of their analysts as 'my
analyst', without any other qualities or functions. They pay a kind of lip
service to the idea that the analyst has a life outside of their sessions –
husband, children, ordinary feelings, dental appointments, etc. – but they
don't really believe it. Not really. Mrs A used to tell me that much as she knew
I must live in a real house and do real things, she had a kind of fantasy which
she could not quite get rid of, that after her session I sort of went into the
closet in the consulting room and waited there, having been 'put away' until
her next session. She knew it could not be true . . . but still.

These recent sessions that I told you about in detail at the beginning, with
the attack on America, came at the point where she was beginning to be
able to recognize that I am a real person, and thus to feel left out and
jealous on weekends and at breaks. One way we could think about the
attack on America – or the attack on an American – material I described
above is the way it was an attack on her growing recognition that I do have
real links – maybe a husband and children, but in this case my own history
and background and loved experiences and loved objects. When she says,
'You *must* see things as I do, feel the same as me about what America is
doing', she is really saying, 'I cannot bear that you have different connections with *them*, which don't include me. If I have to know that you are
separate from me, I will hate you.'

As I say, these sessions came at a point in Mrs A's analysis when she
was struggling with all these different feelings: loving and hating the same
person, bringing different bits of her objects together in her mind, recogniz-
ing things about herself which were painful to know about – in other words,
an increasing capacity to have a fuller, more inclusive sense of herself and the
important people in her life. So she did not simply stay in this paranoid
place where she is good and the American is bad. She had to deal with her
ambivalence.

She began to deal with it, I think, in her dream – the dream in which she is
singing loudly to placate or appease or please Mrs Kelly. She was trying to
make things better – but she was trying to do so in a way which could not
work: she had to sing louder and louder, and it wasn't really a successful way
of making up for the damage she felt she had done. What she was doing was
what is called manic reparation. She was trying to repair things, to repair her
felt-to-be-damaged objects, but trying to do it without actually acknowledging inside herself – without really knowing about – how vicious her attack

had been *and had been meant to be*. She had been trying to make reparation without taking on board the very real hatred and destructiveness of the attack.

We all know about manic reparation and we all engage in it sometimes. The wish to buy my mother the best birthday present she's ever had, or to cook the biggest, most delicious meal ever, or to throw the greatest party, or write the best paper – all these are ways we try to convince ourselves that we are good, valuable, worthwhile, to set against our awareness that we sometimes attack and damage the people we love – that it is in our very nature to do so.

Manic reparation does not work, because deep down we know it is not truthful. It is a denial of psychic reality. For Mrs A, singing the Irish song did not work, no matter how loudly she sang. On the other hand, facing all of this in her analysis, slowly, painfully getting to know about the variety and multiplicity and complexity of her feelings – her bad feelings as well as her good, but her good feelings as well as her bad – did help her to bring different parts of herself together, and different parts of her object together in her mind. By the time she could tell me about Leonard Lewis – the fighter and the folk singer, she was moving back into a real depressive position.

I spoke earlier about Mrs A having been like a baby who had lost her mother's arms and her attention, and felt she was falling to pieces. It is my belief that when I began to pick up the pieces of her experience, and to bring them together by understanding why she felt as she did and why her world had begun to feel so persecuting to her, she felt she was once again being held by my 'mental arms'; and that she had been given back her own 'mental skin'. This is the beginning of a process of internalization – she begins to internalize not so much *me* as my function of thinking with her. *I* gather the pieces of her mind together, *she* begins to take that quality inside herself and have a mind which can think for herself and make links for herself. So that she could then be grateful to me for helping her feel better, annoyed with me for not getting there sooner and for going away the following week, and aware of her own contribution to the imperfect but meaningful place we had got to. Gradually, over time, this internalization establishes a sense of a good object firmly inside her mind – it becomes an 'internal object'.

I want to address a different issue now. It is the question: why do we call it *the depressive position*? What does *the depressive position* have to do with depression? A very simple answer – and one which addresses only the psychological aspect of depression and leaves aside any biological causes and concomitants – is to suggest that severe depression can be described as a consequence of an individual's not having been able to work through the depressive position; that is, not having been able to establish a solid enough sense of good relations with his internal objects.

Let's go back to the beginning. Into the apprehension of the small baby floats a new idea: the world is not black and white, good and bad. The world is beginning to get complicated. Goodness is not my possession. Badness is not all located outside me. Disturbingly, I too can be a source of badness. A new reality becomes inescapable: I cannot protect the one I love and need either from the dangers of the outside world or from the destructive power of my own hatred. This is a moment at which the boundaries between what is Good and what is Bad have become porous. The shocking though gradual recognition that badness – anger, cruelty, rage, envy, jealousy – exists as a part of himself, they are *his* emotions, leads in the infant and then later in the adult to a state of mind we call depression. We all know what it feels like. It is a feeling of badness inside, a sense that one is without any experience of internal goodness. As the child's sense of itself becomes integrated and its sense of the world becomes more realistic, it will go through an experience which is an infantile version of depression.

However, the fact that his murderous rage does not *actually* murder his mother, and that the murderous rage soon gives way to tender feelings of concern, teaches the child a very important lesson: that his objects recover, and perhaps even more important, that he recovers his love for them. It teaches him that his love is stronger than his hate. This is the beginning of the working through of the depressive position – the repeated experience that one's objects in one's mind, one's internal sense of one's objects, have survived one's hatred of them. As adults, our inner resilience depends very much on our sense that we can restore and repair our objects in our mind.

But sometimes circumstances are so devastating that these ambivalent feelings cannot be tolerated. The mind simply cannot contain them, at least not without the most sensitive help. I saw a documentary film on television some years ago about the painter Frank Auerbach. Auerbach is a great painter, as was obvious in a recent retrospective of his work at the Royal Academy in London. One of the most striking features of Auerbach's painting is that he paints the same subjects over and over again: a handful of sitters painted repeatedly over a lifetime; a small patch of the world – the streets and buildings around his Camden Town studio – his neighbourhood, which he paints again and again. He describes himself as always working – desperately sometimes – to get onto his canvas the precise moment, the *reality* of the person or the place. He pursues this goal remorselessly, literally 364 days of every year, year after year. He does almost nothing else. He is compelled to do it.

A number of critics have discussed Auerbach's way of painting in terms of his history, and knowing about his history gives us some insight into what he may be attempting to do. In the documentary I mentioned, Auerbach described his childhood as perfectly ordinary – a comfortable, upper middle class, happy Jewish childhood in Vienna. But in 1939, when he was just under 8 years old, his parents sent him to England to protect him from the Nazis.

He received a few letters from them at the beginning, but of course very soon the letters stopped coming and he never heard from or saw them again. Asked about this tragedy, he looks puzzled and bemused: 'I don't think I thought much about it,' is how he described himself in the film. 'It was just the next thing that happened.' And then, still within the interview, he suddenly remembered that his mother had packed a small suitcase for him to take to England. He remembered that it had had clothes for him to wear that year, but also bigger clothes, marked with a red cross, for him to wear the following years, as he grew bigger without her. And she had packed some tablecloths and linens, he remembered, for him to have when he grew up. He had lost the suitcase with its contents years ago, he said. He did not know what happened to it.

Auerbach paints because he is a painter. But I would like to suggest the possibility that he paints in the way he does because he carries forever the heavy ghosts of his unrememberable parents and childhood home. And that he has forever to try to capture and hold on to, to get down once and for all, and to get it down right, the faces he loves and the places he loves: that nothing can interfere with this because nothing matters more than his desperate attempts to remember, to restore, to repair, to record and to recreate what has been lost.

References

Klein, M. (1935) 'A contribution to the psychogenesis of manic-depressive states', *International Journal of Psychoanalysis* 16: 145–74; reprinted in *Contributions to Psychoanalysis* (London: Hogarth Press, 1948) and *Love, Guilt and Reparation and Other Works 1921–1945* (London: Vintage, 1998).

Suggestions for further reading

The paper in which Klein first describes the depressive position is, as noted above, M. Klein (1935) 'A contribution to the psychogenesis of manic-depressive states', *International Journal of Psychoanalysis* 16: 145–74; reprinted in *Contributions to Psycho-analysis* (London: Hogarth Press, 1948) and *Love, Guilt and Reparation and Other Works 1921–1945* (London: Vintage, 1998).

For Klein's further thoughts about the depressive position and a moving account of the relationship between mourning and depression, read M. Klein (1940) 'Mourning and its relation to manic-depressive states', *International Journal of Psychoanalysis* 21; reprinted in *Contributions to Psycho-analysis* (London: Hogarth Press, 1948) and *Love, Guilt and Reparation and Other Works 1921–1945* (London: Vintage, 1998). For a discussion of manic reparation see H. Segal 'Manic reparation', in *The Work of Hanna Segal, A Kleinian Approach to Clinical Practice* (New York: Jason Aronson, 1981; reprinted London: Free Association Books and the Maresfield Library, 1986); also P. Roth (1999) 'Absolute zero: a man who doubts his own love . . .', *International Journal of Psychoanalysis* 80: 661–70.

For examples from psychoanalytic practice and a clear description of the depressive position, see R.D. Hinshelwood, 'The depressive position', in *Clinical Klein* (London: Free Association Books, 1994). For a helpful and brief discussion of the relation between Freud's work and the work of Melanie Klein, see R. Caper, 'Melanie Klein's place in psychoanalysis', in *Immaterial Facts. Freud's Discovery of Psychic Reality and Klein's Development of his Work* (New Jersey: Jason Aronson, 1988), pp.123–30.

Chapter 4

Envy and its relationship to guilt and projective identification

Kate Barrows

The malignant power of envy was recognised long before the discoveries of Freud and his followers. It is, after all, one of the seven deadly sins, and in the opinion of Chaucer:

> [It is] the worst sin that is. For all other sins are directed against one virtue: but envy is against all virtues and all goodnesses: for it is unhappy about all the bounties of his neighbour ... there is first sorrow of another man's goodness and of his prosperity and then ... joy of another man's harm: and that is properly like the devil, that ever rejoiceth him of man's harm.
>
> (Chaucer 1958 [1388]: 691).

The singular feature of envy is that it attacks goodness without any other positive aim. Unhappiness about the goodness and good fortune of others and pleasure in their misfortunes can only lead to damage and destruction, whereas all other 'sins', however self-seeking, serve to obtain an object of desire, so that possession is a primary aim. For instance, jealousy may lead to attacking a rival rather than the person we love or at least want to possess. This was acknowledged in French law by the recognition of a *crime passionel* (crime of passion) where the sentence for a murder motivated by jealous love was less severe than it was for a murder committed for any other reason. Jealousy involves a third person or element: something or someone that we want to possess, whereas in envy we destroy what we also desire or admire. The only apparent gain is that in spoiling the source of envy we may hope to rid ourselves of the envy itself, for it is an emotion which it is particularly hard to bear.

Before going further it is important to distinguish between two different uses of the term envy. The first is often employed in everyday terms to describe the pangs which sometimes accompany great admiration, and the recognition that someone has a capacity or skill which we either do not have at all, or at least not in such great measure. This does not necessarily lead to an attack on the admired person: we may admire someone's artistic capacities with a pang of envy, but nevertheless feel inspired by their gifts and feel that our view of the world is enhanced by them. This has been termed 'emulatory envy'. The term was first used by Lois Munro, expressing her appreciation of Klein's first presentation of her seminal paper on envy (Klein 1957). Munro felt awe-inspired, and experienced the kind of envy that is both painful and productive; indeed, her definition of emulatory envy sprang from her experience of it (I. Menzies Lyth, personal communication). It differs from the more disturbing, damaging form of envy which cannot endure the untarnished existence of that which is admired.

Psychoanalysts have found this second type of envy to be one of the greatest hindrances to progress in analysis, because the envious patient attacks the insight which he needs and deprives himself, as well as the analyst, of the satisfaction of understanding and hence of the possibility of change. After a helpful session, in which new insights have been gained, a patient may come back in a startlingly negative mood, complaining that it is all no use and is not going anywhere. An envious part of them has attacked the progress which has been made, unable to bear that the analyst was able to help them. However, the envious attack not only affects their view of the analysis but also damages their own capacity to hold on to new insights and build upon them. An envious attack upon another person also damages the self.

Milton eloquently described the tortured and panic-stricken internal state which resulted from Satan's envy:

> Me miserable! Which way shall I fly?
> Infinite wrath and infinite despair?
> Which way I fly is Hell; myself am Hell,
> And in the lowest deep a lower deep
> Still threatening to devour me opens wide
> To which the Hell I suffer seems a Heav'n.
> (Milton 1667: 80, lines 73–78)

Satan's attack on God's creativity and on Adam and Eve's love and untarnished sexuality leaves him without reliable internal objects, inner resources, and therefore defenceless against being consumed by the bottomless pit of his own devouring envy. The sensation of spiralling downwards, out of control, can be the result of extreme envy, for in his mind the individual attacks the very people whose support he needs so that there is nothing inside him to prevent his headlong fall.

Satan disguised himself as a serpent, and the ways of envy are often subtle and hidden. For instance, envy is often accompanied by a particularly insidious form of identification, in which the envious person attempts to take over the qualities and identity of the envied person, and to use that person as a rubbish bin to put their unwanted feelings into. To take a simple example, if we bump into someone else's car, we may deal with it by blaming them, by insisting that they were going too fast or that they weren't looking where they were going. If we are particularly eloquent and moralistic about it, we may even succeed in making them feel guilty. We have got rid of our guilt, and we have also colonised their innocence, taking over their enviable position of blamelessness. But in the process, this blamelessness has been stripped of its innocence and has become superior and unpleasant: the colonised identity has changed in quality, tarnished by the envious takeover. This manoeuvre has been described by psychoanalysts as a type of 'projective identification' and its hallmarks are the subtle degrading of the quality that is appropriated, and a lack of sympathy for the feelings which have been projected and disowned.

Destructive envy is most painful to be aware of, and when it comes to light it can give way to intense feelings of guilt and shame. This may explain why we can be expert at attempting to hide it from ourselves and others. It can feel easier to carp on about someone's faults, for instance, than to realise that we envy them their attributes: we may say that the concert we went to was very good, *but* the orchestra played too fast; the new neighbour is very good-looking, *but* perhaps rather overweight; our friends have been kind to us *but* perhaps a little patronising – these sort of criticisms can sour our appreciation while serving to make us feel less envious. Of course, there is also a place for healthy criticism, and in analysis as in the rest of life it is important to distinguish between valid criticisms and those based on envy.

Another way of avoiding knowing about our envy can be by projecting it into others, by using our attributes or possessions to make others feel bad that they have less. We may flaunt our riches or our successes in a way that is consciously or unconsciously designed to provoke envy. For instance, a beautifully slim young woman was overheard saying to her painfully over-weight colleague that she just could not put on weight however hard she tried.

A subtler form of projection also takes place when we avoid the limelight or eschew success or happiness for fear of being envied. This is a particularly English character trait – we can be expert at dumbing ourselves down, insisting that we are no good at things and that we do not have much to offer. We eat humble pie in the hope of avoiding the envy which we imagine others might feel at our good fortune. This can go to extremes in competitive situations, and students seeking help before exams are often more afraid of success than they are of failure – if they succeed they imagine that they will be the butt of others' envy. Indeed, good fortune or success are likely to evoke some envy, but if the fear of envy paralyses us, this suggests that our own projected envy is at work, the envy which we have been unable to acknowledge and now attribute to others.

Central to our understanding of envy and its vicissitudes is its relationship to guilt and projective identification. This is illustrated in the literary example which follows.

Amadeus

Before going on to talk about the development of psychoanalytic views on envy and projective identification, I would like to discuss a play which exemplifies some of these processes: *Amadeus* by Peter Shaffer (1980). In this compelling play Shaffer dramatises the way in which envy can wreak devastation, and illustrates in detail some of the features which have long interested psychoanalysts.

At the start of Shaffer's drama, Salieri is the Court Composer in the Austrian court and since his childhood he has longed to be a successful composer. When Mozart is heralded as a young composer of extraordinary brilliance, Salieri is filled with despair and envy:

> I looked on astounded as from his ordinary life he made his art. We were both ordinary men, he and I. Yet he from the ordinary created legends – and I from legends created only the ordinary.
>
> (Shaffer 1980: 78)

He is honest enough to recognise that he can hope to become nothing better than mediocre, though he does have the capacity to recognise Mozart's genius and to be profoundly moved by his music. To make matters worse, Mozart is portrayed as childish and scatalogical, pouring forth a stream of obscene jokes as well as being supremely tactless and arrogant towards Salieri. Had Mozart been a personality who inspired respect, it might just possibly have been easier for Salieri to bear his genius, but the fact that Mozart behaves like a grotesque child shows Salieri that the young composer has done nothing to deserve his extraordinary gifts.

Salieri, on the other hand, thinks that he has driven a bargain with God. At the age of 16, desperate to succeed, he promised God that he would behave in a respectable and honourable fashion in exchange for being able to produce brilliant music. He has honoured his side of the bargain but God has not rewarded him, and here is Mozart behaving in a ridiculous fashion and yet able to produce music of incomparable beauty. This undermines Salieri's resolution to be good and honourable. He berates God (p. 56):

> Until this day I have pursued virtue with rigour. I have laboured long hours to relieve my fellow men. I have worked and worked the talent you allowed me. You know how hard I've worked! ... Solely that in the end, in the practice of the art which alone makes the world comprehensible to me, I might hear Your Voice! And now I do hear it – and it says only one name: Mozart! ... Spiteful, sniggering, conceited, infantine Mozart! – who has never worked one minute to help another man!

He is tortured by the unfairness with which God distributes his gifts, and Mozart's misdemeanours exacerbate his sense of grievance. It is as though Mozart is free to flaunt the salacious passions which Salieri has decided to renounce.

An inability to bear the inevitable unfairness or inequality of life is crucial to envy. This is nowhere so pronounced as in the realm of natural talents and attributes – qualities which are given and cannot be bought or even earned through hard work. In his disillusionment, Salieri decides to change his tactics completely and sets about undermining Mozart (p. 76):

> Obviously I would not need to plot too hard against his operas in future. I must concentrate on the man. I decided to see him as much as possible: to learn everything I could of his weaknesses.

This is one of envy's subtle ploys: to go for the weaknesses of the envied person in order to undermine their strengths. How tempting it can be to pick on another person's faults in order to diminish the qualities which we envy.

One of Mozart's weaknesses is women. He seduces Salieri's best young singing student, Katerina. Salieri, though lusting after Katerina, had remained faithful to his unattractive wife as part of his pact with God. He is incensed at Mozart's hedonism and decides to get his revenge. He invites Mozart's new wife – aptly named Constanza – to tea. In exchange for promises of promotion which he could arrange for the young genius, he demands sexual gratification. Much to his chagrin, Constanza refuses to be blackmailed. In humiliation and fury Salieri makes sure that Mozart will have no popularity and no financial recompense.

Over ten years, during which time Mozart is producing the bulk of his work, Salieri consistently turns people against him and prevents him from getting steady employment. Mozart now has a young family to support and is living in a garret. His marriage and his sanity deteriorate under the strain. He finds himself, little by little, slowly but surely, put in the position of envying Salieri who has by now become rich and successful despite the relentless mediocrity of his music. Salieri's importance in the court has become inflated, though empty, and Mozart is the outsider. Salieri has now taken the place which should be Mozart's and has projected into him the feelings of envy which were originally his own.

This is a compelling account of the connection between envy and the process of projective identification, whereby the envious person assumes the position which they envy and attempts to get rid of the feelings of envy which they cannot bear. Salieri has changed places with Mozart, taking on the role of successful composer and keeping Mozart literally and metaphorically out in the cold. Envy works in insidious ways. It gradually seeps into Mozart's life, poisoning it, as it poisons Salieri himself: he becomes possessed by it.

There is only one moment of compassion, when he suddenly sees Mozart in a new light (p. 92):

> There was the Magic Flute, there beside me! . . . Mozart the flute and God the relentless player. How long could the Creature stand it – so frail, so palpably mortal? And what was this I was tasting suddenly? Could it be pity? . . . Never!

Just for a moment, he sees how Mozart is as much a victim of fate as he is himself and pities him for being at the mercy of his own talent. But Salieri retreats in horror from this newfound feeling of compassion, whose implications he cannot bear. This moment of pity is pivotal in the play and it illustrates a central feature of envy. Envy often involves a retreat from feelings of compassion, because the envious person cannot bear to feel remorse for the damage wrought by their envy. He turns away from guilt about the damage he has done, and about the feelings of envy which have spoilt his capacity for appreciation. To take responsibility for these feelings would be extremely painful and it would imply a need to try to call a halt to the damage, to attempt to repair it and ultimately to live and let live. However, Salieri cannot prevent his envious feelings from pursuing their inexorable course and he turns his back upon the pity which he cannot sustain. He gradually drives Mozart mad, and destroys his own mind in the process. At last, he and Mozart are the same: 'We are both poisoned, Amadeus. I with you: you with me' (p. 96).

In this dramatisation, an inestimable price has been paid for sameness – the future of a genius, the works that will never be written. It is significant that the attack on Mozart's genius is also an attack on his marriage, his children, and the children he will never have. The link between the attack on creativity and the attack on the couple is fundamental, since coping with envy of the parents and of their creativity and procreativity is central to every child's negotiation of the Oedipus complex and hence to the development of his or her own creativity and relationships. The child has to cope with acceptance of the parents' relationship and the fact that he is excluded from aspects of it, in particular their sexual relationship and their capacity to produce babies. Envy can interfere with this acceptance and the child's capacity to internalise the parents' creative capacities or to use his own. Envy of other people's artistic or intellectual creativity has its roots in this early relationship, and in symbolic terms may lead to attacks on, for instance, the birth of other people's ideas, their 'brain-children', or upon other forms of creativity.

Envy and psychoanalysis

Freud and many other analysts, as I have mentioned, have found envy to be the greatest impediment to the patient's ability to benefit from psychoanalysis:

At no other point in one's analytic work does one suffer more from an oppressive feeling that all one's repeated efforts have been in vain, and from a suspicion that one has been 'preaching to the winds', than when one is trying to persuade a woman to abandon her wish for a penis on the ground of its being unrealisable or when one is seeking to convince a man that a passive attitude to men does not always signify castration and that it is indispensable in many relationships in life.

(Freud 1937: 252)

While in much of Freud's writing the emphasis was upon the woman's envy of the penis, here he was intimating something rather different, namely that in men as in women a difficulty in accepting of another person's potency or productivity is at the heart of the problem. However, Freud was still talking about men's and women's feelings towards men and the penis and not considering that envy of women might also be a problem.

Freud asserted that children know of only one sexual organ. He described how in his view the child's genital organisation differs from that of the adult: 'for both sexes, only one genital, namely the male one, comes into account. What is present, therefore, is not a primacy of the genitals but a primacy of the *phallus*' (Freud 1923). The controversy arising from this view has attracted more attention than Freud's later observations (Freud 1937) about how in men as in women difficulties in recognition of another's potency can get in the way of analytic progress.

Abraham was perhaps the first analyst to describe in graphic terms the mechanism which people will use to avoid awareness of their envy, of 'that which they do not possess'. Interestingly, in the example which I will cite, what is envied is the analyst's knowledge and capacity for understanding. He described the envious patient as follows:

> They tend to *exchange parts*, just as a child does when it plays at being father. They instruct the physician by giving him their opinion of their own neurosis, which they consider a particularly interesting one, and they imagine that science will be especially enriched by their analysis. In this way they abandon the position of patient and lose sight of the purpose of their analysis. In particular, they desire to surpass their physician, and to depreciate his psycho-analytical talents and achievements. They claim to be able to 'do it better' . . . the presence of an element of envy is unmistakable in all this.

(Abraham 1919: 306; my emphasis)

Abraham vividly identified the change of roles which was later to be described by Klein (1946) in terms of projective identification. With the gentle humour so characteristic of his writing, he described the obsessional neurotic who, after a few months of analysis, generously albeit condescendingly declared:

'I am now beginning to see that you know something about obsessional neurosis' (p. 307).

Abraham (1919: 307) stressed the envy of the father, his penis and his mental capacities, though he did also allude to the notion of envy of the breast. However, it was Klein who gave the fullest account of envy in her seminal book, *Envy and Gratitude* (1957). Her conceptualisation was based on her work on the fundamental importance of the relationship between love and hate, and the part played by projective identification as a means of getting rid of unbearable feelings. She pointed out how the spoiling of the good object can lead to confusion (pp. 184–5):

> The infant who, owing to the strength of paranoid and schizoid mechanisms and the impetus of envy, cannot divide and keep apart successfully love and hate, and therefore the good and bad object, is liable to feel confused between what is good and bad in other connections . . . For envy, and the attitudes it gives rise to, interferes with the gradual building up of a good object in the transference situation. If at the earliest stage the good food and the primal good object could not be accepted and assimilated, this is repeated in the transference and the course of the analysis is impaired.

This can lead to a vicious circle of attacks on the good object, a consequent inability to take it in or to keep it separate from the bad object, and an increase of envy compounded by an underlying feeling of the subject's own worthlessness: 'His own unhappiness and the pain and conflicts he goes through are contrasted with what he feels to be the analyst's peace of mind – actually his sanity – and this is a particular cause for envy' (p. 222).

Klein described the process of projective identification in a number of earlier papers. In the first of these, where she introduced the subject, she suggested that unwanted parts of the self are disowned and projected into the object, leading to confusion between the object and the self, between good and bad (Klein 1946). She was later to add that in some cases projective identification may also entail taking on the identity of the object (Klein 1955). The concept of projective identification has been much discussed and developed by psychoanalysts, and has proved central to post-Kleinian thinking, but there is not space to do justice to these developments here. (They are discussed in Chapter 13.) However, I think that the link between envy and projective identification deserves particular attention, as it is often through the process of projective identification that envy wreaks its damage and then maintains its hold on the personality.

As already described at the beginning of this chapter, we use projective identification to colonise the qualities which are envied and to get rid of our unwanted feelings of envy and inferiority. But the qualities appropriated in this way will always be tarnished and will often bear the stamp of exaggeration or even caricature. Someone who is 'holier than thou' may make us feel inadequate, or a know-it-all culture buff may succeed in making us feel like an ignorant philistine, yet there will be an exaggerated quality to their superiority which gives the game away and suggests that projective identification is at work, that we are *supposed* to feel envious and bad about ourselves. The insecurity which is often associated with envy has been projected as well as the envy itself. Having been enlisted in the service of an envious attack, projective identification may then be used defensively, to protect the envious person from awareness of his/her envy and the guilt associated with it. The identification with the envied person or quality then becomes fixed, the righteousness becomes entrenched, and the supposed inferiority or badness of the other more extreme.

How is envy to be overcome if it can lead to such a vicious circle? This is where feelings of love, remorse and compassion are crucial. When they enter the picture, there can be some hope of overcoming the damaging effects of envy:

> The urge to make reparation and the need to help the envied object are also very important means of counteracting envy. Ultimately this involves counteracting destructive impulses by mobilising feelings of love.
>
> (Klein 1955: 220)

The ability to feel concern for the other and the wish to make reparation is integral to the depressive position (described more fully in Chapter 3). It entails taking responsibility for damaging feelings and doing what one can to put things right.

Where there is a vicious circle of envy and projective identification, it can be hard to break the cycle, and difficult to achieve a reparative solution. The envious person may approach the brink of the depressive position and then retreat, feeling that there is too much damage to overcome, as with Salieri's 'Can this be pity? Never!' Compassion, or generosity towards the other person's capacities can help to ameliorate envy and make it easier to live with, but we may shrink back from a generous impulse.

One of the reasons that it is hard to face up to envy is that it is often accompanied by a very punitive conscience, which undermines the envious person in a similar way to that in which they have undermined the object of their envy. For instance, a 9-year-old girl was very keen to be good at acting and found it extremely hard to bear that her friend was more talented than herself and was chosen as the star in the school play. She succeeded in getting a group of girls to gang up on her friend and ostracise her, to give herself a feeling of superiority. At the same time, she felt deeply guilty and became tense and unhappy. When her mother tried to talk to her about it, she at first said that there was nothing wrong. She was deeply afraid that her mother and father would gang up on her as she had done to her friend, and hate her for being so unkind. Eventually, however, she did manage to talk to her mother and was surprised when her mother did understand about her envy of her friend, and helped her to find a way to make amends. Her mother's actual response was much more sympathetic than she had imagined it would be, for in her imagination it had become imbued with the harshness of her own envy. She expected to be humiliated and made to feel bad in just the way that she had done to her friend. Very often the internal conscience is much more forbidding than the actual figures in our lives, for it has become imbued with the harsh quality of our own primitive feelings. This is a fairly everyday example of a retaliatory conscience which can in some cases be part of extreme psychopathology and has been extensively written about by psychoanalysts.

The relationship between internal and external reality is always complex, however, and is composed of a combination of our own feelings and the real figures in our lives: envy does not occur in a vacuum. We have seen how the envious person may behave, but what are the circumstances which give rise to envy? For instance, Mozart's contempt for Salieri and his infantile behaviour, as well as his lack of sexual restraint, provoked Salieri's feelings of rivalry and of injustice, in that Mozart had done nothing to 'earn' his gifts. So the respect which might have tempered Salieri's envy was lacking, and he all too easily fell prey to hatred and destructiveness. Spillius (1993) has described some of the complexities of situations which may produce or exacerbate envy, rendering it unmanageable:

> Let us suppose that the giver takes pleasure in giving and, further, that he is not, for example, giving in order to establish superiority over the receiver . . . The receiver introjects and identifies with an object who enjoys giving and receiving, and an internal basis for admiration can develop, and hence emulation of the generous giver becomes possible. Let us suppose, in contrast, that the giver actually takes little pleasure in giving, that he is narcissistic and uninterested in the receiver, or that he is outright hostile or inconsistent towards the receiver, or that he gives . . . in order to demonstrate his superiority over the receiver. . . . So, somewhat paradoxically, envy is likely to be greatest when the giving object is felt to give little or badly.
>
> (Spillius, 1993: 1209)

The giver in the second kind of scenario provokes attacking feelings which make envy harder to bear. The giver may even be trying to project his own envious feelings, provoking resentment and hatred of his position. Wealth, good looks and even talent can be used to make the other person feel impoverished, unattractive or lacking in creativity. Our society is one in which envy is manipulated for commercial ends: we can be made to devalue what we have and to feel that we must buy some expensive item or go somewhere exotic to get over feeling so inadequate and perhaps to make others feel the envy which it is so uncomfortable to live with.

A contentious question for psychoanalysts has been about the degree to which a propensity to excessive envy may be innate. Some have emphasised the possibility of an inherently envious personality, an innate difficulty in accepting what life has to offer, while others have stressed the part played by external reality. There is always an interaction between the individual personality and the environment, and in practice it can be hard to tease out the extent to which destructive envy is due to nature or nurture. Psychoanalysts have more to discover about the sources of envy and what the implications may be for the possibility of change.

I would now like to describe a session with a patient which illustrates several of the points which I have been making. There is movement from projective identification to acceptance of some feelings of envy, from the paranoid-schizoid to the depressive position, and connections are made between the patient's adult, adolescent and infantile selves which illustrate how envy can sometimes be traced back to its early roots. One could also question whether I was felt to be provoking the patient's envy, or understanding him in a way that was bearable for him.

Clinical illustration

The session started with me telling the patient that I would be taking six days off in six weeks' time. He immediately told me that *he* would soon be missing some sessions: his mother hadn't seen his new baby and he and his wife wanted to go away. Then there were meetings at the end of the week which would also mean missing a session. He seemed apologetic. I commented on how he had instantly turned the tables and was explaining and apologising to me – how quickly he had got rid of the feeling of being dropped and excluded. He replied that he agreed and added that it was disappointing that he still reacted in this way. He conveyed to me quite sharply that he was disappointed in his analysis because I should have helped him to get rid of the problem by now, and I began to feel guilty and inadequate. (He seemed to feel that it would have been a sign of weakness in himself to mind about my absence or about the sessions which he was missing; instead, he projected into me his feelings of being a disappointment and of being dropped.)

He went on to say that he was thinking with annoyance about some people who were giving a drinks party and how he felt that this prevented *him* from giving a party – they had got in first. I connected this to my getting in first with the news of my absence, which seems to feel like a party I am giving to others, while he would like to be the partygiver. His mood seemed to soften after this and he talked about how his wife had pointed out that all their three children needed him for different things. I said how he felt pleased to be valued by them. He agreed and seemed moved.

He then talked of having run away as a teenager. He described how he was not able to learn at school, and felt rejected by his parents. His father was so scathing of his swearing, his outlandish clothes and his masturbation. I suggested that he might be experiencing my unusual absence as a sign of rejection, as if I were rejecting his angry feelings, his difficulties in learning from the analysis and his masturbation, his 'I am the greatest'. I wondered whether he felt afraid that I was dismissing him, rather than seeing his ability to develop.

He thought of his baby who only feeds from one breast, adding that he couldn't remember which one. He went on to say that he really admired his wife for being able to deal with crying babies. She stays calm, but she is not cold, she understands but does not panic. In contrast, he only just about manages, he carries the baby around and talks to it but inside he is a mass of feelings, and feels panicky and angry with the baby for crying. I suggested that he might be feeling angry with himself for feeling upset about the sudden break in the analysis. I wondered whether he was feeling that he appreciated the extent to which I was able to deal with his upset feelings, like his wife dealing with the baby. He agreed and again seemed moved. But then he said that he felt useless. I said that it was as though I, or his wife, now seemed to have all the capacities, especially the capacity to take on board upset feelings, and he felt as though he didn't have this capacity and couldn't expect to develop it. Either he had it or he didn't, as if there was nothing in between.

He replied that he couldn't develop it because he immediately started to feel that he was seething with furious anger about my having an ability which he would like to have, and he felt like attacking me and like not listening anymore. I said that he'd like to turn me into a bad breast that he didn't want to feed from, that he wanted to turn away from or run away from because he finds it so unbearable if I don't turn against him or reject him. So his anger about being understood was getting in the way of his being able to develop his own capacities. He said: 'It is like that.'

Discussion

This patient's associations during the session led back naturally through his stormy adolescence to thoughts of a baby who can only feed from one breast, and it seems likely that this charted the development of his own envy. This seemed to derive from a feeding relationship in which he felt his envy of the breast or his anger at not being the source of sustenance himself were intolerable for him to bear and perhaps intolerable to his object, who would panic or disapprove or turn away from his aggression and competitiveness.

However, as the session unfolded, he became aware of his 'mass of feelings' and was able to contain his seething emotions rather than trying to get rid of them as he had done at the start of the session, by announcing his forthcoming absence and his disappointment with his analysis. He reacted quickly to the news of my break by projective identification with me as someone whom he felt must be disappointed in him. Then during the session he gradually got in touch with his feelings of appreciation and of the envy which made it hard for him to hold on to good feelings. He recognised the way in which his envy made him feel like destroying me, just when he became aware of qualities in me and his analysis which he valued and also wanted to develop in himself. He seemed on the brink of the depressive position, seething with destructive feelings but managing, unlike Salieri, to hold himself back from destroying the insight which he valued.

The kind of work that took place in this session has to take place many times for lasting change to occur in analysis, the movement from projective identification to contact with the feelings which the patient finds it hard to contain, and the move from a paranoid-schizoid mode of functioning to a state of depressive awareness of his feelings. This patient's envy and competitiveness had deep roots and caused enormous problems in terms of maintaining insight and progress in the analysis, but they did gradually get worked through to some extent so that the patient achieved more stability and self-awareness, as well as a greater capacity to care for others and to recognise what they have to offer.

Conclusion

Envy can affect us at all stages of life, and how it has been dealt with in the earliest relationships will affect its impact later on, though there may also be some chance to work through it anew. The infant's envy of the breast and of the parental couple, the child's envy of the attention received by the next baby, the adolescent's envy of a settled and secure adult life, the adult's envy of the beauty and freedom of the young, the old person's envy of capacities which they are now losing themselves – these can range from the severe to the less pernicious varieties of envious experience which we accept as part and parcel of everyday life.

Emulatory envy manages to spare its object and may even sharpen feelings of appreciation and serve as a spur to development. Destructive envy, however, is perhaps the most painful emotion to be aware of, since it leads to attacks on the very people or qualities that we prize most highly. Small wonder, then, that we have so many ways of avoiding being aware of our envy, and that guilt about it can lead to further denial and to devaluation of the enviable attributes which we find hard to acknowledge. The vicious circle of envy, guilt and projective identification is powerful and can be hard to change. The way in which envy can be overcome is not through denial, which only serves to perpetuate the cycle, but through acceptance and acknowledgement, both of the envy and its object and of the appreciative feelings which it undermines. Perhaps the greatest obstacle to overcoming envy is the fact that since it sullies our view of those upon whom we depend, it can deprive us of the very support and acceptance which we need to help us to overcome it. To reinvest the object that has been devalued may entail calling upon reserves of courage and generosity and a capacity to look envy in the eye and see it for what it is without becoming caught in the vicious circle by turning against the envious part of the self, in fear or disapproval. The envious person needs support in this task, from a forgiving and understanding internal figure, or sometimes from an external one. While the bad thing about envy is that it attacks goodness, the good thing about coming to terms with envy is that this goodness can then be appreciated and enjoyed.

References

Abraham, K. (1919) 'A particular form of neurotic resistance against the psycho-analytic method', in *Selected Papers of Karl Abraham*, London: Hogarth Press, 1973.

Chaucer, G. (1388) 'The Parson's Tale', in *The Canterbury Tales*, London: Dent, 1958, p. 691.

Freud, S. (1923) 'The infantile genital organization', *Standard Edition*, vol. 19, p. 142, London: Hogarth Press.

Freud, S. (1937) 'Analysis terminable and interminable', *Standard Edition*, vol. 23, pp. 250–53. London: Hogarth Press.

Joseph, B. (1986) 'Envy in everyday life', in E. Bott Spillius and M. Feldman (eds) *Psychic Equilibrium and Psychic Change: The Selected Papers of Betty Joseph*, London: Routledge.

Klein, M. (1946) 'Notes on some schizoid mechanisms', *International Journal of Psychoanalysis*, 27: 99–110. Revised version in M. Klein, P. Heimann, S. Isaacs and J. Rivière, *Developments in Psycho-Analysis*, London: Hogarth Press, 1952, pp. 292–320. Reprinted in *The Writings of Melanie Klein*, vol. 3, pp. 1–24, London: Hogarth Press, 1975, Virago, 1997.

—— (1955) 'On identification', in *Envy and Gratitude and Other Works, 1946–1963*, London: Hogarth Press, 1975.

—— (1957) 'Envy and gratitude', in *Envy and Gratitude and Other Works, 1946–1963*, London: Hogarth Press, 1975.

Milton, J. (1667) *Paradise Lost*, London: Penguin, 1989.

Shaffer, P. (1980) *Amadeus*, London: Penguin, 1993.

Shakespeare, W. *Othello*, in *Complete Works*, London: Oxford University Press, 1971, pp. 943–76.

Spillius, E. Bott (1993) 'Varieties of envious experience', *International Journal of Psychoanalysis* 74: part 6.

Suggestions for further reading

Sigmund Freud is well known for his contentious view that children know of only one sexual organ, the phallus (Freud 1923). He also suggested that women's frustration at not possessing a penis, and man's passivity in relation to another's potency could prove the greatest obstacle to analysis (1937).

Karl Abraham (1919) gave more attention to envy and the effect which it can have upon an analysis. He suggested that envy can originate in the feeding situation, and he described the mechanism of 'exchanging parts', used to avoid envy (London: Hogarth Press, 1973).

Melanie Klein wrote the most comprehensive psychoanalytic study of the subject of envy (1957), describing in detail envy in infancy and how this can impair the development of a good relationship to the mother, as well as having a profound impact upon adult relationships.

The concept of envy and its clinical relevance have been much discussed by post-Kleinians, and envy has been given an important place in many accounts, including studies of human nature as well as of psychopathology. Betty Joseph wrote a paper (1986) on the impact of envy in everyday life, describing the ways in which it can prevent the individual both from having good relationships and from having access to their own positive feelings. Elizabeth Bott Spillius (1993) described the difference between the ruthless envy of the paranoid-schizoid position and envy in the depressive position, which is accompanied by guilt and concern. She also drew attention to the ways in which envy, often seen as a character trait, can also be provoked. The literary references speak for themselves. The section on envy in Chaucer's account of the seven deadly sins is as pertinent today as it was in 1388. Milton's Satan (1667) is one of the most powerful incarnations of envy in English literature and as such he fascinates as well as repelling his reader. His tormented reflections describe the effects of envy on the envious person and we can identify with this self-inflicted torment. Shaffer's Salieri (1980), as we have seen, embodies envy which painfully destroys that which it most admires. Last but not least, Shakespeare's Iago is amongst the most ruthless of envious villains, whose pleasure in destruction seems an end in itself.

Part 2

Symbolization

It has been remarked that the psychoanalytic view of the mental world is a gloomy one. There is an obvious reason for this; like doctors, we deal with what has gone wrong. But there are some defences that are also the basis of the most creative and enjoyable aspects of life, one of which is the human capacity to symbolize, to render our inner world into speech, images and music to convey it to others, either to get rid of it, like the Ancient Mariner, or to share it. The first psychoanalysts were fascinated by how creative artists seemed to have direct access to unconscious processes, and used characters from novels and plays to demonstrate mental mechanisms such as the Oedipus complex – Freud toyed with the idea of naming it the Hamlet complex. More recently, we have become interested in the interaction between reader and text, picture and viewer; the way in which understanding symbols requires an act of sympathy or collaboration. People who are termed autistic or schizophrenic have an impaired capacity to symbolize. Either it is largely lacking and the person cannot understand metaphors, like Temple Grandin, the autistic scientist sympathetically observed and described by Oliver Sacks in the title story in *The Anthropologist from Mars* (1995), or they are too concrete. Associations are swamping because there is no way of distinguishing between inner fantasy and outer reality.

In Chapter 5, Jennifer Johns describes the work of Donald Winnicott, a psychoanalyst and paediatrician, and one of the most widely known British psychoanalysts. Winnicott was never particularly interested in either developing a set of theoretical propositions, or relating what he had to say to existing theory. Instead, he provided a set of peculiarly evocative, lapidary *descriptions* of interactions between mother and babies, and how he saw them replayed in the thousands of mothers and babies who came to see him at his hospital clinic in Paddington Green, and in the child and adult patients whom he treated in analysis. The concepts which he developed – the primary maternal preoccupation which creates a 'good enough mother', the false and caretaking selves, the transitional object, the role of illusion, the importance of play and spontaneity – all point to his interest in the baby's developing capacity to symbolize, a capacity which rests on the relationship between his internal world and the outside environment.

Johns describes how, like many other Independent analysts, Winnicott came from the provincial English middle class, and perhaps his (and their) relative familiarity with the milieu of many of his patients led him to focus on the interaction between their 'inner weather' and the real external world. (Klein's position was more radical; she held that our experience of the external world was dominated by unconscious phantasy and so it could not be directly known.) The chapter describes how Winnicott came to differ from both Anna Freud and Klein in his account of the very young baby, and of how it comes to develop a sense of itself as a person, dwelling within his or her own body, largely in relation to the mother.

It is rare to find a psychoanalytic description of the basis of happiness, of ease, in people. Winnicott at his best finds a way of doing so which is neither persecutory – we don't need to be perfect, only good enough – nor sentimental. In fact, it is important that the mother does not continue to be perfectly attuned to her infant; if she is too good, we can never become separate. Juliet Hopkins has described how difficult life became for a mother and baby when the over-empathic mother had always been able to spare her daughter frustration (Hopkins 1996). Winnicott was interested in the complex and marvellous process by which the psyche is built up, and the importance of the analyst not getting in the way of natural processes of integration and healing. He dealt with some profoundly disturbed, if creative, people, and Johns describes one of his most helpful insights: that the madness, breakdown, which they fear might happen to them *has already happened*. Freud had also discussed this in 'Constructions in psychoanalysis' (Freud 1937).

Winnicott was one of the analysts concerned with that group of patients, often talented and successful, who come into treatment because they do not feel real. He believed that they needed to regress in treatment, and several of his patients have left us accounts of how they were enabled to do so (Guntrip 1975; Little 1985). Many analysts do not agree with this, which raises the question: How idiosyncratic, or universal, should we expect technique to be? As in other professions, it is difficult for the averagely competent to use authentically the techniques of the exceptional clinician.

British psychoanalysis has always been marked by an interest in what can be learned through baby observation, and Donald Winnicott, together with John Bowlby, tried to make psychoanalytic thinking relevant to the treatment of babies and children within the National Health Service (Holmes 1993). They were particularly interested in separation anxiety; the effect on babies and young children of being separated from their mothers or primary caregivers for too long. (Perhaps it is the almost ubiquitous upper middle class English experience of being sent away to boarding school and being told not to cry about it that has led to the characteristically English emphasis on the topic.) Symbolization is one of the main ways of dealing with separation anxiety. Freud observed this in 1920 when he saw his little grandson trying to cope with his mother's absence by hauling a cotton-reel toward him and throwing it away again, saying *fort/da*, or here/gone (Freud 1920).

A rare example of the direct effect of psychoanalysis on social policy arose from the work of Bowlby and his colleagues James and Joyce Robertson on the effect on children of separation. It was in particular the impact of the harrowing films that the Robertsons (Robertson and Robertson 1989) made of children who had been left in hospital and in children's homes without being visited by their parents that led to the change in policy whereby the norm in children's wards in Britain is that parents can visit their child at any time.

Baby observation (or, more exactly, the observation of an ordinary mother and baby couple during weekly visits for at least a year) has been an integral part of the training of psychoanalysts in Britain since 1960. This tradition, influenced by the British tradition of empiricism, started with the work of Esther Bick (1964), who wanted those training in psychoanalysis and in child psychotherapy to observe the normal development of a baby and mother pair in as an 'experience-near' way as possible. Students doing such observations learn much about early development and the importance of the baby's earliest relationships. In addition, they learn about the value and relevance of their own emotional reactions (technically, of their countertransference) to what they observe; and about the importance and difficulty of maintaining their professional role – both of which are vital in the practice of psychoanalysis.

In Chapter 6 Giovanna Di Ceglie describes how being able to symbolize is to use words and images to join the inner and outer worlds. She begins with the metaphor of the house, first in St Augustine and then in the dreams of her patients, where it stands as a potent metaphor for the maternal body and our own, the inner world and the memory. (Women seem to dream of houses more often than men; just as many men dream about cars, whereas women rarely do so.) Freud, too, in his frequent resort to archaeology as a metaphor for psychoanalysis, was thinking about the foundations of the mind. Jung used the metaphor even more so, and it appears in Christian iconography – our eternal home, Christ who is our home.

Di Ceglie describes how the internal world is built up; in particular, how we – uniquely the human species, as far as we know – use symbols to represent something which is not there. Dealing with something we need not being there is one of the earliest and most urgent tasks for the child. Klein linked together the epistemophilic instinct – the urge to know – with aggression, the urge to explore, dominate and penetrate. At a later stage, we need to be able to develop a feeling for metaphor to be able to think. To use language freely implies that we use metaphors and know that they are not real; by contrast, we think of the sort of patient who may refuse to play the violin because it is masturbating in public; or explains the meaning of 'blood is thicker than water' by saying that it is less fluid, it oozes more slowly. Even the most abstract scientific thinking is ultimately done through language, by means of metaphor and metonymy.

Klein, like Winnicott, saw some profoundly ill children, whose unhappiness had resulted in an inability to learn. She postulated that they had been unable to take in a good object; either the object had really not been good-enough, or perhaps adverse circumstances, or a constitutionally envious nature, had made it unusable. Consequently, they felt that their inner world had been invaded by a bad object in the way that people are in horror films. In fact, the imagery of horror films is a vivid guide to our unconscious fears – otherwise they could not be so potent. Unless we feel that our inner objects are reasonably benign, we cannot separate from them; they return to haunt us. More recently, psychoanalysts have begun to consider whether some of the children called autistic or schizophrenic perhaps have suffered from birth from an impaired capacity to relate and symbolize. But even if the deficit is genetic, it does not mean that it is completely untreatable; psychoanalysts such as Valerie Sinason have described successful work with profoundly disabled people (Sinason 1992).

Di Ceglie returns to Bion's evocation of how the mother can contain what the child cannot, and gradually enable it to tolerate and absorb it. The chapter touches, as do several others, on the question of creativity. Many, perhaps most psychoanalysts have had creative artists as patients; but the sources of their creativity, and its function within the psyche, seem very varied. Sometimes they create a benign world as an echo of or longing for it; at other times, the evocation of a bitter, broken image seems a way of expressing or sharing pain or loss (see Roth, Chapter 3 this volume).

The spontaneous capacity of human beings to symbolize is also shown in our dreams. Freud came to be interested in symbolism when he treated the patients whom he and Breuer described in hysterical patients (Breuer and Freud 1895). He was struck by how their symptoms represented their psychic dilemmas in symbolic form. He could see the similarity between this way of unconscious thinking and our dreams. As Susan Budd points out in Chapter 7 on recent developments in the theory of dreams, *The Interpretation of Dreams* is a much wider description of his model of the mind than the title implies (Freud 1900). Dreams, like jokes and slips of the tongue, reveal at the same time as concealing the workings of the unconscious mind.

In psychoanalysis, our increased interest in the patient's relationship with the analyst, and especially that aspect known as the transference relationship, has come to mean that dreams have been increasingly interpreted in terms of what they reveal about that relationship, and of the conscious and unconscious use made by the patient of their dream in telling it in the session. Budd considers that for some analysts this has displaced Freud's original view of the dream as a complex amalgam of powerful and disturbing feelings and wishes from the past with current preoccupations, and she thinks that we have lost something valuable in this change. Freud, who continued to write about dreams throughout his life, was aware that they could be used to illuminate the patient's relationship with the analyst, and that where this was the case it needed attention as such. However, his main interest was in what he called the latent dream, which lay behind the dream as reported, and which could be inferred by means of the dreamer's associations to elements of the reported dream. The dream, paradoxically, is the clearest, the most direct channel back to the forgotten past. She points out that while we may take the ability to dream for granted, in fact dreaming, remembering and recounting a dream is a sophisticated mental achievement; children, like some psychotic patients, find it harder to distinguish between dreaming and reality. To be able to dream and tell our dream implies a relatively high level of mental functioning, arising from a sense of having been held in mind or 'contained' by the mind of another. In an analysis, such containment is represented by the emotional holding of the analyst, and when it fails a patient's dreams may not reach the point of symbolization, being filled instead with images of disintegration or pouring out of fractured containers.

References

Bick, E. (1964) 'Notes on infant observation in psychoanalytic training', *International Journal of Psychoanalysis* 45: 558–66.

Breuer, J. and Freud, S. (1893) *Studies on Hysteria, Standard Edition*, vol. 2, London: Hogarth Press.

Freud, S. (1900) *The Interpretation of Dreams, Standard Edition*, vols 4 and 5, London: Hogarth Press.

—— (1920) 'Beyond the pleasure principle', *Standard Edition*, vol. 18, pp. 3–64, London: Hogarth Press.

—— (1937) 'Constructions in analysis', *Standard Edition*, vol. 23, pp. 255–70, London: Hogarth Press.

Guntrip, H. (1975) 'My experience of analysis with Fairbairn and Winnicott', *International Review of Psychoanalysis* 2: 145–56.

Holmes, J. (1993) *John Bowlby and Attachment Theory*, London: Routledge.

Hopkins, J. (1996) 'The dangers and deprivation of too-good mothering', *Journal of Child Psychotherapy* 22: 407–22.

Little, M. (1985) 'Winnicott working in areas where psychotic anxieties predominate: a personal record', *Free Associations*, 3.

Robertson, J. and Robertson, J. (1989) *Separation and the Very Young*, London: Free Association Books.

Sacks, O. (1995) *The Anthropologist on Mars*, London: Picador.

Sinason, V. (1992) *Mental Handicap and the Human Condition: New Approaches from the Tavistock*, London: Free Association Books.

Chapter 5

The facilitating environment

Jennifer Johns

The title of this chapter refers to a concept developed by Donald Winnicott, a British psychoanalyst who was also a paediatrician, and whose life's work was to do with early psychological individuation and development and the conditions, or environment, within which they occur. In his view, the development of health or ill health depended on many factors, both innate and environmental, and he studied the interplay of these factors both in health and when problems arise. His theories are central to British object relations theory.

Winnicott was influenced greatly by Freud, whom he admired enormously but never met, and later, before going his own way, he worked closely for some years with Melanie Klein, whom he considered the next most important psychoanalyst after Freud. He added to their ideas his own vast experience of observing mothers and babies to create his own very particular way of understanding the infant's inner world. He noted that in his professional life as a paediatrician he had observed over 60,000 mother–baby couples, many of whom had developed fairly normally, so it can be claimed that his ideas about normal development must be taken seriously. In addition to this, he treated a considerable number of psychotic patients in psychoanalysis, and there found evidence indicating that failures in the earliest care of the infant had contributed to their psychopathology:

> The mother lays down the mental health of each child during her preoccupation with the care of her infant. . . . The word 'devotion' can be rid of its sentimentality and can be used to describe the essential feature without which the mother cannot make her contribution, a sensitive and active adaptation to her infant's needs – needs which are at the beginning absolute. This word, devotion, also reminds us that in order to succeed in her task the mother need not be clever.
>
> (Winnicott 1952: 220)

His understanding was that the facilitating environment is not only physical care, in all its varieties, but the emotional climate provided by – most often, but not always – the mother.

First, something about the man himself. Winnicott was born in 1896, the youngest child of a provincial middle-class family. The only boy, he was sent away to school in Cambridge where he later went to the university and studied biology before going to London to become a doctor. His family was such that going away to school seems to have been something of a relief, and perhaps allowed his playfulness to develop. Later he was to emphasise the importance of play in human development and wrote about its significance, particularly in his book *Playing and Reality*, which after being in print for 30 years still sells over 20,000 copies a year internationally, something of a psychoanalytic bestseller.

Winnicott felt that he had been deeply influenced by reading Darwin while still at school. I find it interesting that so early in his own life he should already have been entranced by the concepts of evolutionary adaptation as a result of the relationship with the environment, and the survival of the fittest, since the ideas which he developed as a psychoanalyst are also to do with the relationship between the internal and external, with maturation and adaptation. His medical studies coincided with the First World War, and in 1914, he saw his stable world plunged into destruction. He lost many school and university friends and saw action himself in the navy. Following this exposure to trauma, he went to London to further his studies and by 1919 he had read and been powerfully influenced by *The Interpretation of Dreams* (Freud 1900).

By 1923 Winnicott was consultant in paediatrics at Paddington Green and in Hackney, where he worked for 40 years. He trained as a psychoanalyst with adults and children, during which time he was in supervision with Melanie Klein; and by the time the Second World War broke out he was a respected member of both the medical establishment and the British Psychoanalytical Society. This 'foot in both camps', being both a paediatrician and a psychoanalyst, his two parallel careers, gave him the practical background to write and broadcast widely on matters to do with the welfare of children and families. He both spoke and wrote about early development, growth, feeding, school, siblings, the evacuation of children away from home in wartime, the effects of separation from parents, and subsequent difficulties, particularly delinquency. His information and ideas proved useful to parents, teachers, social workers, probation officers, doctors and all students of human nature.

At the outset of the Second World War, together with John Bowlby and Emmanuel Miller, he had warned publicly of the dangers to children's mental health of the policy of child evacuation, and their predictions were to come true in terms of the large number of children who had been separated from their home environment and who became distressed, difficult and delinquent, requiring serious help and management. It was whilst working with these children that Donald Winnicott further developed his ideas and began the major part of his writing.

Winnicott's views

During the Second World War, in the psychoanalytic world in Britain there was internal conflict, to do not only with different ideas about how to train psychoanalysts, but also with the differing theories of early psychic development as held by Anna Freud and Melanie Klein. Since Melanie Klein's arrival in Britain in 1926 her theories had become largely accepted by British psychoanalysts, but when the pre-war influx of Viennese analysts fleeing persecution arrived, including Sigmund and Anna Freud, they found many of these ideas unacceptable, and much ill-feeling arose, not completely resolved by a series of important debates known as the Controversial Discussions.

To summarise, Donald Winnicott, who had been trained by Klein, was unable to agree fully with her theories about the inner world of the baby. He also valued Anna Freud's ideas about the importance of the internal world of the toddler and older child and had his own ideas about the earliest stages of life, finding it difficult to accept that the internal world of an infant could initially be so defined, and so frequently conflictual and persecuted, as Melanie Klein believed. Winnicott, whilst not abandoning instinct theory, argued that it is not possible to study the small infant without also taking the environment into consideration. By environment he meant the principal carer for the baby, in most circumstances this being the mother. In the political dispute between Anna Freud and Melanie Klein he took neither side.

Some readers, those more used to thinking of very small babies as already being individual units with a sense of themselves, find his writing elusive, idiosyncratic, often cryptic, describing as it does the emergence of unit status and the beginnings of self out of a relationship. While accepting the vital importance of Klein's thinking, which is concerned with the internal, instinctual struggles of the infant, he focused much more on the emergence of the individual from the earliest relationship; an emergence which he believed could be adversely affected either by impingement or by deficiency of environmental provision. He argued that, rather than starting with any awareness of itself as an individual body, the baby at the beginning exists in a relationship of two bodies, although he cannot know this. Awareness of being a single individual grows out of the recognition of what Winnicott called 'me and not-me'. The infant thus recognises the existence of self and other at the same time, and is then on the way to being capable of achieving a sense of individuality. This sense of individuality in turn lays the foundation for the capacity for mature object relationships. The core of these ideas is explained in 'Primitive emotional development' (Winnicott 1945: 145–56).

The thousands of so-called normal mother–baby couples at different stages of development that Winnicott observed gave him a unique body of data. His experience differed from that of most psychoanalysts, whose theories about development have been derived from psychoanalytic reconstruction of development in adult neurotic and psychotic patients, or through the analysis of disturbed children. It is clear that he very much valued his double career and prospered in both, becoming president of the paediatric section of the Royal Society of Medicine, and twice president of the British Psychoanalytical Society.

In describing the facilitating environment, Winnicott emphasised the importance of the special psycho-physiological state of a woman in late pregnancy and then for a few weeks when her baby is new: the forgetfulness and dreaminess so often observed in pregnancy, and the almost total absorption in her baby of a non-depressed mother during the first few weeks. He called this state 'primary maternal preoccupation' (Winnicott 1956: 300–305). He saw this as an essential element in the normal unconscious processes that prepare the mother for a high degree of attunement to the needs of an infant in a state of absolute dependency. Unlike Klein and Fairbairn, who saw the infant as having a definable ego more or less from birth, Winnicott, like Freud, saw young infants as being at first undifferentiated from their mothers, having no immediate awareness of self or other, inside and outside, fantasy and reality. He recognised that such awareness began to develop very early, and that the degree and speed of development differs from baby to baby.

To emphasise this initial lack of separateness he stated cryptically 'there is no such thing as a baby' (Winnicott 1952: 99), meaning that a baby cannot exist on its own; there is always a mother or mothering person present too. Winnicott makes it quite clear that although in health the actual mother is probably best placed to perform the mothering function, because of the psycho-physiological changes that occur in women in late pregnancy and after delivery of the infant, it is the function itself and the sensitivity of the person who takes on the care of the infant that creates the facilitating environment. Later, there is gradual and necessary failure as the infant develops ego-strength and becomes able to tolerate increasing frustration. In other words fathers or others can perform the mothering function, and of course in difficult circumstances they may have to.

From the infant's point of view, Winnicott saw the internal state as being one of what he called 'unintegration' – that is to say, a state of not yet being integrated as a unit being who could have any sense of self or other, inside and outside, fantasy and reality. He agreed with Edward Glover (Glover 1932: 162) that the early internal world contained 'ego-nuclei', elements which must coalesce to form the beginnings of self. He postulated that it was difficulties in the process of integration which became the basis for later problems, for instance, affecting the severity of the splitting found in the schizoid phase that Klein and Fairbairn described.

Winnicott saw that the process of differentiation happened as a result of an innate maturational tendency, in action automatically provided that there was an adequate environment consisting of sensitive attention and care. Given this environment, he saw the infant as varying in his or her mental state, being at times more alert, responsive and integrated, at times unintegrated but calm, and at times of distress being in terror of losing such integration as had been achieved.

Winnicott described this state, in which the infant cannot distinguish self or other, inside or outside, reality or fantasy, as the phase of absolute dependence, when for the innate maturational process to occur, including the integration of the ego-nuclei, environmental provision must be exquisitely adapted to the baby's needs. Environmental failure at this stage threatens the baby with primitive agonies, or unthinkable anxiety. He saw such failure and the experience of primitive agony as laying the foundation for later psychosis, which he saw as defending against the re-emergence of such overwhelming anxiety. He understood, for instance, the psychological disintegration found in psychotic patients as being a protection against the fear of a return to the primitive unintegrated state, and also saw tendencies towards dissociation as being a result of that process of early integration being incomplete.

In other words, Winnicott thought of psychosis as an environmental deficiency disease, resulting from either a deficiency of environmental provision during the early stage when integration has not been achieved, or from severe environmental impingement, or very early trauma. He also saw that the process of integration involved both the psyche and soma aspects of the baby, which each have to emerge from the undifferentiated state before they can come into a healthy relationship with each other. He believed psychosomatic illness to be a consequence of failure of the process of early integration and the accompanying process he called 'personalisation', the development of the firm knowledge that one's person exists in one's body. He used the phrase 'psyche indwelling in the soma' and saw it as a hallmark of health. Failure of this process, occurring normally during the quiet phases of a baby's existence, given the adequate and quiet experiences of emotional and body care, he thought could lead either to psychosomatic illness or to feelings of depersonalisation in later life.

The developing sense of reality, including that of time and space which is faulty in psychotic patients, Winnicott called 'realisation'. He thought that it followed closely after integration and personalisation, and was dependent on the same provision of reliable, consistent, physical and emotional care. He described the hungry infant as at first creating for himself the illusion of what is wanted, an illusion that can sustain him for a short while. When the required feed is produced by the mother without too long a delay, the infant's sense of being able to omnipotently create the needed object is strengthened, and the actual details of a feed enrich the experience. It is this ongoing and repeated experience, that of the actual feed, breast or bottle matching and enriching the illusion which he called an hallucination, that allows the baby to begin to match up fantasy and reality, and to value reality. For this to happen, the experience provided by the environment mother must be consistent and reliable, and for this reason Winnicott emphasised the importance of a baby being largely cared for by one reliable person at the beginning.

The holding environment

Another term that Winnicott used to describe the function of the facilitating environment mother in the earliest stage is 'holding'. The characteristics of 'holding' are that it should, reliably and at first unnoticeably from the infant's point of view, meet its physiological needs to be sheltered from hunger, cold, etc. and protected from physiological pain. The process will be unnoticeable because the infant does not yet recognise separateness of self and other, and therefore cannot recognise that it is in fact dependent on the other. 'Holding' involves total bodily and emotional care, and adaptation to the microscopic changes in the infant's state. The healthy mother, whose unconscious contains traces of her own good infantile experience, can identify with her baby and his needs, allowing her this sensitivity, whereas the mother whose own early experiences have left painful and conflictual remnants may find herself disturbed by her baby's needs, may experience them as a criticism or attack and retaliate.

About the term 'holding', this ordinary word used by Winnicott to describe the mother's total physical and emotional care of her baby and his needs at the time of earliest integration, has been used slightly differently by other analysts, notably Bion, who used it to describe simply the physical element of childcare. This idea is also sometimes confused with another concept of Bion's, 'containment', which is increasingly used in contemporary psychoanalytic thinking, but belongs to a rather different developmental framework, and involves an infant who is already, in Winnicott's terms, mature and integrated enough to be a unit being who is able to split and project. The concept of containment has, however, enabled something of a rapprochement between Winnicott and post-Kleinian thinking.

So that, in Winnicott's developmental schema, the innate maturational tendency (of the baby to become integrated as a whole ongoing being) is effective insofar as there exists a facilitating environment (which both is and is provided by an emotionally attuned mother) adapting and developing alongside the developing infant. The infant can then integrate and eventually object relate, proceeding from absolute dependence to relative independence. However, things can go wrong at various stages of this developmental path. Winnicott described the fear of breakdown in adult patients as the fear of re-experiencing the conditions previously encountered during failure of the environment in infancy, which he described as various degrees and types of primitive agony (Winnicott 1974) associated with different defence systems. He saw disintegration, for example, as a defence against the unthinkable dread of a helpless return to the unintegrated state. This has clinical importance, since these unthinkable fears will be reached in analysis in the transference. It is during analysis that the feared disaster can be known and understood, despite the fact that the disaster which happened has not previously been experienced, because at the time that it originally threatened in babyhood the individual was not yet integrated enough to experience it.

Thus the facilitating environment initially consists of close maternal attunement and repeated body care, feeding, winding, bathing, changing, which together Winnicott referred to as holding, allowing a baby with normal potential to begin to become aware gradually and simultaneously of its own separateness and that of its mother. In the next phase, once this process is under way, he felt that the 'good-enough mother' would over time gradually and progressively fail to provide quite such sensitive maternal attunement. There would be a slight increase of delays in attention, small frustrations, etc. at a rate at which the growing baby can increasingly tolerate, and this would result in a strengthening of the emerging ego. The baby, now becoming increasingly able to tolerate frustration and increasingly aware that it is a separate being from mother, emerges from 'absolute dependence' to 'relative dependence', and begins to adapt to reality and the painful awareness of all that separateness entails, including eventually the development of concern for the other and the capacity for guilt that Melanie Klein called the depressive position.

To put it another way, if the mother is attuned at the beginning, then the baby's experience is that the beginning of the unpleasant experience that we adults call hunger, a frightening experience for a small being who doesn't know what the nasty feeling is, where it comes from or what it means, is shortly followed by the arrival of mother's breast (and a delicately offered bottle will do just as well) which can be suckled, and by both mouth pleasure and filling the empty stomach the unpleasant hungry sensation recedes. The very new undifferentiated baby can believe in an illusion – that he created the breast himself, in fact it is part of the baby, the baby's possession. After all, it seems to do as it is told, to come when wanted. And the attuned mother supplies the material for that illusion by providing the feed at the right time, willingly, because she wants to. Winnicott spoke of this illusion on the part of the baby as 'primary creativity'. As the baby matures, the 'good-enough' mother begins to lose her primary maternal preoccupation, her complete absorption in the baby, and without noticing it begins just slightly to frustrate her baby. The breast may arrive a split-second later than the baby's wish for it at first, then a minute or so, and much later on this gradual process has developed so that she may even decide that a nappy has to be changed before a feed.

The baby who has had enough very early good experience has had a strong sense of having omnipotently created the object and so has confidence that the breast can be found, and such a baby can tolerate its absence for a short while, knowing that while not there at the moment, it exists elsewhere and will return. The awareness of external reality has begun. The sense of self and other (me and not-me, to use Winnicott's terms) has begun to develop and thus the foundations of object relationships are laid. The baby, beginning to be aware of his own separateness as well as that of the object, starts to believe in his own survival too.

When integration has begun and the 'good-enough mother' is letting her baby down as gradually and delicately as he can stand it, the facilitating environment is still important. Developmental problems can occur at that stage too. If there is such a thing as a 'good-enough mother', there must be such a thing as a 'not good-enough mother', who fails her baby in ways that the baby cannot manage and has to defend against or react to. For instance, Winnicott points out that there are mothers who are so sensitive to their infants that the super-sensitive care of the mother in a state of primary maternal preoccupation is maintained beyond the point at which her baby is mature enough to tolerate some frustration. Since an initially slight but gradually increasing amount of frustration is necessary to provoke ego strengthening, such a mother may be depriving her infant of a needed experience and seducing the baby into passivity.

Thus satisfactory progress through this next stage also depends on the principal caring person who must, while failing the baby on one hand, still have enough sensitivity to recognise something of the new and more integrated messages that the slightly more mature baby can give. Winnicott, whose day-to-day work helped so many mothers through this most difficult stage by means of understanding something of their own inner states, was alert to the dangers both of idealising or attributing pathology to mothers. He also knew what we all know, that parents may be attuned to their infant at one developmental stage and not always so sensitive at another. In addition, there are babies with physical problems whose development cannot ever be within normal limits, and those who are born into tragic situations which put special burdens on those who care for them. Not even the best-equipped mothers can cope with everything, but may need understanding and help at the right time. A mother's capacity to care for her baby therefore depends on many factors, internal and external, and not least on her own early experience. Mothers able to empathise with a tiny baby may consciously or unconsciously regard toddlers as monsters, whereas others can hardly wait for a stage of more independence and find themselves resenting, even hating, the intense demands of the newborn baby.

Winnicott described a special situation arising when a mother fails to recognise quite what her infant is communicating. The degree to which this may happen depends on the mother's own capacity to object relate, to see her baby as separate from herself, how much she is in touch with her own baby aspects, and her level of anxiety. She may well fill this gap in understanding with an interpretation of the baby's needs in terms of her own internal world, thus missing the baby's meaning altogether. When this happens, Winnicott described the infant's response as *compliant*. The infant, still dependent on the mother, and beginning to recognise the reality of that dependence and the seriousness of what it means in terms of acceptance, love, and even survival, will accept the mother's action and her interpretation of what is needed. Winnicott called this her *gesture*, which sometimes ignores the fact that the infant's own gesture, its own communication, has been missed by the mother. This compliance on the infant's part is, in Winnicott's terms, the origin of the False Self. In 'Ego-distortion in terms of the true and false self' (Winnicott 1965: 140–52), he described not only the idea of a False Self, a term already in use in psychoanalysis, but what is also implied in the term, the existence of a True Self. The true self he believed to be capable of spontaneity and play, and developing in health as a result of both the early holding, and maternal meeting of infantile needs, but also the accurate dosing of maternal failure implied by the term 'good-enough mother'.

The true self and the transitional object

In addition to achieving all this, the mother must continue to be fairly accurate in her response to the baby's communications, so that there are no or not very many adaptations to the environment that it has to make at too early a stage. The baby, not having to make adaptations, in other words without interference, has the possibility of realising its true potential as a person. On the other hand, should mother's lack of accurate response to the baby's communications or gestures force or tempt the baby to comply, to apparently accept mother's solution to a problem, mother's way of going about things, in order to maintain the relationship on which the baby is so alarmingly dependent, and please mother, then the true self is hidden and a false self develops, very often apparently successfully. Winnicott described five degrees of false self personalities, from an extreme in which the true self is completely hidden and the false self appears as if it were authentic, and frequently successful, though such people tend to fail in intimate relationships; to that false or caretaking self in individuals approaching health, where some degree of the false self exists in the ordinary restraint necessary for social adaptation and is part of good manners. The intermediate versions often involve some degree of imitation, so that the child is seen as being 'just like' a relative or close friend. He emphasises a particular instance of false self, common in those who are intellectually gifted, which involves a dissociation between intellectual activity and psycho-somatic existence. Such people install the false self in the mind, which does not in their case seem to reside in the body. The 'psyche indwelling in the soma', Winnicott's sign of health, has not been reached. They may for instance be high achieving academic or professional people who nonetheless complain of feeling unreal. Such people are at risk, as the hidden sense of unreality may lead them to self-destruction, to the shock and surprise of those around them.

A patient of mine, a very successful man, who regarded his life as perfect and had worked hard to make it so, came to me for analysis when he had shocked himself by walking past his office in such a state of unreality that he failed to recognise that he worked there. When I first saw him he told me, 'Someone is living a very successful life, but I don't feel it is me.' He had had an infancy which was very disturbed. He was passed from pillar to post from birth until finally, at about six months, he reached a home which cared for him well where he had apparently thrived. He was a very charming man, with a dry and delightful sense of humour, and it was difficult to resist being seduced by his charm into a cosy relationship in which we would both be false and have a lovely but quite unreal time in the analysis. I could imagine how he had survived in the various institutions by being the most delightful baby there.

Without the rescue at six months which allowed him some experience of consistency and holding, he might have become a charming and psychopathic confidence trickster. As it was, the rescuing family had very firm but consistent boundaries and expected him to develop responsibility. He had fought but also adopted their values and became successful but over-rigid alongside his sense of unreality. In his analysis he struggled with his very severe pain and rage, and gradually did become more real. I saw him for about five years before he decided to finish, saying wryly, 'My life is much worse. My house has dry-rot, my business is not so secure, my kids are nowadays getting very troublesome, my wife nags, but it is my life now, and I'm living it.' As his analyst, I was pleased.

In addition to his ongoing observation of young infants and their mothers, Winnicott derived his understanding of early infantile needs from the study of the transference as it develops in adult patients. He compared the need for maternal sensitivity to the necessary sensitivity of the analyst in the care of the regressed patient – the analyst whose care consists both in providing the physical parameters of the analytic session as well as a particular quality of attention. Winnicott thought that regression in analysis was necessary to reach the parts of the true self that might still be available to analysis, though he states very clearly that these cases are difficult.

Finally, I would emphasise that it is the emphasis on primary narcissism, the undifferentiated state, and the emergence from it towards a sense of individuality and therefore the capacity for object relations that particularly distinguishes Winnicott's thinking. His developmental framework includes the splitting of the ego, the projective and introjective mechanisms described by Klein and Fairbairn, but he was more interested in early ego integration, which he felt had to occur first in order for splitting to be able to happen. I have emphasised his description of primary narcissism and the necessity to take into account both the infant and environmental provision when describing development towards a sense of reality, and the transition to object relatedness. It is this which makes it possible for Winnicott to address creativity in the way that he does, through the idea of transitional phenomena. His picture of development is very fluid – the newborn is floating in and out of a state of undifferentiation, and development he sees similarly as dynamic, two steps forward and one step back, except not so strictly patterned.

For many children the use of transitional phenomena in development is significant: that is to say the emotional investment in an inanimate object or an idea, or a pattern of behaviour, that is important for the growing child and is recognised as such by the rest of the child's world. It is in the early stages, as the difference between the baby's awareness of 'me' and 'not-me' begins and strengthens and the illusion of having created the breast can not be held on to any longer, that many babies need a way of bridging the gap between fantasy and reality which might be too much for them, and this is where transitional phenomena have their place. They are a way of temporarily prolonging the fantasy of omnipotence by being something over which the baby feels he has control, when the mother is beginning to demonstrate to her infant that he does not control her. Winnicott described the newborn baby's use of the hand, thumb or even fist to stimulate the mouth and in older babies the use of the hand to hold, stroke, and play with objects, often soft toys or the edge of a blanket. He pointed out that between the stages of undifferentiation and not knowing and the awareness of internal and external reality, which implies separateness and individuation, there is a multitude of possibility. He called this the intermediate area of experience, and placed it:

> between the thumb and the teddy bear, between oral erotism and the true object-relationship, between primary creativity and projection of what has already been introjected, between primary unawareness of indebtedness and the acknowledgment of indebtedness. ('Say: "ta" ').
>
> (Winnicott 1951: 230)

The common patterns of infancy in which the baby first finds his thumb or fist, or an object to suck or stroke, or makes babbling noises, are accompanied by the beginnings of mental activity, that is to say by fantasy. Later in infancy it may happen that the activity or the object becomes necessary when the baby is going to sleep or is anxious, and this need is recognised by his parents, who unconsciously know that it represents a continuity of experience that the baby needs.

This 'transitional object' becomes the first 'not-me' possession, and while it is symbolical of a part-object, the breast, it is important because it is neither the baby nor that object. For this reason sensitive parents know that it is not to be changed or even washed, but must accompany the infant, to be loved or misused as the baby fancies. Winnicott listed the special qualities of the relationship with the object. The object must be reliable and survive. It must, from the baby's point of view, come from neither without nor within. Eventually it will lose its significance, but not be forgotten, not mourned; it simply loses its meaning, again gradually, bit by bit, at that stage when a wider cultural field of experience has appeared. The phase of transitional phenomena begins, Winnicott says, at four to six to eight to twelve months. In other words, no babies are the same, or perhaps he would have said that no mother–baby couples are the same. The object usually gains a name at about the time when babies are beginning to speak. Of course, despite the gradual passing away of the need for the experience which the object represents, we all know that such objects are important at bedtime even for an older child who ignores it during the day, and that an ill child, or a depressed one, or a lonely one, will revert to the previous pattern of relationship with the object or pastime, and through that to the stage at which the needed mother may be, at least in fantasy, more available.

Basic to all of Winnicott's contributions is the concept of the early infant as not having a consistent, ongoing awareness of separateness, of individuality, of inside and outside, of self and other. These awarenesses develop, or fail successfully to develop, slowly, irregularly, in fits and starts, according to many factors, which we as adults can see as both internal and external to the infant. Winnicott saw the environment as being for by far the majority of babies the mother or whoever stands in for her, and was emphatic that her contribution is vital. Much of his paediatric work, as well as his writing for both lay people and fellow professionals such as nurses, social workers, teachers, the clergy and so on, is directed at encouraging the support of young mothers to allow them to do their job of providing the sensitive adaptation to their babies that serves the infant's development best. In 'The mother's contribution to society' he writes that those who are able to might, at the beginning:

> give moral support to the ordinary good mother, educated or uneducated, clever or limited, rich or poor, and to protect her from everyone and everything that gets between her baby and herself . . . This collective task is an extension of the job of the father, of the father's job at the beginning, at the time when his wife is carrying, bearing and suckling.
>
> (Winnicott 1957: 141–4)

References

Freud, S. (1900) *The Interpretation of Dreams, Standard Edition*, vols 4 and 5, London: Hogarth Press.

Glover, E. (1932) 'A psycho-analytic approach to the classification of mental disorders', *On the Early Development of Mind*, London: Imago, pp. 161–86.

Phillips, A. (1988) *Winnicott*, London: Fontana.

Rodman, F.R. (1987) *The Spontaneous Gesture*, Cambridge, MA: Harvard University Press.

Winnicott, D.W. (1945) 'Primitive emotional development', *Collected Papers, Through Paediatrics to Psycho-Analysis*, London: Tavistock, 1958, pp. 145–56.

—— (1949, revised 1953) 'Mind and its relation to the psyche-soma', *British Journal of Medical Psychology* 27, 1954.

—— (1951) 'Transitional objects and transitional phenomena', *Collected Papers: Through Paediatrics to Psycho-Analysis*, London: Tavistock.

—— (1952) 'Psychoses and child care', *Collected Papers, Through Paediatrics to Psycho-Analysis*, London: Tavistock, 1958, pp. 219–28.

—— (1956) 'Primary maternal preoccupation', *Collected Papers, Through Paediatrics to Psycho-Analysis*, London: Tavistock, 1958, pp. 300–305.

—— (1957) 'The mother's contribution to society', *The Child and the Family*, London: Tavistock, 1957, pp. 141–4.

—— (1958) *Collected Papers, Through Paediatrics to Psycho-Analysis*, London: Tavistock.

—— (1964) *The Child, The Family and the Outside World*, London: Penguin.

—— (1965) 'Ego-distortion in terms of true and false self', *The Maturational Processes and the Facilitating Environment*, London: Hogarth Press, pp. 140–52.

—— (1965) *The Maturational Processes and the Facilitating Environment: Studies in the Theory of Emotional Development*, London: Hogarth Press.

—— (1971) *Therapeutic Consultations in Child Psychiatry*, London: Hogarth Press.

—— (1974) 'Fear of breakdown', *International Review of Psychoanalysis* 1: 103–7.

—— (1974) *Playing and Reality*, London: Pelican.

—— (1977) *The Piggle: An Account of the Psychoanalytic Treatment of a Little Girl*, London: Hogarth Press.

—— (1986) *Holding and Interpretation: Fragment of an Analysis*, London: Hogarth Press.

Suggestions for further reading

Winnicott wrote for many audiences, parents, teachers, psychologists and psychiatrists, social workers, nurses and health visitors, and the interested public. In the 1940s and 1950s he published and broadcast on child development, largely aimed at the public and those working with developing infants and children, some of the resulting small books being eventually combined as *The Child, The Family and the Outside World* (London: Penguin, 1964). His first psychoanalytic publication was *Collected Papers, Through Paediatrics to Psycho-Analysis*, (London: Tavistock, 1958). His approach always took in the developmental aspect and this book contains papers on primary maternal preoccupation, primitive emotional development, hate and aggression, and transitional phenomena as well as the relation of mind and body. Further papers on development and on psychoanalytic technique can be found in *The Maturational Processes and the Facilitating Environment: Studies in the Theory of Emotional Development* (London: Hogarth Press, 1965). This has some important thoughts on dependence and independence, on child observation, and on the True and False Self. *Playing and Reality* (London: Pelican, 1974), which appeared just after Winnicott's death, is probably his best known book, and contains some of his most mature and subtle ideas, developing thoughts about transitional phenomena to include his views of creativity and the ways in which an infant or a patient uses or can be helped to use the objects and relationships in his or her life. The Winnicott Trust has continued to publish his work, including such volumes as *Therapeutic Consultations in Child Psychiatry* (London: Hogarth Press, 1971) and *The Piggle: An Account of the Psychoanalytic Treatment of a Little Girl* (London: Hogarth Press, 1977). His way of working with a patient can be seen in *Holding and Interpretation: Fragment of an Analysis* (London: Hogarth Press, 1986).

A useful companion to the work of Winnicott has been provided by Jan Abram, whose *Language of Winnicott* (London: Karnac, 1996) acts as an expanded dictionary of his terminology, with plentiful references. For those who are interested in the man himself there are several biographies, and a book of his selected letters edited by F. R. Rodman, *The Spontaneous Gesture* (Cambridge, MA: Harvard University Press, 1987).

Chapter 6

Symbol formation and the construction of the Inner World

Giovanna Rita Di Ceglie

An introductory metaphor

I would like to start this chapter with a picture of the internal world which I found in St Augustine's *Confessions* (397AD) where he tries to give a definition of memory. He says:

> It is like a great field or a spacious palace, a storehouse for countless images of all kinds which are conveyed to it by the senses. In it are stored away all the thoughts by which we enlarge upon or diminish or modify in any way the perceptions at which we arrive through the senses, and it also contains anything else that has been entrusted to it for safe keeping, until such a time as these things are swallowed up and buried in forgetfulness.
>
> (St Augustine 1967 [397AD]: 214)

Later St Augustine talks of 'hiding places' from which it is not that easy to retrieve thoughts.

I find that this view of the internal world is not very different from the modern psychoanalytic view of the internal world. The internal world is not a mirror image of the external one, nor is it in opposition to it; it is rather the result of an encounter between the two. St Augustine's idea that we enlarge or diminish or modify our perceptions is close to the psychoanalytic idea of unconscious phantasy with which our mind actively interacts with external reality, modifying, interpreting it and taking it in. Therefore the internal world cannot be a mere mirror of the external one. It is a most extraordinary quality of the human mind not only to be able to modify through interpreting external reality, but also to reflect upon the mind itself. It is because we possess a mind which can reflect upon itself that we can entertain the idea of change, the idea that we can change the way we feel and think about our self and the world.

Freud's description of the unconscious has given us, after Copernicus and Darwin, the third great blow to our self-importance, namely that we are not even masters in our own house (using the same symbol of the house for the internal world used by St Augustine). He has also given us, with the psycho-analytic method, an instrument to reach the 'hiding places' of St Augustine's metaphor, so that we can inhabit our house with a certain degree of comfort, and desire to enrich it.

Freud (1916–17) considered the symbolic representation of the house in dreams to refer to the human body, and parts of the house refer to the parts of the body. This meaning acquires a particular importance in the light of Ferenczi's view (1913) that the first symbols arise from the infant's search to find in objects 'his own organs and activities'. When, as in St Augustine's metaphor, we describe the internal world as a house, we make use of a sym-bolic representation: we take for granted that it is not an actual house but *like* a house, which contains furniture or people; our internal world acts to con-tain both conscious and unconscious thoughts. I am not implying here that the house is the only symbolic representation of the internal world. However, there is something so basic and simple about it that makes this representation of the internal world deeply significant and important. It seems to bring together all that we feel about ourselves, and the world, including our sense of belonging, our sense of being at home. It often appears in dreams, and it is impressive how the details of the representation can throw light on, or reveal, both psychopathology and insight into it. One patient, for example, who continuously in her early years of analysis devalued herself and constantly blamed other people for not loving her, brought a dream where she was inside her house which had been burgled of everything valuable; through the window she could even see stolen stuff left on the garden lawn. In the dream she was desperately trying to sort out how the burglars got in, since the windows and doors were closed and intact. The dream offered her a wonderful opportunity for the insight that she must start the enquiry from within and to begin to ask herself why or how she came to deprive or burgle herself of all the valuable aspects she undoubtedly had. When she began to do so in analysis her inner world began to be populated with people and feelings which she had simply wiped out.

Another patient at the beginning of her analysis dreamed of a ruined house which had an orange tape surrounding it to indicate ongoing repairs. The dream represented the work of analysis, which was intended as repar-ation of an internal world experienced and represented as a house in a state of dereliction. On other occasions dreams of houses have guided me to understand the problems which had led patients to seek analysis. One patient I saw for assessment dreamed of a house with doors which had no working locks and, as it happened, that the price to repair the door locks was exactly the same amount as the fee for the preliminary consultation. He had no idea of what that meant, but it was not a bad representation of this man's incapacity to negotiate relationships with people and of his wish to do some-thing about it. He either felt completely invaded or totally isolated. He felt himself to be like a house with no doors working properly. He was terrified of letting homosexual friends bugger him without his really wanting it and feeling totally unable to prevent it. He did not feel in charge of his own body, as anything or anybody could come inside as they pleased.

Another patient dreamed of living in a rented house. Its toilets were either blocked by stuff which should not have been there, or they were overflowing with water, so that they were totally useless. This man suffers from anorexia of the bulimic type. In reality he uses toilets to vomit after his meals, and he uses the analysis in the same way, more to evacuate his internal world than to engage in a process of knowing about it. He is still very far away from being curious about his internal world, but he is intrigued by his dreams and brings them to me because he knows that I value his internal world even if, for the time being, he cannot. He uses my mind as his rented house.

I give these examples to show how dreams can reveal aspects of the internal world through symbolic representation, and how they reveal in an extraordinary synthetic way the essence of the way we feel about ourselves, including our body and our relationship with other people. However, symbolic functioning must include a capacity not only for representing or using words to describe that representation but a capacity for distinguishing the representation from the real object, in the same way that a photo or a picture is not the object that it represents. This concept is clearly expressed by the Magritte painting of a pipe with the subtitle, 'This is not a pipe'.

The absence of the object and symbol formation

The mental function which we call symbol formation is acquired in the course of normal development. It is such an integral part of being and we take it so much for granted that we forget the gigantic developmental leap it involves, and also the difficulties or failures that some individuals have in achieving it.

Research on the development of symbolic thinking has similarities with the research into the evolution of man as a distinct and unique species. It is an area of great interest not only to psychoanalysts but also to developmental psychologists and neuroscientists, palaeontologists and entomologists. It is interesting to see the parallel between the beginning of symbolic thinking in the evolution of our species, and the appearance of symbolic activity in the development of the individual.

Palaeontologists connect the appearance of *Homo sapiens* with what is known as 'the creative explosion'. This has set us apart from any other species inhabiting the earth. Think of those magnificent animals painted on the walls of many caves in various parts of Europe. They go back to 30,000 years ago and mark the beginning of a new species. Although it will not be possible to fully know the meaning of those pictures on the walls, one thing is certain: those people could think of an absent object, experience its absence and represent it. Those animals, formerly only objects of consumption, become in those caves objects of imagination.

To return to the development of this capacity in the history of individual development: there is a time when the infant shows the beginning of a creative explosion. Piaget, in his book *La formation du symbol chez l'enfant* (1945), clearly identifies the appearance of symbolic activity with the beginning of play. He calls it '*le symbol ludic*'. He differentiates this from any other form of mental activity such as imitation. With imitation, the infant uses play activity to introject something or somebody objectively present in external reality; with the appearance of the '*symbol ludic*' the infant evokes an absent object which has already been assimilated and which is not present. For example, he observed a baby girl who got hold of the tail of a toy donkey and said laughing 'na-na, na-na' which means sleep. Pleasure was produced by the evocation of the pillow, the experience of falling asleep with her soft toy. It is the capacity to associate to objects in their absence which has been developed in this example. The baby will shortly be able to evoke an absent object or state without the help of present objects associated with them.

Piaget's formulation of the '*symbol ludic*', related to absent objects, is consistent with the psychoanalytic thinking underlying object-relations theory. In 'Beyond the pleasure principle', Freud (1920) linked a child's play with the absence of the mother in the context of exploring the role of pleasure in mental life. His observation of the child's play has become known as the *fort-da* game: Freud observed his 18-month-old grandson, who would throw a wooden reel attached to a string over the edge of his cot accompanying the action with the sound *o-o-o-o* taken to mean *fort* – 'gone' and then he would pull it back and happily welcome it with *da* – 'there'. Freud thought that the pleasure the boy experienced in playing the game derived from his mastery of the situation, as the game symbolised the departure and return of his mother. Through the game the child transformed a situation over which he had no control, his mother's absence, into one where he could make an object appear or disappear as he pleased. Freud was not primarily concerned with the process of symbolisation, but nonetheless observed its empowering force in dealing with an experience of absence.

Winnicott (1951) saw the beginning of thinking as occurring in the infant when the transitional object is created, which he defined as the infant's first possession of a not-me object. This object is particularly important at times of separation or at bedtime. Winnicott considered the transitional object as expressing our attempt as infants to grasp a reality outside ourselves, which I think involves the experience of absence. The transitional object can be a blanket or a teddy bear or any other object; it is the infant's way of dealing with the absent breast by creating a substitute or a reminder.

The presence of the object and symbol formation

Symbol formation can be deficient, which has induced many psychoanalysts to ask questions not only concerning how and when symbols appear, but also to formulate hypotheses as to what might go wrong in normal development to bring about the failure to form symbols, the essence of thinking and communicating. I am talking here of psychotic or autistic patients, amongst whom dreaming, playing or talking is grossly impaired, and also of people who may dream, but the dream is not evocative of any other object or experience. The dream has a quality which we would describe as 'concrete' rather than 'symbolic' of the patient's subjective experience; such dreams cannot be associated to nor interpreted. In these cases dreams cannot be an object of curiosity; they are rather something to be got rid of or evacuated as quickly as possible.

Where people experience inhibitions in certain areas of life, for instance, children who cannot play or people who cannot work, their thinking becomes concrete. It seems that the play or the activity stirs up too much anxiety and therefore has to be blocked. A toy or a game is not a representation of something else, but has the quality of the immediate concreteness of a primary object. If we take the game of chess as an example, we know that on one level the game is about killing the queen and checkmating the king, representing unconscious wishes towards our parents. It is a different matter if the queen and king are not experienced as representations. In international football matches people feel patriotic pride at their victory over the opposition team; the match is a symbolic representation of a war. However, for football hooligans the match ceases to be a representation of a war and it becomes a real one. Similarly, Winnicott reported the case of a child whose soft toys were his children and no one was allowed to refer to them as toys. The toys were not *representing* his children: they *were* his children. It was Winnicott himself who, referring to the analytic situation, said that for some people the couch stands for a good experience but for some it *is* the good experience. I think that the same can be said of bad experiences as well.

I was able to see this clearly during the treatment of a patient in her early thirties with difficulties in her relationships. She experienced a vague sense of dissatisfaction about life slipping away. She also could not formulate to herself what she was looking for, but felt that she was searching for something. What struck me was her frequent reference to the fact that her house was in a state of neglect. It quickly became evident that the analysis became both the derelict house where everything went wrong as well as an extremely idealised one where nothing had to change. I was constantly in the wrong, words did not seem to have a common meaning, separations were beyond comprehension and what became clear was that she believed it was me who needed analysis and not her. The power of her projections of her needy self into me was such that I often had the fantasy of lying down on the couch and letting her sit in my chair!

Analysis with this patient had a completely different quality from the work I do with other patients. There was no room for exploring or interpreting, as either generated intolerable anxiety. She had to be protected from any awareness of being a separate person. Separations did not leave us intact; instead they were experienced as mutilations. Either they left her intact but I was deprived of something she now had which she felt I would want to have back, or the other way around. It became clear to me that the analysis could not represent the spacious house but instead revealed her failure to achieve such a representation. On the other hand, I was meant to house what she experienced as unbearable and incomprehensible. It was clear that what needed repair was not the internal world as such but its very foundations.

It is unclear what it is that goes wrong in the course of development to bring about such disturbances of symbol formation. What is clear is that we need as infants to inhabit the mother's physical and mental space, and that it is within the mother–child relationship that development can take different paths. Rey (1979) described the construction of mental space as a representation created in the mind of the child by the physical and emotional space provided by the mother, a kind of marsupial space from which the infant will emerge with its own resources differentiated from those of the mother. His formulation is similar to Winnicott's idea of the 'holding environment' (1960). Winnicott believed that with the holding environment the infant, whose psychic and somatic experiences are inextricably interconnected, begins to make links between motor, sensory and functional experiences. Through these links he begins to have a sense of being a person with a limiting membrane equated with the surface of the skin which enables the child to have a sense of inside and outside.

It is not easy to grasp the complexity of both the physical and psychical mechanisms involved in such a process of differentiation from our maternal house, as well as in the process of introjection of it, and different authors have explored different and equally important aspects of it. Rey (1979) and Winnicott both emphasise the concomitance of physical and emotional factors.

Klein and the internal house

Melanie Klein concentrated her work on the way the infant must manage powerful feelings of love and hatred towards the mother; she formulated her view of symbolism in 'The importance of symbol formation in the development of the ego' (1930). In this paper she described the case of a little boy who could not play. She related his inhibition to his unresolved aggression towards his mother from whom he could not move away by finding substitutes in external reality, as these substitutes would be experienced as being as terrifying as some aspects of the original object, namely his mother's body. Klein concluded that it was for this reason that the process of discovering reality and managing feelings had come to a standstill.

Klein's paper is especially interesting because in it she related the pathology of the boy to an experience of early infancy marked by lack of emotional and physical intimacy with the mother. In the same paper, she links the concept of the epistemophilic instinct to symbol formation. For Klein, this inborn curiosity towards the breast or the inside of the mother's body, which Freud considered as part of infantile sexuality, is bound up with powerful wishes to destroy it, as well as with wishes to spare it from our aggression. If these two feelings are not integrated, the process of learning will be jeopardised to a greater or lesser extent.

With Klein, the infant is not a passive recipient of maternal care: the infant is actively involved from the beginning in a process which should ultimately lead to the introjection of the maternal home. The so-called 'introjection of the good object' is in fact the introjection of a good relationship, first with the breast or aspects of the breast and then with the mother as a whole person, with the father and siblings, so that a whole world is built up inside. This world is not an exact copy of the external one, but it is the result of an encounter between powerful internal feelings and phantasies and actual experiences.

The introjection of the so-called good object is ultimately what enables the process of separation to take place successfully. This is not difficult to grasp: if we can retain inside a good experience and a sense of belonging to a good object, we are better equipped to deal with the experience of absence of that object. It is a different matter when what has been introjected is a negative experience. To give an example, a woman in her early thirties came to see me for a consultation. She complained that she had felt compelled to think all the time about her mother and that this was ruining her life. She was married and lived in a different country from her mother; she had left her parents but in her mind she had not separated from them. Without the concept of inner reality it would be impossible to make sense of what this woman was talking about. In her mind she was tangled up within an extremely demanding, insatiable mother. We can say that something impeded the introjection of the good object. It was also clear that she experienced the burden inside her concretely. She conveyed to me that she was not reporting an experience, but rather speaking of a thing inside which she did not know how to get rid of.

Love and hatred, and their corollaries jealousy and envy, influence the process of introjection of good experiences. This was particularly evident in this patient. Her experience of having had a good session was very precarious, not just because she lost it when the session was over, but because it seemed to turn into something else, like 'having being taken for a ride' or cheated, because of the contaminating effect of these primary emotions. We can see how such a quick transformation, often taking place unconsciously, weakened the patient's capacity to take in good things which are so essential at times of frustration.

In Kleinian thinking, the integration of our internal world and symbol formation go hand in hand and the process is never achieved once and forever. Hanna Segal developed Klein's ideas of symbol formation further in 'Notes on symbol formation' (1957), when she distinguished between *symbolic equations* and *symbols proper*. In *symbolic equations* the symbol substitute is felt *to be* the original object; *the symbol proper* is felt *to represent* the object. Segal linked a capacity for symbol formation to the transition from a state of unintegration to a state of mind of greater integration and awareness of the mother as a separate person. Following Klein, she emphasised the reparative aspect of symbol formation based on a desire to spare the original object from aggression. She sees in reparation the foundation of creativity. The symbols themselves are for Segal a creation of an internal object, which bears connections with the original, primary maternal object but which is also recognised as different.

Containment, transformation and symbol formation

It is not easy to convey the tremendous leap forward that the transition to symbol making involves; it is interesting that symbol formation is both brought about by separation as well as what makes separation possible in the first place. It is in fact the delicate area of experiencing the absence of the breast that Bion sees as the platform where the infant embarks either towards thinking or towards the avoidance of thinking.

Bion (1962a) attributed the beginning of thinking to two fundamental ingredients: the infant's capacity to bear frustration in regard to absence; and the maternal capacity for containment and reverie. Bion's theory of thinking seems the most revolutionary way of studying the mother and baby interaction in relation to the development of symbolic functioning. Although profoundly rooted in Freud and Klein, his model of development, based on the relationship between the container and the contained, has added a new dimension to a view of mental development based on the progression from non-integration towards integration. The evolution from one state to the other, with Bion, can only occur through a process of *transformation* involving two people in interaction with one another.

Bion came to thinking about mother and baby relationships through work with severely psychotic adult patients who present with disturbances of symbolic thinking (1962a, 1962b). He related the psychotic mode of functioning to a psychological disaster in the first link with the mother. In Bion's theory the baby in normal circumstances communicates to the mother anything that is unmanageable or incomprehensible, such as his fears and puzzling bits of emotion. These cannot yet be used to furnish the internal world; they are the raw elements, or β-elements as Bion called them, which can only be expelled. If the mother is capable of receiving these elements, if she 'houses' them, a *transformation* occurs in her mind. What was unbearable becomes bearable, and by dealing with the baby appropriately she gives back to him those elements, now made more bearable by their sojourn in her.

Through this experience, the baby will be able to introject not only the transformed elements but also the function of containment and transformation itself. What was meaningless and raw and unusable for furnishing the inner world becomes, with time, meaningful and good for use (Bion 1926b). Certainly the idea of containment and transformation of unbearable and meaningless elements into bearable and meaningful ones is at the core of analytic work. The concept is also an invaluable tool in dealing with mental phenomena wherever we encounter them, in the classroom, clinic or any other institution.

Symbolon and symbol formation

To go back to the house metaphor, Bion's model tells us why we need to rest in our maternal home before we can have our own. Segal's paper shows that our first symbols are truly our own creations. I would like to add that the first symbols are acts of freedom and love towards our original objects and towards ourselves, in our desire to develop as unique individuals whilst maintaining a sense of belonging to our origins. This aspect is captured by the Greek word *symbolon*, which means a sign of recognition. The *symbolon* was an object which was broken in two by two people, each retaining one half. After a long absence from one another, when reunited they would match the two pieces together as a sign of recognition of their relationship. The *symbolon* is a representation of our need to grow and separate without losing our sense of belonging to our origins. I believe that without the *symbolon* we would not manage separation. However, it is also true that without separation we would not be called upon to exercise the function of creating symbols and with them to furnish our internal home.

References

Bion, W.R. (1962a) 'A theory of thinking', in W.R. Bion *Second Thoughts*, New York: Jason Aronson.

—— (1962b) *Learning from Experience*, London: Heinemann.

Ferenczi, S. (1913) 'Stages in the development of the sense of reality', reprinted in *First Contributions to Psychoanalysis*, London: Hogarth Press, 1952.

Freud, S. (1916–17) *Introductory Lectures on Psychoanalysis, Standard Edition*, vol. 14, London: Hogarth Press.

—— (1920) Beyond the pleasure principle, *Standard Edition*, vol. 18, pp. 3–64, London: Hogarth Press.

Klein, M. (1930) 'The importance of symbol formation in the development of the ego', *The Writings of Melanie Klein*, vol.1, London: Hogarth Press.

Piaget, J. (ed.) (1945) *La formation du symbole chez l'enfant*, Neuchâtel: Delashaux & Niestlé.

Rey, J.H. (1979) 'Schizoid phenomena in the borderline', *Advances in the Psychotherapy of the Borderline Patient*, New York: Jason Aronson.

Segal, H. (1957) 'Notes on symbol formation', *International Journal of Psychoanalysis* 38.

St Augustine (1967 [397AD]) *Confessions*, Harmondsworth: Penguin.

Winnicott, D. (1951) 'Transitional objects and transitional phenomena', *Collected Papers: Through Paediatrics to Psychoanalysis*, London: Tavistock.

—— (1960) 'The theory of the parent–infant relationship', *International Journal of Psychoanalysis* 41.

Suggestions for further reading

Ernest Jones's 'Theory of symbolism' in his *Collected Papers in Psycho-analysis* (London: Baillière, 1918), is the classic paper on the origins of psychoanalytic thinking on symbol formation after Freud's first formulation in *The Interpretation of Dreams* (1900) *Standard Edition*, vols 4 and 5; and the *Introductory Lectures on Psycho-Analysis* (1915–16), *Standard Edition*, vol. 15.

Melanie Klein's paper (1930) 'The importance of symbol-formation in the development of the ego', in the *Writings of Melanie Klein*, vol.1 (London: Hogarth Press) roots symbol formation within object relations theory. Here symbolism is considered essential to creativity and as an essential feature of psychic development. Klein's ideas are further refined and expanded by Segal (1957) in her seminal paper 'Notes on symbol formation', reprinted in *The Work of Hanna Segal. A Kleinian Approach to Clinical Practice* (New York: Jason Aronson, 1981). Amongst many original theoretical developments of the concept of symbol formation and the structuring of the internal world, Bion's paper 'A theory of thinking', in *Second Thoughts* (New York: Jason Aronson, 1962) and *Learning from Experience* (London: Heinemann, 1962) are suggested. Interesting developments of the concept can be found in Meltzer's paper 'The relation of anal masturbation to projective identification', reprinted in *Melanie Klein Today*, ed. Elizabeth Bott Spillius, (London: Routledge, 1988); and Roger Money-Kyrle's paper 'Cognitive development' in his *Collected Papers*: Clunie Press, 1978). For recent explorations of symbol formation and body representations, the following paper is suggested for Italian speakers: 'Strutture e funzioni del corpo nella formazione del simbolo' by Domenico and Giovanna Rita Di Ceglie (2001) *Psicoanalisi, Rivista della Associazione Italiana di Psicoanalisi* 5, 1. *The Cradle of Thinking* by Peter Hobson (London: Macmillan, 2002) is an interesting exploration of the origins of thinking and research into autism.

Chapter 7

Recent developments in the theory of dreams

Susan Budd

In a sense, psychoanalysis began with dreams. *The Interpretation of Dreams* was first published in 1900, followed quickly by two books, on jokes and on the psychopathology of everyday life, in which Freud demonstrated how his new theory of the processes of the unconscious mind could be used to explain a great deal of everyone's everyday behaviour.

His stress throughout was on the normality and ubiquity of activities like dreaming, forgetting things, making mistakes, telling jokes, and so on, which are rooted in the unconscious mind. We've all got one, and the way it makes us think and behave unites us with those outsiders, those others, young children, primitive peoples and the mentally ill, from whom we spend much of our lives trying to distance ourselves. I often think that much of the hostility to psychoanalysis expressed by academics and public figures stems from its anarchic, banana-skin effect on our wish to be seen as properly grown up, balanced, judicious, full of *gravitas*; our dreams especially can be wonderfully debunking productions. A patient comes in and tells us that they dreamt that we invited them to tea and then we hadn't got any to offer so they kindly cooked us a hamburger, or that they arrived in a consulting room which was full of our badly behaved children and turned into a sandpit. We can enjoy these subversive images together, and also notice the relief that both analyst and patient feel in being liberated momentarily from our customary roles in the consulting room.

It is strange, given the high value that Freud placed upon dreams – 'the royal highway to knowledge of the unconscious aspect of the mind', he called them – that a century later, many psychoanalysts take no special interest in dreams, and do not think that they offer us any special access to the inner world or demand any particular interpretative technique. This change is not particularly new: Freud himself was noticing and regretting it by the 1920s.

Vicky Hamilton's recent study (1996) of how a group of English and American analysts of different theoretical persuasions actually put psycho-analytic theory into practice found that analysts differ widely in their atti-tudes to dreams. Some find them not particularly interesting and hard to work with. Others find them enjoyable and fascinating. (Unsurprisingly, the second sort of analyst is told far more dreams.) But few contemporary psychoanalysts think that dreams are a uniquely valuable source of information about the patient's psyche. This is because of the overwhelming contemporary emphasis on the central role of the transference interpretation. Hamilton thinks that this is part of the contemporary restriction of psychoanalysis to a focus on the patient's present relationships, particularly that with the analyst, at the expense of the earlier aim to recreate the patient's psychic history, laid down in sedimentary layers that the dream, like a geological bore, brings up in condensed and scrambled images the forgotten and concealed psychic past:

> The focus on the here-and-now transference interpretation has changed analysts' use of dream material. When dreams are interpreted as manifestations of disguised thoughts and feelings about the present transference relationship, dreams are understood along a horizontal as opposed to a vertical dimension. Relational, present-time interpretations flatten and extend laterally the condensed and dispersed associations to dream content. The dream, like the mind, loses depth both historically and as an imaginative elaboration of everyday experience. And with this loss, the fragility, specificity, and complexity of dreams disperse into more simple affective and relational transactions. . . . If analysts are no longer concerned with the detailed histories of their patients, the idiosyncratic imagery of dreams has less to reveal about the mind of one of the two participants in the analytic relationship. And perhaps that means that imagination is, after all, less central to the analyst's creativity than is his capacity for empathic or projective identification.
>
> (Hamilton 1996: 283)

Hamilton regrets this change, as I do. How has this situation come about? Let us begin at the beginning.

The Interpretation of Dreams is a stiff read. When teaching psychotherapy students, I try to console them with the thought that it is not only about dreams, but also contains Freud's theory of how the mind works, yet they still find it tough going. Unlike Jung, Freud did not consider that dreams were in themselves sources of any unique wisdom or insight inaccessible by other means. He thought that dreams allow us to sleep by discharging in veiled form primitive impulses stirred up by the previous day; his attitude to dreams was more like that of Scrooge, telling Marley's ghost that he was really caused by a speck of indigestible mustard. But what fascinated Freud was the process of symbolic transformation by which an unconscious wish is translated into a conscious thought. The contents of the unconscious, being derived from infantile wishes and bodily drives, he did not think particularly remarkable. He saw the dreaming mind as continuous with and working in a very similar way to the waking mind. Most of our perceptions and mental activity are not accessible to consciousness whether we are asleep or awake. Dreams for the psychoanalyst are akin to daydreams, hallucinations, visions and jokes.

Theoretically speaking, Freud's views on dreams were based on the topographical model, and never clearly modified to fit in with the later structural model. His account of the formation of a dream was that of a lengthy system of transformations and translations undertaken by the dreaming mind to smuggle forbidden ideas past the censor. The forbidden wish can appear in consciousness or in the dream because it is heavily disguised. So the classical technique of dream interpretation involves putting the process of forming a dream into reverse.

Classically, the analyst works back from the manifest dream, or more accurately the dream as it is remembered and reported in a session, by gathering the patient's associations to each element of the dream, putting them together with the events of the previous day and his knowledge of the patient's life, and decoding from its symbolic language the dream thoughts, the latent dream, which lead back to the particular infantile wish, generally sexual and often on one level about the relation with the analyst, which threatened to disturb sleep and so produced the dream in the first place. The metaphor that Freud used is that of the archaeologist deciphering hieroglyphics that refer to events long ago, buried in the mists of time. He saw the unconscious as striving to speak in a kind of visual language, full of puns and reversals.

Freud realized that people have generally been interested in dreams because they wonder if they are significant; in particular, if they predict the future. He made only one reference to this. The preconscious mind, he thought, recognizes things that the conscious mind denies. So if we dream that a friend is dead, and shortly afterwards discover that he is indeed fatally ill, this is because the preconscious knows more than we wish to know. We have pushed away from consciousness all the clues that tell us that there is something wrong. Since Freud, Jung certainly, and many other analysts implicitly, have seen the manifest as well as the latent content of the dream as informing us about the patient. The early analysts spent a good deal of time on dreams; the impression one gains from some accounts of sessions is that dreams provided the most important sort of material (Sharpe 1937).

The surrealist artists and poets who enthusiastically adopted psychoanalytic ideas in the 1920s and 1930s saw the dream as a means of access to the irrational layers of the mind. They tried to represent dreams by means of automatic writing and pictorially. They followed Freud in seeing the dream as reflecting a crazy unpredictable world, in which reality is discontinuous. But unlike him, they thought this world a valuable counterweight to rational thought. Dali explicitly used Freudian dream symbols in pictures in which he tried to explore his mental difficulties. In an exhibition of Dali's work at the Tate in Liverpool, his homage to Freud was represented at the beginning of the exhibition by Freud's analytic couch.

Figure 7.1 Salvador Dali, 'The Accommodations of Desire', 1929. Copyright © Salvador Dali, Gala-Salvador Dali Foundation, Design and Artists Copyright Society, London, 2004.

In *The Accommodations of Desire* of 1929 (Figure 7.1), the thoughts appearing repeatedly on each of the discrete pebbles remind us of Freud's principle of over-determination in dreams – the same thought appears over and over again. It has a flat, pale-brown background, which many surrealists use to suggest dreams and which I will return to later. The picture is concerned with the horror of a woman's genital, which is either swarming with ants, or a lion's mouth. The lion is derived from Freud's view that wild beasts in dreams symbolize forbidden desires, and it reappears several times in various forms, illustrating the mechanisms of displacement and reversal, together with other vaginal images – the vase – and as part of the protective father whom the painter is seeking. Dali's paintings of this period often contain a protective male figure who is both his father and Sigmund Freud. In 1938, Dali had visited Freud, who wrote afterwards:

> Until now, I have been inclined to regard the surrealists, who have apparently adopted me as their patron saint, as complete fools (let us say 95%, as with alcohol). That young Spaniard, with his candid, fanatical eyes and his undeniable technical mastery has changed my estimate. It would indeed be interesting to investigate analytically how he came to create that picture.

(Ades 1995: 82)

But although in the popular mind psychoanalysts interpret dreams as one can the painting by playing a game of spot the symbol, in fact very few analysts now work in this classical way. It is rather stultifying, it tends to bracket off the dream from the rest of the analysis, and we often feel it is not the most important thing to focus on in a session.

Why is this? Why have we changed? Partly it is the impact of modern dream research, which has confirmed many of Freud's views, but not others; we now think the dream is not always based on a forbidden wish. Dreams stand on the frontier of the mind and the brain; they have both somatic and ideational roots. This has been known for a long time; Lucretius commented in *De Rerum Naturae* that children who wet their beds often dream of pissing into chamberpots; the dream protects our sleep from the need to get up and go and find one. The research undertaken in sleep laboratories on the relationship between dreams and various kinds of sleep shows the complexity, and the importance, of the dream in our psychic life (UCL 1999).

Partly, psychoanalysts have changed their attitude to dreams for the same reasons that have changed our technique in other areas. Patients and dreams seem to have changed; we focus now much more on the interaction between patient and analyst, and the dream, for bad or good, is the patient's possession. Many of us now see the manifest content of the dream as significant in its own right, and not just a clue to hidden wishes. I shall discuss these changes in turn, but I would like to say from the outset that many of the changes that we have made in our ways of seeing and using dreams Freud had made as well. As so often, it is his early work that is taken as definitive, but he was to go on writing about dreams and changing his mind for another 40 years.

Changes in patients and in dreams

It has often been said that psychoanalysts do not see so many of the 'good neurotic' patients as Freud did – or do we analyse them differently? Certainly hysterics, of whom Freud saw so many in his early years, are on the whole good and vivid dreamers, and we now see more character disorders and schizoid personalities. Modern patients do not often produce the kinds of dreams that Freud had. Modern dreams mostly seem to be shorter and more fragmentary, and this is because the dream is undoubtedly a cultural as well as a neurobiological product. It is not just a kind of mental garbage. Dreams are very specific to each individual, but they are also products of the social order. The visions of schizophrenic patients as recorded by asylum keepers had a predominantly religious quality until the mid-eighteenth century, when they began to be replaced by images of sexuality and of machines. But the modern world is both short of time and pays no official attention to dreams; patients in treatment tend to find their dreams changing and becoming richer as someone else takes an interest in them. It is comforting that Ella Sharpe

(1937) thought that the shortest, fragmentary dreams are often those which most repay attention.

Dreams vary in the extent of their cunning disguise. Sandor Ferenczi was the first to remark on how the forbidden wish is often extraordinarily transparent in the dreams of the unsuspecting person who insists, on meeting us at a dinner party or other social occasion, that we tell them what their recent dream means (Ferenczi 1916–17). Freud thought that if an analysis is going well, patients can be increasingly left to interpret their own dreams. I remember a young woman, going through a negative patch in analysis, who dreamt of sitting in the Royal Free Hospital casualty department, and recalled hearing the previous day of a boy who had shot himself in the eye with an air rifle. She then burst out, 'If I shot myself in the tongue, I wouldn't have to talk to you.' This account of her unconscious wish was entirely convincing to us both.

Freud took the ability to dream for granted. We now think that to be able to have a dream, tell it and think together with someone else about what it shows is a considerable mental achievement. The most important thing that we have to be able to do to enable us to dream successfully is to know the difference between a dream and reality. This is similar to being able to be in and use an analytic session by keeping a frame round it. Some authorities believe that deeply psychotic patients do not dream, because their waking life is full of hallucinations and dreamlike confusion. Young children confuse the contents of their minds with physical reality; they wake, and ask indignantly where the sweets are that you had put on the shelf, or think that the gorilla really is lurking behind the curtains. The mental world is not yet out there, or representational; the inner reality of dreams is also part of the external world. In the same way, very disturbed patients struggle to separate dreams from reality, and may feel that hallucinations and dreams are real and they must act them out. If the analyst appears as hostile or friendly in the dream, they will find it difficult in the session not to react as if the analyst really were like that. Their dreams often seem to reflect their anxieties directly, without the elaborate symbolic disguise of the dreams of the more normal person.

The first challenge to Freud's theory that we dream to enable us to go on sleeping was the nightmare or anxiety dream; the dream that wakes us so violently that we find it hard to sleep. The well-known painting of *The Nightmare* by Fuseli, painted around 1782, was one of the early icons of the Romantic movement. It is said that Freud had an engraving hanging in his waiting room. It depicts the ancient view that the choking anxiety of a nightmare is caused by a demon sitting on the chest, which will sexually invade the body of the dreamer and try to take over her mind. Ernest Jones thought that these sorts of dreams were caused by a specific kind of homosexual anxiety which was commoner in the sixteenth and seventeenth centuries (Jones 1916), but it seems more likely that here we are looking at a physiological universal.

If we look at images of nightmares from other cultures we can see the same themes appearing: the pressure on the chest, the sense of there being other beings inside one's head, the animals who invade us. Presumably the similarity of these images across time and space stems from the universal human experiences of inhabiting the same bodies, having the same sorts of experiences in early childhood, experiencing the physiological states of anxiety and fear in the same way, and so on. Even in cultures where dreams are believed to predict the future rather than revive the past, patients vividly dream of past traumas as they do in the west. Such dreams are doubly frightening for them, since they fear that the trauma is not only past but will come again in the future. The dreams of borderline patients commonly depict the body or the inner self being invaded by a parasitic being, just as many horror films do. But to dream even this is an accomplishment. The worst nightmares are those with imageless sensations of terror: in them we experience a horror without being able to symbolize it.

There was plenty of evidence for this amongst the shell-shock patients of the Great War, whose treatment gave such an impetus to psychoanalysis. Night after night, soldiers would experience again the horrifying events that had led to their breakdown. Modern research into traumatic dreams shows that as people begin to recover from horrifying experiences, images of the terror begin to appear in their dreams. Finally they begin to dream that they can master the horror – escape from the burning building, flee from the assailant – and then they can use the process of symbolization to begin to sleep. In Hanna Segal's terms (1986), they are moving from a symbolic equation to a true symbol.

In the same way, the drawings of sexually abused children will at first show broken fragments, or tearing and scratching of the paper, and then begin to show in symbolic form and increasingly directly what the bodily invasion felt like. Ferenczi, who worked with some very damaged patients, told of a woman who every night would experience imageless sensations related to her early traumas, wake, and then have a dream in which the sensations were represented in images, which would allow her a refreshing sleep (Ferenczi 1931). Indeed, many of us have the sense that a good night's sleep involves satisfactory dreams, even if we do not particularly remember them (Parsons 1997). We could say that the dream does indeed represent a wish; but it is a wish to dream, to represent our psychic life in image or narrative.

The evidence from dream research is equivocal about the merits of post-traumatic dreams as a method of mourning and coming to terms with the past. Some studies show that the best way of surviving horrifying experiences is to repress them so deeply that we never even dream of them. Others suggest that for the mildly depressed, dreaming is indeed a way of coming to terms with distressing events, and their dreams during a single night show progressively more pleasant themes, and a lighter mood on waking.

It was Jung who pointed out that dreams can be analysed in series. He believed that they show the unconscious mind returning over and over again to a central dilemma or theme in the life of the dreamer, and some dreams certainly are of this type. I shall return to this again when I talk about symbolism in dreams. Ronald Fairbairn, who produced a revised meta-psychology for psychoanalysis in a series of papers in the 1940s and 1950s, saw dreams as being like cinema shorts; they represent in condensed form our self-narrative (Fairbairn 1944). His analogy is interesting. The cinema has drawn extensively on the psychoanalytic view of dreams, and perhaps is the medium most capable of representing the dreaming experience to us.

Freud always implicitly assumed that there is a distinction between reality-based thinking, located in the ego, and psychotic thinking, such as dreaming, which is dominated by unconscious processes. Melanie Klein was less interested in dreams as such because for her all thinking was more permeated by unconscious elements. She thought that we cope with unacceptable ideas less by repression than by splitting the ego, and in our dreams our divided minds often appear represented by different levels, or different rooms in a house.

We can see these two approaches reflected in visual representations of the mind. For example, in Goya's familiar engraving of *The Sleep of Reason Brings Forth Monsters* the dreamer, slumped forward in sleep, is separate from the monsters that appear in the background, even though the advance made by the Romantic movement was intermittently to realize that these monsters come from another part of oneself. But the dreamer will awake, and they will disappear into the underworld. Melanie Klein was working in a more modern idiom, in which there is no such reassuring division between the sane waking world and the world of dreams; dream images are part of the divided inner self. Consider Figure 7.2, *Cerebral Palsy*, produced in 1906 by

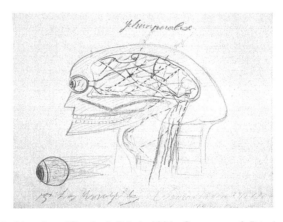

Figure 7.2 Louis Umgelter, 'Cerebral Palsy', 1906. Courtesy of Prinzhorn Collection, Heidelberg University and Hayward Gallery, London.

Louis Umgelter, a mental patient suffering from alcoholism and dementia praecox. (It forms part of the Prinzhorn Collection of art produced in European mental asylums between the start of the last century and the 1920s, on show at the Hayward Gallery, London as part of the exhibition of 'Art and Psychosis', December 1996 to February 1997.) Like many of the other drawings in the exhibition, it showed the space inside the head as fragmented, muddled, divided. It is not an unsophisticated production; it reflects the medical diagrams that the patient must have seen of the inside of the head. It is rather reminiscent of the 'X-ray' images of Australian aboriginal art, produced by a culture in which all reality starts in dreams; we are literally dreamed into existence. These artists must be aware that kangaroos and men do not really look like this inside; these are pictures of psychic space.

Many modernist artists and thinkers in the twentieth century have been excited by the direct access that some mental patients and primitive peoples apparently have to the unconscious. The Nazis took the opposite point of view. They condemned modern art precisely because it resembled either primitive art or that of the insane. They exhibited some of the Prinzhorn paintings together with modern art as examples of the degenerate, primitive and savage developments in painting that they were trying to stamp out. Indeed, some of those artist/patients were to die in the concentration camps.

Dreams and the transference

The second major shift in British psychoanalytic thinking that has affected our attitude to dreams has been the increasing focus from the 1950s onward on transference–countertransference issues. In its extreme form, the analyst focuses on the events of the session as it proceeds, scanning the material for the projections and introjections that both block and express the interaction between analyst and patient. Here, the dream is less important for its content than for its place in the session. Is it seen as a gift? Is it an escape? Is it a part of the self being evacuated? Is it a repository for things that cannot be talked about otherwise? Why is it being told at this moment, and in this way? Is the dream the patient's secret possession to which he alone has the key, or does he hand it over passively as something whose meaning belongs to the analyst? How does the relation between analyst and patient find reflection in the dream?

At the same time as this change was occurring, because of the influence of Melanie Klein there was also an increasing focus in British psychoanalysis on the death instinct and on experience in very early childhood. This meant that the unconscious content of dreams came to be seen as very traumatic and overwhelming to the ego. The early unconscious fantasies that were uncovered were of being attacked by a cruel and archaic superego, which makes us feel terribly ashamed of memories of childhood experiences – wetting the bed, for instance. I think that this situation is well represented in medieval paintings of hell. The doom paintings found in so many churches remind us of the archaic fantasies that Melanie Klein found to haunt young children. God is the superego dividing us into the good, who cannot do anything except stand around looking relieved, and the bad, who are punished by cruel demons, a fusion of the superego and the id. The demons in Bosch and other painters are the images of nightmares; their vividness derives from the energies of the id. Such nightmarish figures, part man and part animal, often seem to be devouring and shitting out figures through every orifice. The mouth and the anus are equated, as in the child's earliest oral fantasies about birth. The internal angry feelings have been externalized into a multitude of angry persecutors. The blessed, cut off from that 'seething cauldron of impulses', seem lifeless and monotonous by comparison.

Many analysts came to believe that these unconscious phantasies are ubiquitous; because they underlie all thought and feeling, therefore dreams are a less important and special means of communicating them. Also, if the analysis of the transference is seen as the most important thing, dreams, which take place outside the session, are less interesting in themselves than in the way they are used in the session. Vicky Hamilton, in the passage I cited earlier, thinks that in this way we flatten out the dream and lose its capacity to surprise us or make us see things anew.

Freud emphasized all his life that we do not really know what a dream means, any more than we can ever know the unconscious mind. The dream, he said, has a navel that joins it to the underworld; the most important part of the dream will always be too deep for us to capture it, because we can never know the unconscious. But if we focus on the transferential aspect of the dream, we tend to interpret from a position of the person who knows, rather than being able to hear about the dream from its author and be surprised by it. The modern tendency is to focus on the telling of the dream as part of the relationship between analyst and patient, and not systematically to ask for associations to the dream. This increases the likelihood that the analyst will be felt to know about the patient's mind through empathy rather than through listening to associations, which remind us that the connections which the patient makes to the images in their dreams are to some extent unique to themselves.

I think that dreams, even fragments of dreams, are valuable in analysis precisely because they are produced outside the session. Not only can we notice how the analysis is progressing through changes in dreams, but also things come to light in dreams that have been unconsciously censored in the session. This can happen in surprising ways. I remember a patient who had been in analysis with me for some years who had recently sold a valuable family heirloom. His dream was apparently a simple wish fulfilment; he dreamt that the sale had been more successful than it was. But in recounting it, he was struck by the light in the dream, which reminded him of the light, soft but brilliant, of the winters in Teheran when he was a child. As he went on reminiscing, most unexpectedly a girl appeared, with whom he used to play in an overgrown apricot orchard and enjoy exploring both sexual and aggressive feelings in a way that he had, until that moment, completely forgotten. This led to recognition of another aspect of his transference to me. Would we ever have reached this material other than via a dream?

For normal and neurotic people, the dream has an imaginative 'as if' sort of quality. By means of it, they can explore areas of themselves, or feelings about the analyst, which feel hard to acknowledge. 'It was only a dream' they say, just as people say 'it was just a joke'. I find myself reminding them that it was them, after all, who dreamt it, but the untraumatic dream seems a gentle and convincing way of showing them some of the unconscious aspects of their minds. Lewin (1946) wrote an influential paper in which he compared the dream to the projection of an image on a neutral surface, a screen like a cinema screen, which was originally the mother's body. I think that the flat, pale-brown surface found in many surrealist paintings is alluding to this. If we can view the dream as something outside ourselves, as if it were happening on a screen we were watching, we do not feel that we are disrupted and invaded by it. It is when the image seems to fragment, or crumple, or become uncannily still, or when people dream of falling forever, or disintegrating, liquefying and pouring out of their skin, that the containment function of the analyst and the maternal presence seems to fail and the screen, or the skin-ego we imagine round ourselves, is pierced. Then the dream seems to be less separate from us, and becomes more frightening.

I have often been struck by the importance of the spatial dimension in the dream and in the unconscious. Patients seem strongly subliminally aware of the shape of the analyst's consulting room and its relation to other spaces, and in their dreams they seem very conscious of the analyst being behind them. Rear-view mirrors in dreams are one way of showing how they wish to check up on us. Seating arrangements in dreams often show the associations created by the unusual situation in which one person lies down and looks at a blank wall, while the other sits out of sight and sees only the top of their head. One patient came in with a dream in which I appeared as the shark behind the sofa.

The final section of my account of how our views on dreams have changed is the interpretation of symbolism in dreams.

Symbolism in dreams

Freud sometimes interpreted as if there were a universal symbolism, and sometimes not. He starts out *The Interpretation of Dreams* (1900) by saying that he is not thinking in the eastern European tradition of the Dream Book; i.e., the assumption that you can look up in a book what a particular dream means because there is a fixed and universal symbolic language. But in his interpretations of dreams he sometimes asserts that a given image has a fixed meaning: boxes and hollow closed spaces standing for the vagina, etc. Jung thought that there was a universal language of mankind revealed in myths, visions and dreams because dreams were messages, not only from the self but also from the collective unconscious. Freud, who was always anxious after his rift with Jung to dissasociate himself from him, can be seen in the case history of the Wolf Man (1918) veering back and forth as to whether there was indeed a phylogenetic inheritance of unconscious fantasy, or whether our dreams refer back to our specific histories.

In an influential paper, Ernest Jones (1916) argued that the situations symbolized in dreams are quite limited: they refer to the universal human experiences of living in our bodies, birth, death and procreation, and our earliest family relationships. Energy flows from these ideas via the channel of symbolism to all other ideas. But symbolic systems themselves shift and change, moving in and out of consciousness. Even Victorian paintings can sometimes puzzle us with their imagery. *The Daydream* is a beautiful water-colour of William Morris's wife Janey, painted in 1880 by Dante Gabriel Rossetti, by that stage using laudanum and much obsessed by her. The paint-ing contains at least two symbolic orders, the first of which would be more apparent to the Victorians, the second to us. The first is the language of flowers, or perhaps the Pre-Raphaelite view of the medieval world, of why it is that the woman is holding honeysuckle, and what the particular species of bush is that surrounds her. This would have been in the conscious mind of the painter and his contemporaries, but these symbolisms are now largely forgotten. I can only speculate about why he chose these plants. We know that Rossetti dreamt all his life of a dark-haired beauty in whom he could bury himself: whose daydream is this? However our post-Freudian eyes register the sensuous dreaminess in the face – Victorian genre painters had an extra-ordinary capacity to render human expression – and notice the phallic quality of the stick she is caressing.

It is certainly true that many dreams seem to contain ideas of the human body. A patient troubled about his potency dreamt of driving through a dark threatening underground passage to a safe car park. Another told her Kleinian analyst of a dream of marching soldiers; they were marching, she said, 'eight abreast'. An analyst tells of his patient's dream of a multitude of red and white soldiers fighting; quite astonishing because the next day the patient was diagnosed as suffering from leukaemia. Patients certainly seem to recover images of birth in analysis, and the sea does often stand for the mother in whose amniotic fluid we all swim. These ideas of the body are subject to different kinds of symbolic disguise, showing and denying at the same time.

There is a famous painting by René Magritte, which exists in various versions, called *The Treachery of Images*. On a flat, pale-brown dream screen floats an image of a pipe, painted in the hyper-reality of an advertisement, or an illustration in a children's book. Underneath is written 'This is not a pipe'.

Magritte wanted to use his painting to challenge everyday notions of the solidity and familiarity of reality. He uses his skill and every pictorial device to make us believe that this is a pipe. But he writes underneath that it is not a pipe. And of course it isn't but if it isn't what is it? It illustrates Freud's idea of negation – the thing which is denied is the thing that is. And yet it is not. It reminds us of the oddity of dream images. Somebody comes in and says 'Last night I dreamt of a woman who looked like my mother, but it wasn't her – she was in this room, but it was also the garden shed at home', and we know what they mean.

Like other analysts, I have been struck by the importance of the animals who appear in dreams. People who dream of small smashed fragments of animals, multitudes of insects, invertebrates who have a hard shell and a soft inside like snails, seem to be telling us about their sense of a fragmented self, or one with a tough armour to protect its lack of internal structure. Wholer patients seem more likely to dream of vertebrates. I remember a most important crucial dream of a patient who dreamt he was inside a gorilla suit in which he could act in a freer, more spontaneous way, and this dream was a turning point in his ability to come to terms with his animal nature.

Hanna Segal tells a story of a psychiatrist interviewing a mental patient who was a violinist, and asking him why he never played the violin any more. He replied that he didn't want to masturbate in public. That is, the analogy between a woman's body and a violin had become too concrete; he couldn't liberate himself from it. If we cannot know that a symbol is not what is symbolized, we cannot think.

Figures 7.3 and 7.4 are two levels of symbolism around the same idea. Figure 7.3 is a photograph by Man Ray from 1924 called *Le Violon d'Ingres*. It alludes to the wonderful Ingres painting *La Baigneuse*, which beautifully conjures up a woman's passive flesh, and to the similarity between the shape of her back and of the violin, both of which can be brought to life by the fingers. The second image (Figure 7.4) is another Magritte, *Le Viol*, painted in 1934. It is an image he drew many times slightly differently, and which other artists have used as well. It is a much more disturbing picture; we expect to see a face and see something different. It is even more perturbing to babies, whom we now know to be pre-wired, so to speak, to notice and read the human face. Like the medieval pictures of demons, this painting equates bodily orifices with each other. In this particular version though not in others, the woman's head and neck also resemble a penis. Magritte maintained he named his pictures at random, but *Le Viol* not only sounds like violin again, as if that association was in his mind, but it also means 'The Rape'. It puts the spectator in the position of the rapist, who obliterates the woman's face beneath his perception of her body, and may also confuse her body with a penis. It also alludes to the deep unconscious where the sexes and bodily parts get muddled up, where women's bodies contain penises anyway.

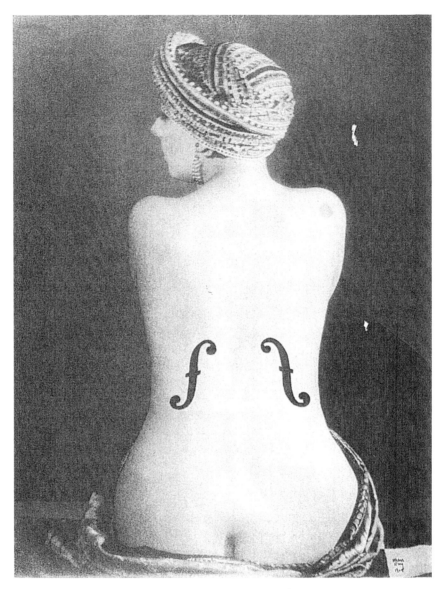

Figure 7.3 Man Ray, 'Le Violon d'Ingres', 1924. Copyright © Man Ray Trust/ADAGP, Paris and DACS, London, 2004.

In Ella Sharpe's (1937) book on dreams, based on lectures given to students at the British Psycho-Analytical Society in the 1930s, she points out that the mechanisms of transformation of dreams, which are related to the mechanisms of defence, are akin to literary ideas. Dreams exhibit synonyms and

Figure 7.4 René Magritte, 'Le Viol', 1934. Copyright © ADAGP, Paris and DACS, London, 2004.

similes, they pun, they take the part for the whole and so on. Charles Rycroft and other authors in the Independent tradition such as Marion Milner valued the dream for its creativity, its capacity to turn thoughts into narrative and images. They equated the dream far more to creative play than to a disguised wish. Indeed Freud, in his paper on the creative writer and day-dreams (1908), speculated that the reason we are so fascinated by and envious of artists and writers is because they seem to us to play all day.

Analysts do not now always look behind the manifest content of the dream for the hidden symbolism. We now think that the dreamer may be directly representing his current adult dilemmas in life. Freud came round to this view in 1920 when he distinguished dreams from above from dreams from below, perhaps recalling the classical distinction between the dreams that come through the gates of ivory and of horn. Indeed, the manifest content of his own dreams as recorded in *The Interpretation of Dreams* are full of his adult dilemmas; his responsibilities as a doctor, his intellectual and political ambitions. This change brings the psychoanalytic view of dreams nearer to the romantic view that they are worthwhile in their own right as a part of our creative imagination, our capacity to reflect and fictionalize. Many dreams seem semi-lucid, scarcely transformed by the dream work. Patients report that they edit them; say to themselves in their sleep, it's only a dream, it should end this way, and dream again, and so on.

Recent dream research suggests that we should not abandon the idea that dreams refer to past memories saturated with powerful feeling. Clear evidence for dreams is found only in the higher mammals, together with a perceptual code and long-term memory, which gives us the ability to store memories, retrieve them, and thus learn from experience. Their evolutionary significance may be as a pre-verbal method of recalling past difficulties to us as we mull over present dangers. As Freud thought, a dream image is apparently a layered one, consisting of a day residue superimposed on a stored long-term memory, the links between them being made at a pre-verbal level by auditory, visual or emotional similarities or puns.

Men and women have always known that there is something very important about dreams, and will doubtless go on wondering how to interpret them, inside psychoanalysis and out. There is something inexhaustible about them, just as Freud said. Doubtless as psychoanalytic theory and technique changes, the way that we are told dreams and the way that we interpret them will change as well. It is comforting to reflect that dreams themselves are not quite so plastic. I end with a typically caustic observation from Freud's 1923 remarks on dream interpretation: 'I think that in general it is a good plan occasionally to bear in mind the fact that people were in the habit of dreaming before there was such a thing as psychoanalysis' (Freud 1923).

References

Ades, D. (1995) *Dali*, London: Thames and Hudson.

Fairbairn, R.D. (1944) 'Endopsychic structure considered in terms of object relation-ships', *International Journal of Psychoanalysis* 25, reprinted in *Psychoanalytic Studies of the Personality*, London: Routledge and Kegan Paul, 1952.

Ferenczi, S. (1916/1917) 'Dreams of the unsuspecting', republished in *Further Contributions to the Theory and Technique of Psychoanalysis*, New York: Brunner/Mazel, 1926.

—— (1931) 'On the revision of *The Interpretation of Dreams*, Part 3 of Notes and Fragments', in *Final Contributions to the Theory and Technique of Psychoanalysis*, New York: Brunner/Mazel.

Freud, S. (1900) *The Interpretation of Dreams*, *Standard Edition*, vols 4–5, pp. ix–630, London: Hogarth Press.

—— (1908) 'Creative writers and day-dreaming', *Standard Edition*, vol. 9, pp. 141–54, London: Hogarth Press.

—— (1918) 'From the history of an infantile neurosis', *Standard Edition*, vol. 17, pp. 1–122, London: Hogarth Press.

—— (1923) 'Remarks on the theory and practice of dream interpretation', *Standard Edition*, vol. 19, pp. 109–24, London: Hogarth Press.

Hamilton, V. (1996) *The Analyst's Preconscious*, New York: Analytic Press.

Jones, E. (1916) 'The theory of symbolism', reprinted in *Collected Papers*, London: Baillière, 1948.

Lewin, B. (1946) 'Sleep, the mouth and the dream screen', *Psychoanalytic Quarterly* 15.

Parsons, M. (1997) 'Do we think our dreams? Do we dream our thinking?', Unpublished public lecture.

Segal, H. (1986) 'Notes on symbol formation', in *The Work of Hanna Segal: A Kleinian Approach to Clinical Practice. Delusion and Artistic Creativity*, London: Free Association Books.

Sharpe, E. (1937) *Dream Analysis*, London: Hogarth Press.

UCL (1999) Papers presented to the Ninth International Psychoanalytic Conference on Psychoanalytic Research, London: University College London.

Suggestions for further reading

The seminal work is, of course, Freud's (1900) *The Interpretation of Dreams, Standard Edition*, vols 4 and 5, which contains his theory of the mind at that time. Vol. 5 also contains 'On dreams', which is a shorter version more specifically on dreams. He takes up, with careful discussion, the question of whether there can be telepathic dreams in 'Dreams and telepathy', *Standard Edition*, vol. 18; and concedes that not all dreams are unconscious wishes in 'Remarks on the theory and practice of dream interpret-ation' (1923) *Standard Edition*, vol. 19. Ernest Jones enlarges on his theory in 'Freud's theory of dreams' and put forward an influential 'Theory of symbolism' in his *Collected Papers* (London: Baillière, 1948).

Melanie Klein considered dreams merely an aspect of the continuous flow of unconscious phantasy: for expositions, see Hanna Segal's 'Notes on symbol forma-tion' and 'The function of dreams', reprinted in *The Work of Hanna Segal* (London: Free Association Books, 1981); and Donald Meltzer (1981) 'The Kleinian expansion of Freudian metapsychology', *International Journal of Psychoanalysis* 62. Ella Freeman Sharpe in *Dream Analysis* (London: Hogarth Press, 1937) and Charles Rycroft in *The Innocence of Dreams* (London: Hogarth Press, 1979) treat dreams as imaginative products, and show their connections with literature and other ways of looking at them; as does *Dreams and History: The Interpretation of Dreams from Ancient Greece to Modern Psychoanalysis*, eds. Daniel Pick and Lyndal Roper (London: Brunner-Routledge, 2004).

Part 3

Sexuality and the formation of identity

The reader may be wondering at this point what has happened to Freud's original insistence that it is the suppression of sexual and aggressive drives which gives rise to the unconscious. English psychoanalysis has now moved from what has been termed a 'one-body' psychology, or conflict between drives or drive derivatives and other parts of the psyche. Instead, we think of even inner conflicts in terms of a 'two-body' psychology. We stress the way in which instincts are experienced and conceived of in relation to other people: 'My mother wouldn't have liked me to do that.' 'You shouldn't tempt me.' There is an endless interweaving between and within our psyches, splitting off the bits we cannot tolerate, dealing with them via other people's psyches; our conflicts may be dealt with or amplified in relation to each other. In an age of relative sexual freedom and effective contraception, we can see more clearly that human sexuality is less problematic in itself than in the unconscious phantasies it arouses, and in the way it makes us relate to others and contributes to our sense of identity.

In Chapter 8, Eglé Laufer is concerned with the sexuality of adolescence, a period when sexual anxieties are heightened as we move towards a secure adult sexual identity. Freud's views on how the child came to have a sense of being a boy or a girl led on to the question of gender identity and how it is acquired. Laufer shows how repeatedly psychoanalysts and others have raised the question as to whether gender identity is primarily built upon the internal experience of the body and its physical vicissitudes, or on the identifications made with the parents, or on the parents' and society's reaction to the body. She describes some of the American empirical studies of children and of identity, and the work done on transsexuals, who know and feel that they belong to the opposite gender. One of Freud's seminal ideas was that where a secure sense of sexual identity does not develop, the capacity for thinking is also hampered. Many psychoanalysts, including Laufer, dissent from the current view that gender and the awareness of the body are largely mediated through language, and therefore by culture. They see an individual's crisis over sexual identity as part of borderline pathology. Jeanine Chasseguet-Smirgel, for example, defined sexual perversion as the inability to acknowledge the differences between the sexes, the generations, and our own desires and others (Chasseguet-Smirgel 1985; also see discussion in Chapter 15, this volume). The question as to what is a variation in sexual orientation or desire and what is a perversion is a heavily politicized one (Lewes, 1995; O'Connor and Ryan 1993); as is the question of whether sexual orientation is genetic or acquired, and whether that acquisition is the result of psychic experience or physiological endowment (Ridley 2003; Raphael-Leff and Perelberg 1997).

Freud's views, as Laufer describes, immediately came under attack from feminists, both psychoanalysts and others, many of whom insisted that little girls too are born knowing themselves to be such, not having to come to femininity through seeing themselves as 'deficient' boys. But Freud believed that all of us have to develop a sense of which gender we are and, separately from this, a capacity for attraction to our own sex, the opposite one or to both. Interest in the development of sexual identity is less marked in English psychoanalysis than in the United States, as a result of the influence of Klein and her followers. Klein, in setting the Oedipus complex very early – at 6 months or so, compared to Freud's 5 years – was looking at very early anxieties, those of being engulfed, annihilated, exploded or shat out, which do not resemble the adult's conception of sexuality.

In Chapter 9, on femininity, Dana Birksted-Breen revisits some of these themes and their treatment in modern American and French psychoanalysis. She describes how the early debate on penis envy reified the concept, and how the question of whether femininity is born or made was taken up again in both France and the United States, but not in English psychoanalysis. It has been the influence of feminism, structuralism and Lacan which has drawn English psychoanalysis back to these questions. Birksted-Breen describes how Lacan returned to aspects of Freud that had largely been neglected, especially to the importance of the father figure as the one who detaches the child from his or her early state of merger with the mother, and enables him or her to move into using language and acknowledging the existence of society as outside and antithetical to the self. (If you saw *Greystoke*, a film based on Edgar Rice Burrows's *Tarzan*, you may remember the pivotal scene in which Tarzan, a human orphan raised by great apes, meets his fellow man for the first time. His entry into culture is marked by his learning to say the word 'razor'. It would have fascinated Lévi-Strauss that 'razor' marks both a cultural and sexual division: animals and wild men do not shave; women do not have beards.) For Lacan, Freud's original concept of penis envy is not about physical difference, but rather is used to explain the sense of lack in both sexes; the sense of something forever missing and incomplete.

Birksted-Breen develops the thesis that masculinity and femininity can be understood as biological or psychoanalytic concepts. Each perspective occludes the other, but at the same time both must be descriptions of aspects of the same human subject. The developmental view of human sexual identity leaves out the extent to which psychic development is based on inner, not outer, reality. The structural view neglects the fact that we inhabit bodies, and that our sense of self must be predicated on them: 'The ego is first and foremost a bodily ego' (Freud 1923). A visit to any art gallery confirms that perceptions of the human body are variable and change over time. Why do many more adolescent girls suffer from eating disorders than boys? Why do more men present with sexual perversions? To what extent do patterns of pathology change over time – will gym culture and increased male grooming result in a growing similarity between the sexes of desirable body images and consequent psychic dysfunction?

However, with Freud's formulation of the idea of the Oedipus complex, psychoanalysis moved on to a three-body psychology: there is ourselves, the one we love, the one we hate, and the relations they have with each other and how we feel about that. We have included two chapters on the Oedipus complex, partly because it was impossible to choose, and partly because they show how differently the idea can be developed from Freud's original account. In Chapter 10, Michael Feldman goes back to Sophocles' account of Oedipus and reminds us of the true horror of incest. If the parents cannot give the child a sense of the proper relations between adults and children, men and women, young and old, the child is left confused and its capacity to think is damaged. Psychoanalysis was often seen in the early and mid-twentieth century as legitimating permissive theories of childrearing and education; yet in many ways it is their sternest critic. Anna Freud, for example, once remarked that the worst thing that parents could do to a child was to leave it at the mercy of its own instincts.

Feldman takes up the Oedipus complex in terms of Klein's emphasis on splitting as a means of defence. The young child relates to two people, or things, in the outside world by either feeling jealous and excluded, or trying to make an exclusive relationship with one – the good one – at the expense of the other, which then becomes hated, and more and more powerful and threatening. Like Blake's Upas tree, the hated object is immensely powerful because it is watered and fed by the child's malign feelings. He illustrates from his case material the difficulty that we all have in acknowledging the sexual relationship between our parents – Freud's Primal Scene – and how throughout our lives, we re-enact our difficulties in coming to terms with being second-best. Things are even worse, of course, if the relationship between the parents *in reality* is bad, or non-existent, and the child is turned to as if it were a parent or a partner. Increasingly, we look for the ways in which experiences such as these have impaired the capacity to think, experiences to which, like Oedipus, we would rather turn a blind eye: we do not want to see or to know.

In his account of a session, we can hear Feldman listening to a woman who feels her husband is somewhat selfish and inconsiderate, and who exerts pressure on the analyst to be on her side. Like her mother, she feels she must be good, and be seen to be good; but she can only be so by constantly fending off a more complex reality that makes her very anxious. He describes a familiar clinical situation, one in which he is being strongly pressured to agree with his patient's version of events. It is very difficult to maintain his freedom of mind: neither to agree nor disagree with his patient, but to show her how she feels that whoever is not with her is against her, and that if she is not agreed with she is bad. In using a conception of the Oedipal triangle based on the child's very early experience, the theory has been extended: it is both about the birth of sexual identity and our jealousy over being left out, excluded (Steiner 1989).

In Chapter 11, Gregorio Kohon looks at the Oedipus complex from a very different perspective. He points out that Freud's formulation of the Oedipus complex implied theories of castration anxiety and penis envy. Since psycho-analysis takes over terms and endows them with a special meaning, there is a constant tendency to reinterpret them, and they become blurred by general use. He tackles a question which interested Freud but which later analysts often ignore: if an unconscious idea, such as the Oedipus complex, is uni-versal in mankind and is a primal fantasy, where did it come from? Memory, instinct, or phylogenetic fantasy? The latter idea interested Freud, but he moved away from it after its enthusiastic adoption by Jung. In the case his-tory of the Wolf Man, we can see him debating with himself as to whether the little boy really would have needed to see his parents having intercourse to form the fantasy (Freud 1918). There is not a 'correct' version of the Oedipal myth: it cannot be systematized, it exists in many variants, and has been interpreted in many ways. Laplanche and Pontalis (1968) discuss the complex distinctions between various theoretical traditions.

Kohon shows how Klein's view of unconscious fantasies differed from Freud's, and how Laplanche and Pontalis have offered a different view again. All these theories are based on the original helplessness of the infant, but the French school has laid more stress on the role of language in understanding. Kohon outlines how the baby reacts to not having everything he wants when he wants it, by substituting wishes – hallucinations – for action, and these unconscious wishes then form the basis, the territory, of psychoanalysis. The mother feels all-powerful, loved, hated, and the child comes to realize that he/she cannot satisfy the mother's sexual needs.

Kohon separates this process in humans from that in animals; it is unconscious phantasy which makes us human. The Oedipus myth is not about actual people or social arrangements; anthropologists such as Malinowski, who attempted to show that the Oedipus complex is culture-bound, were missing the point. All societies have myths that address the difference between the sexes, between ourselves and what is not ourselves: the absent, the missing, the obscure objects of desire. In this way of looking at things, to become a human being, a member of a family and of society, involves accepting lack and loss, and the need to acquire language. Like Feldman, however, Kohon argues for the complex relations between the child's body, the child's actual experience, and fantasy.

References

Chasseguet-Smirgel, J. (1985) *Creativity and Perversion*, London: Free Association Books.

Freud, S. (1918) 'From the history of an infantile neurosis', *Standard Edition*, vol. 17, pp. 3–123, London: Hogarth Press.

—— (1923) *The Ego and the Id, Standard Edition*, vol. 19, London: Hogarth Press.

Laplanche, J. and Pontalis, J. (1968) 'Fantasy and the origins of sexuality', *International Journal of Psychoanalysis* 49: 1–18.

Lewes, K. (1995) *Psychoanalysis and Male Homosexuality*, New Jersey: Jason Aronson.

O'Connor, N. and Ryan, J. (1993) *Wild Desires and Mistaken Identities*, London: Virago.

Raphael-Leff, J. and Perelberg, R.J. (1997) *Female Experience: Three Generations of British Women Psychoanalysts on Work with Women*, London: Routledge.

Ridley, M. (2003) *Nature via Nurture: Genes, Experience and What Makes Us Human*, London: Fourth Estate.

Steiner, J. (ed.) (1989) *The Oedipus Complex Today*, London: Karnac.

Chapter 8

Gender identity and reality

M. Eglé Laufer

Gender identity is a relatively recent term in psychoanalytic writing. Even the concept of identity itself was not used by Freud when he conceptualised a model of the structures of the functioning mind. He used the concept of ego, in German *Ich*, as comprising both the self, on the one hand, and on the other the agency of the mind containing functions such as perception. This agency relates directly to external reality, in order to ensure the individual's survival while simultaneously trying to mediate between the demands of the id and the authority of the super ego. It is for this reason that I have taken as the theme of this chapter the relation to reality when discussing the nature of gender identity. The relationship between gender identity and reality can be seen to be of fundamental significance in the treatment of the seriously disturbed adolescent. For these adolescents, the developmental task of having to find a way to integrate the newly developed sexual body into their internal reality can lead to a temporary break with external reality if the psychic implications of acquiring an identity as sexually male or female creates an unbearable state of conflict and anxiety.

We know that such adolescents may respond by attacking their own bodies or by extreme attempts at controlling the changes that are taking place, as in anorexia, for instance. They may regress to infantile states of clinging to the mother as if unconsciously needing to cling on to their pre-pubertal state, and so on. All these pathological responses to puberty have as their common theme a denial of the reality of the gender identity into which they feel their body is compelling them, and which is in conflict with the identity they have established unconsciously as part of their inner reality. These findings raise the issue as to whether we should be speaking of two distinct identities – a conscious one and an unconscious one – that may not be in accordance with each other.

What brings us nearer to the concept of self as seen by Freud is when he talks of the identifications with external objects which have become internalised as part of the process of losing or giving up of the object. In *The Ego and the Id* (1923) Freud says, referring to his earlier paper 'Mourning and melancholia' (1917), that he supposed that 'in melancholia, an object that is lost has been set up again inside the ego – that is an object cathexis has been replaced by an identification' (Freud 1923: 28). In referring to this in *The Ego and the Id*, he says:

> At that time we did not appreciate the full significance of this process and did not know how common and typical it is. Since then we have come to understand that this kind of substitution has a great share in determining the form taken by the ego and that it makes an essential contribution towards building up what is called its 'character'.
>
> (Freud 1923: 28)

Perhaps, in speaking of character in that sense, Freud is getting quite close to self or identity, although neither is equivalent to character. Identity seems to me to contain the additional quality of self-awareness; thus the ability to see oneself first as a separate person that differs from others – despite the identifications which are part of that identity and are experienced as part of the individual's identity as in 'I am like my mother/father', for instance.

This chapter arose from being asked to present a lecture on gender identity in a series of introductory lectures on psychoanalysis. At the time I felt uncomfortable with the title. I was not sure what of the experience of self was to be included in the term gender identity. How can one have an identity that is not based on gender and what would then be included and what left out by limiting identity to gender identity? Psychoanalytically, my introduction to the subject was based on Freud when he wrote about femininity. In this paper Freud (1933) goes into a more general discussion than in his earlier papers, where he had spoken of female sexuality only in developmental terms and comparing it to that of the boy. In that earlier work, when discussing female sexuality he considers how the little girl develops into a sexual woman, and posed questions related to sexual development and its relation to normal and pathological states. But this came under great criticism from some psychoanalysts, notably Ernest Jones, who concluded his argument with Freud's views with the statement that women are born not made – meaning that they begin life as female and one does not have to explain how they become a woman as Freud had done.

This same issue was taken up by some child analysts, notably Margaret Mahler, by focussing on the question of timing – that is, when does the child first become aware of itself as differing from others because of its perceived anatomical difference and is able to think of itself as either male or female? Freud had put this as late as about 3 or 4 years old, and used the idea of the child's perception of the difference of its own genitals from that of the others as that which forces the child to be aware of the nature of its own genitals, as well as being central to that which creates the necessity for the dissolution of the Oedipus complex. That is, he saw the awareness of its differentiated genitals as the point in development when the child has to give up the fantasy of seeking to possess the mother as its exclusive sexual object. For the boy it creates an awareness of his father's bigger and more powerful penis compared to his own, which he would need in order to compete with the father for the mother's love, while in the case of the girl, the awareness of the absence of a penis forces her to turn away from the mother as her sexual object and turn to the father, thus making the mother into her rival. But that did not tell me how gender identity is defined in the adult or how it develops. In fact, does it exist in a defined form beyond the anatomical sense, and if so what of it is based from within the individual person and how far is it perceived like a mirror image from the external world, as in Freud's defining of the visual impact on the child of the 'anatomical difference'? When Freud originally developed his ideas, at the beginning of this century, on the significance of sexuality in the psychological functioning of man, he saw sexuality as fundamental to man's need to find ways of dealing with his genetically determined biological instincts in such a way that *he could survive* in the external world as an individual, as well as ensuring the *survival of the species* through procreation.

Freud showed that far from this only becoming a problem once the person has reached adulthood and is sexually mature and capable of procreation, sexuality in its broader instinctual meaning is there from birth, and is already operative within the mother–infant relationship, where it ensures the infant's survival as well as its capacity for pleasurable experience. He included the oral instinct within the realm of sexuality and showed that the infant's search for an external object to suck was determined not only by its inner tension of hunger and the need for satisfaction, but that sucking becomes driven by the search for pleasurable experience, and becomes a source of sexual pleasure independent of the satisfaction of hunger. Taking the infant's first sexual experience of the mother and the breast as his starting point, Freud traced the significance of sexuality in the child's early dependent relationships on its parents until their resolution at the Oedipal stage. In his clinical work he showed how the manner in which the child had been able to resolve its Oedipal wishes, that is, how it was able to resolve its earlier phallic desires directed at the parents, formed the basis of his sexual life in adulthood. He linked the outcome of this development to either a normal adulthood or showed how it could lead to a pathological outcome, for instance, the symptoms of hysteria or obsessional neurosis. Within this theoretical construct, he did not examine the issue of identity, either of gender or in a broader sense. Instead he focused on those issues which helped him to reconstruct the course of early development. He addresses the question of how did the little girl acquire an awareness of herself as a woman, and what formed the instinctual basis for her sexual desires and conflicts? But in doing so he postulated – and it is this which gave rise to so much attack and controversy – that despite their anatomical differences, the boy and the girl have the same instinctual drives and hence the same desires in their earliest relationship to the mother. It is only at the point at which they have to deal with the perception of the differences between male and female genitals that their sexual developmental paths diverge. He presented this view in 1925 in his paper 'Some psychological consequences of the anatomical distinction between the sexes'. In this, he discusses the sexual development of children, male and female, in terms of the *object* of their sexual drive – that is, to whom does the child look for gratification of its sexual desires?

Freud argued that whilst the mother and her breast remain the sexual object for both, the psychic representation of sexual desire and fantasies is not differentiated by gender. Thus he defined the difference between the boy and girl as being determined by the problem of how does the female child then succeed, as she has to eventually, in giving up her first sexual object which is the mother, i.e. a woman, and look to her father for gratification so that she will eventually regard a man as the object of her desire? For the boy he saw no problem regarding his development into a male heterosexual.

We can see that Freud was risking infuriating everyone by defining the difference between the boy and the girl through posing such a question. In society at large, such questions should not be asked at all since the answer is considered to be 'self-evident'. Asking the question was experienced as another assault on the assumption that we know what constitutes 'normality', perhaps even seeing it as a part of normal gender identity and therefore what is acceptable and different from 'abnormal' identity and unacceptable. The first assault had been the idea that what were regarded as the child's most innocent pleasures, like thumb sucking, could be defined as an expression of the same desires that were experienced by adults in their sexual lives. Freud was now felt to be questioning another idea, which was generally regarded as inborn and therefore natural, that girls are biologically attracted to men as sexual partners and that any deviation was to be seen as unnatural and therefore socially unacceptable.

Those who had followed Freud so far in his thinking about sexuality, such as Ernest Jones, were angry at what they saw as Freud's implication that the little girl had no inborn or instinctual sense of her own genitals and hence of her own worth, but needed the awareness of her difference from that of the boy in order to define herself. This was then also taken up by the early feminists who branded Freud as a male misogynist. In this controversy we begin to see the idea of a gender identity emerging, even in the need to define it. Is there an inborn awareness of one's own sexual identity, or does it have to be acquired through the impact of the external world? And how can the girl not only achieve an identity of her own but also one that she can value and not see in terms of what she is missing?

Evidence was produced by child analysts using observations of small children as well as from the analyses of female patients by those opposing Freud's proposition, showing that little girls are aware of possessing a vagina. They showed that their fantasy world and play was preoccupied with representations of inner spaces and cavities which could be filled while the play of boys was filled with more active and thrusting fantasies. Feminists indignantly objected that Freud's argument was determined by his own view of male superiority and that it bore no relation to the experience of being a female. If women saw themselves as inferior and possessors of a penis as superior, then this view had been imposed on them by men. Freud responded to such criticisms by insisting that however much the observations being used to contest his theory of sexual development might be correct in themselves, they neither conflicted with his views of the development of infantile sexuality, nor were able to explain other clinical observable problems of female development which his theory took into account. He insisted that however much the little girl may have vaginal awareness, either through self-exploration or as an inborn body schema, this did not invalidate his criterion that the sexual *instinct* is initially defined by its *active* seeking for an object that ensures survival and pleasure, and the sexual desire that defines sexuality is therefore the same in the boy and the girl. For the boy, the penis then becomes that part of the body which he comes to identify as the active agent in satisfying his desire – while Freud argued that the clitoris plays a similar role for the girl. The child, male or female, experiences pleasurable sensations in its genitals and the fantasy which becomes attached to these sensations by the child is initially related to the mother as sexual object. According to Freud, it is when the girl perceives the clitoris is small and insignificant in comparison to that which she distinguishes as belonging to the boy that she sees herself and her body *not only* as belonging to a different class but *inferior* and hence incapable of fulfilling her sexual desires. That is to say, she blames her genitals for her incapacity to become mother's exclusive sexual partner, whilst still believing that the boy or the father can satisfy his desires and possess the mother. Freud saw the sense of herself as inferior to boys as defining the core of the girl's experience of herself, i.e. the basis on which her personality or self then develops. His conviction of the validity of this hotly debated concept in my view does not come from his own sense of male superiority, nor as supporting the then prevailing social attitude to women, but from his persistence in adhering to the instinctual bedrock of human experience as that which explains and unites the physical experience, the body, with the mental experience, the mind. But what is of interest in relation to the concept of gender identity is that Freud does seem to relate its formation to the visual impact of 'the other' as different from themselves rather than in relation to bodily experiences that participate in the formation of the 'body ego'.

Freud next approached the question of the difference between male and female in a paper written as a lecture to a general audience entitled 'Femininity' in 1933. In that lecture he talks of 'the riddle of the nature of femininity' as being a subject having 'a claim on your interest second almost to no other'. He cites as an observable fact that the first distinction we make on meeting a human being is whether they are male or female and he adds that 'you are accustomed to make the distinction with unhesitating certainty' (Freud 1933: 113).

He goes on to describe how we base our judgement on the appearance of the individual and infer the anatomical distinction, but that it still leaves undefined what it is which constitutes femininity and what masculinity. This time he goes out of his way to acknowledge that, as he says, 'the material is different to start with in boys and girls' (1933: 117) and distinguishes well-known and established differences in the character of male and female infants and small children. He emphasises some positive differences which favour the girl (such as that they seem to be more intelligent and livelier than boys of the same age – they go out more to meet the external world and form stronger object cathexis than boys), but he adds: 'These sexual differences are not however of great consequence: they can be outweighed by individual variations. For our immediate purpose they can be disregarded' (1933: 117). He then takes up once again his theory that 'the little girl is a little man' (1933: 118):

> With their [the boy's and the girl's] entry into the phallic phase, the differences between the sexes are completely eclipsed by their agreements. In boys, as we know, this phase is marked by the fact that they have learnt how to derive pleasurable sensations from their small penis and connect its excited state with their ideas of sexual intercourse. Little girls do the same thing with their still smaller clitoris. It seems that with them all their masturbatory acts are carried out on this penis-equivalent, and that the truly feminine vagina [i.e. as sexual organ] is still undiscovered by both sexes.
>
> (Freud 1933: 118)

Freud emphasised the role of infantile masturbatory activity not only as a source of pleasurable experience, as in thumb sucking, but also as a way of dealing with the frustration experienced as the result of the absence of the primary object. This was later taken up by Hoffer in 'Hand, mouth and body ego integration' (1949) where he tries to show how such activity also acts as a means of establishing the relationship to the child's own body and thus as separate from that of the mother.

This was further developed by Melanie Klein (1928) who showed how the child's sexual fantasies relating to parts of its own body become associated with a sense of being a good or bad child, loved or hated, dirty or perfect, and so on, and therefore how the child experiences itself. Here I think we can begin to see a sense of a separate bodily self emerging which is then given a character or identity through its relation to the breast. Returning to the issue of gender identity, and the need to decide whether identity is to be regarded as something *primarily* determined through external sources such as visual perception of differences and judgement based on visual perception by the other, or from the identifications made with the original objects, the breast and then the parents, we can now add, or by internal experiences arising from the child's own body and its own activities in relation to it. Freud, as far as I can see, seems to have considered the issue of gender identity, if he had to define it, as based primarily on the internal instinctual sources and the pleasurable experiences accompanying the instinctual impulses in relation to the object. That is why he says 'we are now obliged to recognise that the little girl is a little man' (Freud 1933: 118) during the stage preceding the dissolution of the Oedipus complex. But this can be understood as being similar to having a male character, that is a phallic character through the identification of the clitoris with the father's penis in the same way as he also described different character types, by defining them as oral characters or anal characters.

However, Freud was also aware that the issue of how to define male and female was not so simple. He had described man's bisexuality from his earliest theories of psychological functioning onwards. He based this originally on the biological structure of the infant but he also extended it to mean that each one of us, irrespective of our actual biological gender, contains identification with both sexes – a man develops not only on the basis of his male identifications but also on the basis of feminine ones and a woman takes on masculine identifications as with the father as part of her normal psychological development independently of anatomical differences. The way a person functions or perceives him or herself is also dependent on the preponderance of one set of identifications over the other and may not be in accordance with the person's biological gender.

However, Freud did not consider many questions related to the development of a sense of self or of an identity; nor until much later did other psychoanalysts. It was first taken up as an issue by Heinz Hartmann who had emigrated to the USA from Vienna. In developing the theory of ego psychology he pointed out that Freud had not differentiated between what Freud termed the ego and the self. In German the word for ego is *Ich*, which means both. The way in which Freud used the term ego made it clear that he was in fact using it in both senses, but Hartmann thought that they needed to be differentiated. Without going into more detail, Hartman's views of ego psychology affected psychoanalytic thinking about the development of a sense of self and later of identity and the history of their development from infancy. Geographically this interest was most pursued in the United States.

Research programmes were set up to observe mother and infant interactions, notably those by Margaret Mahler and her co-workers, in order to determine the mother's influences on the infant and the point at which the child could be assumed to have acquired a sense of self and of separatedness from the mother. More recent work such as by Roilph and Gallenson (1981) has focused on the issue of how and when does the child acquire a sense of a separate gender identity. Clinically, some aspects of emotional disturbance were defined in terms of disturbances in the person's sense of identity and distinguished from the psychoneuroses or psychotic states. Erik Erikson (1956) is the analyst who specifically used the concept of identity to define normal or pathological stages of psychological development, by using the concept of an identity crisis. He viewed stages of normal development in terms of the individual's mastery of an identity crisis. He defined certain specific points in a person's life cycle as periods of potential 'identity crisis' where the person's sense of identity is experienced as being at risk through the need to change, leading him or her to question his or her own identity in some fundamental aspect. He defines one such point in the person's life cycle, for instance, as that of becoming an adolescent on reaching physical puberty.

The child on reaching puberty has to find a new way of defining his identity and an answer to the question 'Who am I?' The answer has to contain a solution to the sense of being a sexually mature male or female, and as such is related to the inner pressure arising from the newly awakened instinctual forces in the body. In posing the question 'Who am I?' it implies the adolescent seeking of a definition of his identity via the perceptions of the external world. Other psychoanalysts in the USA, notably Greenacre (1958) and Jacobson (1964), were also concerned with the question of the early development of a separate self and of the infant's sense of separatedness from the mother. They related disturbances in the sense of identity, which they saw as potentially arising during those early periods in the development of the infant, to the more severe mental disturbances in adulthood, such as borderline states. The perversions in particular were also seen as related to confusions in a person's sense of identity and terms such as identity diffusion were used in the clinical descriptions of such patients. However, these states were also described in terms of the person's loss of fixed body boundaries and the subsequent loss of the sense of identity, and linked to clinical states described as fantasies of merging with another object, or fantasies of being both male and female. These states were seen as being used by the patient to defend against the anxiety related to acquiring a sense of separateness or a fixed identity. Their sexual behaviour, in that it enacted these fantasies, protected them from the fear of being separate and alone – or of having a genital only of one sex. The inability to relinquish the fantasy of being able to possess both male and female genitals arises from a need to defend against the sense of loss of the mother's body.

The emphasis on normal development in contrast to these pathological states was centred on the importance of the child's achievement of a sense of self and, in Mahler's terms, of individuation from the mother. Phyllis Greenacre, speaking at a panel meeting held in the United States on the subject of the concept of identity in 1950, defined it in these terms:

> The term 'identity' has two significant faces – an inner and an outer one. It means, on the one hand, an individual person or object whose component parts are sufficiently well integrated in the organisation of the

whole so that the effect is of genuine oneness or unity. On the other hand, in some situations identity also refers to the unique characteristics of an individual person whereby it can be distinguished from other somewhat similar persons or objects. In the one instance, the emphasis is on likeness and in the other on specific differences.

(Greenacre 1958: 612)

Applying this definition to gender identity brings out once more the difficulties arising from such a concept. Is it to be defined by the subject himself through observable differences from others of a different gender, or is it defined by the person's own sense of 'likeness', i.e. by identification with another who is perceived as belonging to one's own gender?

In addition, Greenacre stated:

Most adults seem to accept their own identities unquestioningly or at least without much contemplation except under rather unusual circumstances such as when coming out of an anaesthetic, being alone in a foreign country . . . Otherwise only young children, philosophers, artists and certain sick individuals concern themselves constantly with questions of their own identity.

(Greenacre 1958: 612–16)

Much the same can be said of most people's basic sense of which gender they belong to biologically. But we also know that most normal people experience some considerable degree of anxiety about the extent to which they are regarded as masculine if male or feminine if female. In ordinary language the use of the terms 'an effeminate male' or a 'masculine woman' show how we do not ascribe a gender identity purely on the basis of biological gender, but are aware that the way in which a person had developed psychologically from birth has affected the manner in which they relate to other people in a way that is independent of their biological gender and yet is connected with it.

A homosexual who seeks as a sexual partner a person of the same biological gender may wish to play the role of the opposite sex in the relationship, even though he or she has rejected the opposite sex as the object of sexual desire. Here an identification with the opposite sex has taken the place of seeking a sexual partner of the opposite sex. Disturbances which show evidence of a confusion of gender identity are those of transvestite sexual behaviour or of fetishism. Here, the male can only feel safe to satisfy his sexual desire with a heterosexual partner, as long as, in the case of transvestism, he can identify himself with a woman by getting inside her clothes; or in the case of fetishistic behaviour by endowing the woman partner with a particular object that allows the man to identify her as possessing the equivalent of a penis in his mind. Thus subject and object of desire remain the same and undifferentiated. All of these sexual behaviours can be viewed as defending the person against the acceptance of the idea that there are two separated classes of persons – male and female – and against the anxiety aroused by the acceptance of difference.

We can therefore hardly speak of there being a fixed gender identity other than the biological one. What we can define is a sense of gender identity – an identification of oneself as belonging to a given sex that is characterised differently for each person according to the earliest identifications that resulted from the child's relationship to his first sexual objects, the parents.

Both male and female infants share this fact that the first object of their sexual drives is female, as Freud argued, but in addition the loss of this object results in it becoming the child's first object for identification. The girl in that sense has the easier task in acquiring an early sense of her female identity through identification with her mother's body, although this may then be the basis for an intense conflict for the girl at puberty when she feels compelled to reject the identification of herself with her mother's sexual body. For the boy, however, the identification with his mother is already a source of conflict in early childhood, since it is felt as a threat to his being able to develop and maintain a sense of his separate male identity, thus making the boy more dependent on the actual presence of the father for identification and in order to defend against his anxiety of losing his penis through his identification with the mother. Without such a strong male identification, the boy will also be more at risk in adolescence, since he will not be able to detach himself from his desire for the mother as sexual object without feeling threatened by the revival of his feminine identification with her. These problems of conflicting identification and the anxiety they create and the defences that an individual has to hold on to in order to deal with such anxieties play an essential part in any emotional disturbance, and are one of the main reasons for some patients to seek psychological help.

More recently a new problem has come to the attention of analysts which calls for explanation, that of the transsexuals. These are people who, contrary to our expectations, do not experience themselves as having any anxiety or conflict about their gender identity, but insist that they need to have their bodies changed so that they can be the sex that they both *know* and *feel that they belong to*, irrespective of their biological gender. The question these individuals raise for psychoanalytic theories of mental development is how to explain the absence of conflict or anxiety they appear to show about their gender identity. Their only concern is that others shall agree with their view that the body they have is a mistake, so to speak, that needs to be rectified. From their mental viewpoint they tell us that they have felt themselves *to be* of a different gender than their biological gender from very early childhood – from as long as they can consciously remember being aware of belonging to any gender.

I said this presents psychoanalysis, or certainly me, with a new problem because, as I implied by my choice of title, I regard gender identification as bearing a particular relationship to reality in the sense that the biological body lies on the boundary of an inner subjective somatic reality of experience shared with and relating the person with objects in the outside world.

In my work with adolescents I work with the assumption that if there is a conflict between the adolescent's unconscious or conscious sense of their sexuality and the somatic experience of their own body, that the extent to which they then defend against allowing the somatic perception of the body into consciousness, in order to avoid having to deal with the conflict the somatic reality provokes, must also affect their relationship to external reality. For instance, a boy may find it impossible to be in the presence of a girl because unconsciously he fears that this might lead to sensations in his penis. Instead he becomes convinced that girls are persecutors who are trying to shame him. This belief to which he adheres affects his sense of reality in his relationship to girls, so that he can then feel as if he is punishing them by avoiding them, and can avoid awareness of his male identity.

However, Robert Stoller, the American psychoanalyst who has extensively investigated the early history and psychological functioning of transsexuals has found that their sense of reality appears totally intact and that they are not suffering from any particular state of anxiety or conflict, but that their belief in their 'right' gender identity is unshakable. Stoller found that in each case of male transsexualism which he had investigated in detail, the man had not only always thought of himself as being a girl, but that this belief had been actively encouraged by the mother. Stoller was not able to establish how far back the influence of the mother's encouragement went, or the many subtle forms it might have taken during the mother's handling of the infant's body, but he found no reason to doubt that the child had accepted the mother's demand for a child of a different gender. Thus he deduced that each individual has a *core* gender identity which is established within the early mother–child relationship, and in the establishment of which the mother's expressed wishes or fantasies play a crucial role. Stoller also investigated children whose biological sex had been wrongly diagnosed at birth. These children – if they were brought up to believe themselves to be as the sex they were assigned – had a core gender identity different from their biological sex.

More recent studies on the early development of gender identity in normal children have confirmed some of Stoller's findings (Stoller 1968) and have convinced other analysts that the early gender identity developed at round 18 months is primarily dependent on the influence that the mother brings to bear unconsciously or consciously within the early mother–child relationship. Perhaps the present concern and anger directed at society for the role it is seen to play in assigning gender identity to children via education, or to adults via the mass media, etc., is also an expression of the anxiety that one can be 'forced' to accept criteria from outside that determine our gender identity rather than feeling that we are able to make a free choice.

This brings me back to the beginning of the dilemma. Because although the child can be said to have a free choice to make whatever identifications he chooses, what or who he will become, in another sense there is no such choice. Unconscious forces determine the child's identifications, just as the actual biological body and the somatic experiences associated with the drives determine our inner reality and relationship to our internalised objects. To assert that women are born as 'women' and not 'made into women' once the child can distinguish itself from another class of being does not really answer the problem.

In work with severely disturbed adolescents – that is adolescents whose sense of reality is impaired and who though not psychotic have psychotic-like experiences – what has impressed me is the presence of behaviour which represents a compelling drive to attack or destroy their newly matured sexual bodies. Drug addiction, self-harming such as cutting, anorexia or bulimia, involving oneself in fights or suicide all have in common an attack on the adolescent's own body. The newly matured sexual body appears to have become the object of the adolescent's destructive impulses, and the behaviour represents the conflict that reaching puberty, that is, the point at which differentiation into male or female has become a new reality, creates for the adolescent. No longer able to function using his earlier unconscious identifications to defend against anxieties of loss and separation, he is forced by his changing body to deal with the identifications that he feels the reality of his body is forcing him into. Perhaps some of the present ways in which adolescents behave and dress, asserting as they do a freedom of choice independent of their actual sex, express these conflicts in a less self-destructive manner by defying external reality, whereas the disturbed adolescent feels unable to deal with them other than by attacking the body that he sees as containing the reality which is denying him his freedom of choice. In this presentation, I have tried to show some of the difficulties and confusion that exist when we try to define the concept of gender identity.

References

Erikson, E. (1956) 'The problem of ego identity', *Journal of the American Psychoanalytic Association* 4: 56–121.

Freud, S. (1917) 'Mourning and melancholia', *Standard Edition*, vol. 14, London: Hogarth Press.

—— (1923) *The Ego and the Id, Standard Edition*, vol. 19, London: Hogarth Press.

—— (1925) 'Some psychical consequences of the anatomical distinction between the sexes', *Standard Edition*, vol. 19, London: Hogarth Press.

—— (1931) 'Female sexuality', *Standard Edition*, vol. 21, London: Hogarth Press.

—— (1933) 'Femininity', *Standard Edition*, vol. 22, London: Hogarth Press.

Greenacre, P. (1958) 'Early physical determinants in the development of the sense of identity', *Journal of the American Psychoanalytic Association* 6: 612–16.

Hoffer, W. (1949) 'Hand, mouth and body ego integration', *Psychoanalytic Study of the Child* 3, 4: 49–56.

Jacobson, E. (1964) *The Self and the Object World*, New York: International Universities Press.

Klein, M. (1928) 'Early stages of the Oedipus conflict and of superego formation', in M. Klein *The Psychoanalysis of Children*. New York: Norton, 1932.

Roilph, H. and Gallenson, E. (1981) *Infantile Origins of Sexual Identity*, New York: International Universities Press.

Stoller, R. (1968) *Sex and Gender: The Development of Masculinity and Femininity*, New York: Jason Aronson.

Suggestions for further reading

The General Introduction in Dana Birksted-Breen, *The Gender Conundrum* (London: Routledge, 1993); and E. Jacobson 'Review of recent literature on the problem of identity', in E. Jacobson *The Self and the Object World* (New York: International Universities Press, 1964), pp. 24–32.

Chapter 9

The feminine

Dana Birksted-Breen

Few people have been perceived in such opposing lights as Sigmund Freud: hailed as revolutionary by some and despised as reactionary by others. The feminist anarchist Emma Goldman describes her attendance at his lectures in Vienna at the turn of the century:

> His simplicity and earnestness and the brilliance of his mind combined to give one the feeling of being led out of a dark cellar into broad daylight. For the first time I grasped the full significance of sex repression and its effect on human thought and action. He helped me to understand myself, my own needs.
>
> (Goldman 1970: 173)

Revolutionary or reactionary? This is a specially conflictual question when it comes to Freud's writings on female sexuality. In the post-1960s phase his work was adopted eagerly by French feminists but condemned as the root of all evil by American feminists.

One of the reasons lies in the complexity of Freud's theory and the distortion which occurs when only one aspect is emphasised at the expense of others. Further damage is done by the popularisation and misrepresentation which has often occurred. Concepts taken out of context become denuded of their proper meaning and the total theoretical context in which they were developed. This is the case with his concept of 'penis envy' which everybody will have heard of and most likely dismissed as the prejudice of a phallocentric man of the Victorian age. This is the case not just in our day of political correctness but ever since Freud put forward this concept as central in feminine development in his paper on 'Some of the psychical consequences of the anatomical distinction between the sexes' in 1925; he attracted furore for his ideas in what came to be known as the Freud–Jones debate in the 1920s.

Before dismissing it let us be clear what this concept refers to. For Freud penis envy is part of a set of object relationships. Freud pointed out that the girl's first love is the mother and that in her penetrative strivings towards her the little girl starts as a little man. So why should she ever turn to her father and to other men in a feminine way? Freud suggested that it is the recognition of sexual difference and the perception of a lack in herself, the lack of what could make her the object of her mother's desire, which makes the girl turn away from her mother in anger and towards her father in the hope of getting from him what she feels she lacks: the baby, representing the missing penis. Hence it is on the basis of her early disappointment that she engages on a heterosexual path.

For this theory to make sense it is important to understand that for Freud the recognition of sexual difference, which brings with it the fear of castration for boys and envy of the penis for girls, refers to a primal phantasy – in other words, that it is an innate phantasy which gives meaning to the perception, and not the perception, which is meaningful in itself. So, penis envy for Freud refers to more than a state of mind; it refers to the whole psychological organisation which will define the girl's relation to men and to women and to her choice of homosexual or heterosexual love object. For the passage from homosexual to heterosexual choice to take place, awareness of lack must be sufficiently accepted to allow for the passage from the wish to possess the penis as a masculine attribute of the self, to the wish to possess the penis in a receptive way.

As I mentioned earlier there was immediate disagreement with Freud about these ideas, in particular by Karen Horney (1926). Other women analysts accepted his view: Helena Deutsch (1946), Marie Bonaparte (1936) and Janette Lampl de Groot (1927), although they rigidified his theory, losing the more creative dynamic aspects of it.

Those opposing Freud's view, championed by Ernest Jones (1935), accused Freud of taking a phallocentric view whereby he underestimated the importance of the female organs. They argued for a primary femininity. That is, they believed that little girls know about the vagina from early on and also have an innate heterosexual drive. In other words for them heterosexuality was not a problem but something which occurred naturally, because of a biological given. These analysts suggested that if the vagina is often not acknowledged it is due to a defensive denial out of deep-seated anxieties concerning the inside of the body. For Melanie Klein (1932), for instance, this anxiety pertains to the girl's own wish to attack the inside of the mother's body and steal her babies or the penis she thinks to be inside her body. Josine Muller (1932) gave as evidence her observations of children which clearly suggested that little girls know about their vaginas and had vaginal sensations. Freud however was not impressed by this and did not feel that it called for a revision of his theory since in any case, in his view, vagina and anus were not sufficiently differentiated in children of this age. The dispute was heated and remained unresolved. There was a loss of interest in the subject in the mid-1930s when Freud's attention was drawn away from female sexuality to other preoccupations, death and the death instinct, in the build up to the Second World War which was to throw the world into total upheaval and destruction. It was not until the 1960s that a new Zeitgeist, with the general questioning of existing social roles and structures and the rise of the feminist movement, once again brought the topic of female sexuality to the forefront. The original debate was reawakened with greater complexity and in a different register with protagonists mainly in France and the USA. In England interest was never fully renewed after the 1930s amongst psychoanalysts, because interest shifted away from sexuality to separation anxiety and to the earliest phenomena in mental life.

In France, Chasseguet-Smirgel (1964), in an important collection of papers, suggested that it was time to re-examine the theories of female sexuality while retaining Freud's approach to the unconscious. The authors of this collection do so from a perspective inspired by Klein's ideas. As Klein did, all the authors of this collection suggest that the girl has an awareness of the vagina from the beginning and that envy of the penis derives largely from conflict with the mother and from the girl's wish to escape from her control and power. Penis envy as the wish to possess the male organ as an attribute is thus a revolt against the mother. Catherine Luquet-Parat (1981) adds to this the idea that it is a defence against the fear of being penetrated, the girl's way of denying her vulnerability. Joyce McDougall (1981) suggests that the girl's wish for a penis can also stem from her wish to have the means to repair her mother, and that this is one factor in homosexual relationships. Bela Grunberger (1981) writes that the mother–daughter relationship is essentially frustrating 'because neither is a satisfactory object for the other' (p. 76) and he sees women's narcissism as an attempt to make up for this maternal deficiency rather than making up for the absence of the penis as Freud had described. Janine Chasseguet-Smirgel (1981) suggests that if the vagina is not known in early childhood it is because of a particular form of feminine guilt which she calls 'incorporation guilt'. In order to keep the father ideal when the girl turns away from her mother, the girl has to repress her aggressive instincts in relation to him. It is for this reason, she says, that women find it difficult to achieve in fields which take on an unconscious phallic significance, because it is experienced in the unconscious as castrating the father.

However Freud's original ideas were by no means buried and the debate was certainly not over. While the authors of this collection were in agreement with Jones's and Klein's perspective, a completely opposite tack was taken by another French psychoanalyst, Jacques Lacan. He, on the contrary, upheld the Freud side of the original Freud–Jones debate. His careful re-reading of Freud's texts lead him to suggest that the real Freud is the one who wants to keep psychoanalysis separate from biology. Psychoanalysis is above all the "talking cure", and Lacan upholds that it is to language that we must return for an explication of the problem. Basing himself on the structural linguistics of Ferdinand de Saussure and the structuralism of the anthropologist Lévi-Strauss, Lacan suggests that the unconscious is structured as a language with its specific rules such as those we find in dreams as described by Freud: displacement, condensation and conditions of representability. Moreover, he suggests that the unconscious is intimately linked with language. It is the father who introduces the law of the language system – what Lacan calls the law of the father. At that moment of the introduction of language there is a rupture in the unity of mother and child and an entry into culture. For Lacan it is a misunderstanding to look for the subject's truth beyond language. Psychoanalytically speaking, the body does not count for Lacan and therefore feminine only exists as a division in language, in opposition to masculine and not as something in itself. The human subject is determined by language. Lacan endorses Freud's notion of phallic monism, whereby only the phallic organ, penis or clitoris, is known by the child. Psychoanalysis for Lacan addresses itself to the structures of the mind, and is not about development or biology. He is not interested in prediscursive phenomena, that is phenomena before the acquisition of language. In these structures he gives a special place to the father and the phallus as evidenced in language. These refer not to a person or an organ but to what he calls after Ferdinand de Saussure, a 'signifier', that is something which arbitrarily relates to the signified. He writes:

> In Freudian doctrine, the phallus is not a fantasy, if what is understood by that is an imaginary effect. Nor is it as such an object (part, internal, good, bad etc.) in so far as this term tends to accentuate the reality involved in a relationship. It is even less the organ, penis or clitoris, which it symbolises. And it is not incidental that Freud took his reference for it from the simulacrum which it represented for the Ancients. For the phallus is a signifier.
>
> (Lacan 1982: 79)

For Lacan the father introduces the law of the language system and it is in this language system that castration refers to the representation of lack, since clearly the girl has nothing missing in reality, and that the question of 'feminine mystery' comes to be embodied in the question 'What does the woman want?' In the language system woman represents the Other. (The Other sex for Lacan is always Woman for both male and female subjects.)

To summarise: in France, the Freud–Jones debate was still alive in this opposition between Chasseguet-Smirgel following the Jones perspective, and Lacan following Freud's view. Meanwhile in the USA, interest in female sexuality was also reawakened with the rise of the feminist movement, but there an opposite tack was taken. The pragmatic ethos of that culture led to a belief that if one could solve the physiological aspects of female sexuality, or if one could observe closely the development of the girl the problem would be solved. Mary Jane Sherfey (1966) made use of Masters and Johnson's findings on the physiology of the female orgasm to question Freud's theory, and many other psychoanalysts used child observations to validate or invalidate certain aspects of the theory.

Roughly ten years after the French collection of papers, there was an American collection edited by Harold Blum (1976). In the American studies, the girl's envy of the penis is on the whole thought to be an impediment to femininity rather than initiating femininity as Freud had described with the change of object. Also, while the authors of Chasseguet-Smirgel's collection consider penis envy to be mainly defensive, the American authors tend to describe it as occurring naturally. Most (except Roiphe and Galenson 1981) do not see it as exerting crucial influences on feminine development. These authors also describe 'a true early genital phase' preceding a phallic one. Stoller calls it a 'primary femininity', which is a conflict-free source of femininity (1976). This conception of an early conflict-free femininity is part of the more general American ego psychology. In this perspective, there are cognitive functions independent of unconscious conflicts and sexuality. This is at fundamental variance with the French and British approach for whom there are no areas free of conflict and sexuality. Melanie Klein, for instance, describes how knowing and the desire to know are intimately connected with component aspects of the libido and of sadism. Another American psychoanalyst who writes about femininity, Judith Kestemberg, also talks about an early inner-genital, pre-oedipal phase followed by phallic phases with drives first towards the mother and later towards the father (1980). For her, femininity is made of these three different aspects which go to make up what she refers to as the three faces of femininity: the maternal (the early inner genital phase), the determined (with drives towards the mother), and the seductive aspects (with drives towards the father).

Some of the divergences in theory between American, French and British perspectives are the result of important theoretical differences in psychoanalytic theory generally. In particular there is the question of what makes up psychoanalytic data. While the American writers base many of their conclusions on the observation of babies and children, many French and British psychoanalysts believe that the raw material for psychoanalytic theory can be collected only in the consulting room. Green (1986), for example, deplores the reduction of the structural dimension of psychoanalysis to the merely genetic. He points out that direct observation cannot account for the essential dimension of psychoanalysis which is to do with how the environment is interpreted and internalised. Direct observation without theoretical hypotheses is unintelligible and cannot supply new knowledge to psychoanalysis (Diatkine 1979). These two different perspectives, synchronic (that is, structural and ahistorical) or diachronic (historical), have coloured the theory of female sexuality. At one extreme there is Lacan's understanding of femininity from a purely linguistic dimension as a representation of lack, as subordinate to the law (a synchronic approach). At the other extreme, there are the observational studies of the ego psychologists who describe the girl's early knowledge of herself as being a girl and how this will be confirmed by any direct observational study (a diachronic approach).

Let us go back to Freud for a moment. Having discovered the unconscious (or rather invented the unconscious, as Roustang (1982) prefers to say since the unconscious is a hypothesis not a tangible entity), Freud looked for an understanding of sexuality which did not assume that unconscious processes would automatically parallel biological processes. It is in this that he differed from all other writers on the subject who assumed a natural heterosexual drive at the root of femininity. He pointed out that the first love partner to the girl is a woman, the mother who nurtures and suckles her. Why, he asked, would the girl ever wish to give up this first love to turn to her father and later other men? He writes:

> It would be a solution of ideal simplicity if we could suppose that from a particular age onwards the elementary influence of the mutual attraction between the sexes makes itself felt and impels the small woman towards men, while the same law allows the boy to continue with his mother.
>
> (Freud 1933: 119)

Freud suggests however that it is not biology but the girl's intense disappointment with her mother, a disappointment which takes its full force when she recognises sexual difference and feels she has been shortchanged by her mother, which makes her turn from her mother towards her father from whom she hopes to get a baby to replace the missing penis. While I think that Lacan was right to emphasise this aspect of Freud's theory, to emphasise that Freud was keeping psychoanalysis separate from biology, I believe that this is only half the story because Freud also states that the ego is foremost a body ego, in other words that it is shaped by the body, and this means male or female body. It is part of the complexity of Freud's work that his theory has been seen by some as ascribing an inescapable biological destiny to man and woman, while others have understood him to uphold the revolutionary belief that, psychologically speaking, we are not born man or woman, and that masculinity and femininity are constructed over a period of time and are relatively independent of biological sex. I believe that this duality is there in Freud's work, not because he was confused or changed his mind or developed his ideas, but because an inherent tension exists at the heart of the matter, which is why this opposition is not going away and why the debate is still alive half a century after his death. It is in relation to women that the disjunction between biology and psychology is greatest in Freudian theory, and the debate on female sexuality therefore comes to embody that tension.

When talking about the meaning of masculinity and femininity, Freud says that psychoanalysis cannot elucidate the intrinsic nature of what in biological phraseology is termed masculine and feminine. He uses the German verbs *Verblassen* (to fade, to pale) and *Verflüchtigen* (to evaporate, to vanish) which convey the sense that as one tries to grasp the nature of masculinity and femininity they get out of focus and cannot be grasped. This I believe describes how the two points of view, biological and psychoanalytic, are out of focus because they do not completely overlap. At the same time, like the two images in binoculars which are out of focus, they are connected even if disjointed. It is the very duality and opposition – femininity constructed around lack and dissatisfaction, and a femininity related to the specific female bodily experiences – which to my mind constitutes the feminine unconscious.

While Freud, the man, emphasised lack and castration, which also lies at the heart of the masculine unconscious, Melanie Klein, the woman, emphasised the positive aspects. While Freud stressed the primordial importance of the father and his penis, Melanie Klein stressed the primordial importance of the mother and her breast and womb, and of the child's phantasy of the penis inside the mother. Freud looked at the girl's feminine anxieties and development in relation to the father; Melanie Klein looked to the role of the girl's relationship to her mother as the impediment to her feminine development. But there are two parents in everyone's unconscious. Both parents, and one's place in relation to the intercourse between them, have to be negotiated and this also leads to defensive manoeuvres. The girl has to negotiate the dual perspective of what I call negative and positive femininity. Positive femininity refers to the mental representation of her internal organs and her potential for maternity. Negative femininity refers to absence and lack. It is the absence of the phallus as representative of power and completion. It is from this perspective that one can understand the phallic defence so frequently adopted by a certain kind of female and male patient to parry the sense of helplessness and vulnerability. But also the phallic defence protects women from psychotic anxieties connected with their feminine organs. The unconscious significance of the penis as phallus, which stands for power and wholeness and is used in the phallic defence – the macho attitude as defence against vulnerability – has to be differentiated from other meanings of the penis in the unconscious, namely its linking and structuring functions (Birksted-Breen 1996). The psychic possession of a good internal penis is necessary for both men and woman as is psychic bisexuality for a good mental functioning. While the phallus allows for no need and hence no intercourse, a balance of masculine and feminine internal good objects with the recognition of mutual need for each other is what sustains health and relationships. In other words masculinity is equally important to women as femininity is important to men. Some women find it impossible to compete with men and have to make themselves stupid because masculine achievement is felt to be stolen from the father or castrating of the father.

For men the problem of accepting their femininity is somewhat different. Freud thought that women are more bisexual than men because of their original love for the mother. Sylvia Payne in the 1930s pointed out that although it was true that the boy could continue his attachment to women, he nevertheless had the important and not easy task of changing from a passive relationship to the mother who feeds, to an active position in relation to women. In the 1960s psychoanalysts began to understand that the early close relationship to the mother is one which threatens the development of a masculine identity. The refusal of femininity (a point in common for both sexes, Freud had noted) came to be understood less as bedrock and more as a defence against fusion with the mother and loss of identity. The phallic defence I referred to earlier, the macho attitude, is often a fear of that fusion with the mother in both women and in men. It is a rejection of the mother and the wish to assert a separate and independent identity. Each sex has its own specific problems in accepting the feminine in themselves. Women resort to attacks on their own body in an attempt to wipe out the mother and the feminine in themselves, as in anorexia nervosa for instance. Their body marks their relationship to their mother and to the mother in themselves. Men overvalue the penis and denigrate the feminine in order to feel different and separate from their mother. It is however the originality of psychoanalysis to show that the power of the psyche is such that the actual body may be of little significance compared to the fantasy body. This is clear for instance in the case of male anorexics who also try to get rid of the mother in themselves by starving their bodies.

One consequence of Freud's theory of the non-recognition, even unconsciously, of the vagina until puberty is that the female genitalia as such have no effect on ego functions. This, as we have seen, is at variance with most other theorists for whom there is always unconscious knowledge. Erikson was the first to write about the centrality of inner space on women's ego-functions (1964). In observing children at play he found that there were sexual differences in the organisation of play space which paralleled the morphology of genital differentiation. More recently, Bernstein (1990) discusses the role of specific genital anxieties derived from the characteristics of the female genitalia on the girl's psychic development, in the same way that castration anxiety and phallic fantasy are elaborated by boys. She suggests that the genital anxieties of girls are not nearly as focused and tidy as boys' anxieties. She suggested that the girl's experience with the unfocused, open, penetrable nature of her genital creates difficulties in forming mental representations of her body that have clear boundaries and sharp definition. She also suggests that this unfocused representation of the genitals complicates the formation of ego boundaries and a firm sense of self. If we take seriously Freud's idea that the ego is foremost a bodily ego, then I think we do need to consider the differential influence of the male and the female body. At the same time, in psychoanalysis we are always talking about the representation of the body not the actual body, and about the fantasies associated with it. The fact that femininity is often associated with mystery and with a lack of definition may have some basis in the morphological reality of the female genitalia but obviously goes far beyond that.

Lisa hated women's bodies which she said lacked definition, and putting on weight meant to her spreading out and therefore psychic disintegration. She hated her body because it showed time, because it reflected her mortality and hence her imperfection. This made her open to a terror of death. So she exercised compulsively and kept a strict diet in order to keep herself lean. When her body was lean she experienced it as a masculine body and she felt she had boundaries, a sense of unity and an identity. She believed that the male body did not change over time and so in this way she thought her sense of identity could be preserved. Unchanging meant to her immortal. We can see here how far we are from biological reality, but how the reality of the female body with its cycles and the mother's pregnancies, which indicate the passage of time and turn the child's world upside down, are markers for these fantasies.

While for Freud feminine development started from the acceptance of lack, I have found that in the analysis of women the acceptance of lack often reveals a terror of the feminine which has to be worked through before femininity can be established. One woman, for instance, who gave up a phallic defence felt that something was still missing. 'I think of my mother and you and other women as having a shape even though my mother is old and bent, but I feel shapeless . . . I could put up with having a masculine shape or a feminine shape but the problem is having neither.'

I have found with other women too that during their analysis giving up a masculine stance did not automatically equal feeling feminine, although as in the classical theory it did initiate a movement towards femininity which then confronted them with rivalry and envy of the mother, something previously defended against. While for Freud however there is a primary non-recognition of the vagina and womb, I found that my patients' 'missing' female organs which they reported when they accepted the missing penis were keeping at bay severe anxieties about the damaging potential of those organs. Barbara was terrified when the gynaecologist spoke of the cavity inside her and she pictured coffins disappearing to be incinerated. The hole of death and destruction she felt she had inside her originated in her relation to both her parents, the depriving mother whose 'insides' she hated for producing more babies, and the father whose penis she wanted to destroy for not making up for this deprivation. By constructing a masculine image of herself, she could avoid the fear of the hole of death inside her.

In conclusion, I do not think Freud was phallocentric when he brought to light the importance of lack in the female unconscious but he was phallocentric in falling short of exploring the 'positive' side of femininity. I use the word 'positive' here not to imply an affectively positive experience but to mean femininity in its reference to more than absence (of the penis). It is a reference to the experiences, anxieties, and conflicts relating to the internal female organs with their anatomic biological characteristics underpinning fantasy elaborations. I suggest that a woman's sexual position can be traced only by considering both dimensions: her position in relation to sexual difference and her lack, and her position in relation to her female body, and the interplay of these two dimensions with each other and with the relationship to both parents.

References

Bernstein, D. (1990) 'Female genital anxieties, conflicts and typical mastery modes', *International Journal of Psychoanalysis* 71: 151–65.

Birksted-Breen, D. (1993) *The Gender Conundrum*, New Library of Psychoanalysis, London: Routledge.

—— (1996) 'Phallus, penis and mental space', *International Journal of Psychoanalysis* 77: 649–59.

—— (1999) in D. Bassin (ed.) *Female Sexuality, Contemporary Engagements*, New York: Jason Aronson.

Blum, H. (1976) *Journal of the American Psychoanalytic Association* 24 (supplement): 157–93.

Bonaparte, M. (1936) 'Passivity, masochism and femininity', *International Journal of Psychoanalysis* 16, 3: 325–33.

Chasseguet-Smirgel, J. (1964) *Recherches psychanalytiques nouvelles sur la sexualité féminine*, Paris: Editions Payot. Published in English (1981) as *Female Sexuality*, London: Virago.

Deutsch, H. (1946) *The Psychology of Women: Psychoanalytic Interpretations*, London: Research Books.

Diatkine, R. (1979) 'La psychanalyse de l'enfant', *Nouvelle Revue de Psychanalyse* 19: 49–64.

Erikson, E.H. (1964) 'Womanhood and inner space', in *Identity, Youth and Crisis*, New York: Norton, 1968, pp. 261–94.

Freud, S. (1925) Some of the psychical consequences of the anatomical distinction between the sexes, *Standard Edition*, vol. 19, London: Hogarth Press.

—— (1933) *New Introductory Lectures, Standard Edition*, vol. 22, London: Hogarth Press.

Goldman, E. (1970) *Living My Life*, New York: Dover.

Green, A. (1986) *On Private Madness*, London: Hogarth Press.

Grunberger, B. (1964) 'Outline for a study of narcissism in female sexuality', in Chasseguet-Smirgel, J. (1964) *Recherches psychanalytiques nouvelles sur la sexualité féminine*, Paris: Editions Payot. Published in English (1981) as *Female Sexuality*, London: Virago, 1981.

Horney, K. ([1926] 1967) 'The flight from womanhood', in K. Horney (ed.) *Feminine Psychology*, London: Routledge and Kegan Paul.

Jones, E. (1935) 'Early female sexuality', *International Journal of Psychoanalysis* 16: 263–73.

Kestemberg, J. (1980) 'The three faces of femininity', *Psychoanalytic Review* 67, 313–36.

Klein, M. (1932) 'The effects of the early anxiety situations on the sexual development of the girl', *The Psycho-Analysis of Children*, vol. 2 *The Writings of Melanie Klein*, London: Hogarth Press.

Lacan, J. (1982) 'The meaning of the phallus', a a a a a a a a a a a a a a a a
    Sexuality: Jacques Lacan and the Ecole Freud' a a a a a a a a a a
Lampl de Groot, J. ([1927] 1985) 'The evolution of the Oedipus complex in a a a a
    J. Lampl de Groot *Man and Mind: Collected Papers*, New York: International
    Universities Press, pp. 1–11.
Luquet-Parat, C. (1964) 'The change of object', in J. Chasseguet-Smirgel *Recherches*
    psychanalytiques nouvelles sur la sexualite féminine, Paris: Editions Payot.
    Published in English (1981) as *Female Sexuality*, London: Virago.
McDougall, J. (1981) 'Homosexuality in women', in J. Chasseguet-Smirgel *Recherches*
    psychanalytiques nouvelles sur la sexualité féminine, Paris: Editions Payot, pub-
    lished in English (1981) as *Female Sexuality*, London: Virago. 1981.
Masters, W. and Johnson, V. (1966) *Human Sexual Response*, Boston: Little, Brown.
Muller, J. (1932) 'A contribution to the problem of libidinal development of the
    genital phase in girls', *International Journal of Psychoanalysis* 13: 361–8.
Roiphe, H. and Galenson, E. (1981) *Infantile Origins of Sexual Identity*, New York:
    International Universities Press.
Roustang, F. (1982) *Dire Mastery: Discipleship from Freud to Lacan*, Baltimore: Johns
    Hopkins University Press.
Sherfey, M.J. (1966) *The Evolution and Nature of Sexual Identity*, New York:
    International Universities Press.
Stoller, R.J. (1976) 'Primary femininity', *Journal of the American Psychoanalytic*
    Association 24 (supplement): 59–79.

Suggestions for further reading

A more detailed discussion of the literature can be found in the Introduction to
D. Birksted-Breen (ed.) *The Gender Conundrum* (London: Routledge, 1993). A land-
mark book which both reviews the early writings and presents some other ways of
thinking about female sexuality is the book edited by J. Chasseguet-Smirgel in the
1960s and later published in English under the title of *Female Sexuality* (London:
Virago, 1981). For a look at more recent publications I can suggest D. Bassin (ed.)
Female Sexuality: Contemporary Engagements (New York: Jason Aronson, 1999),
which gives a view of current American perspectives. On this side of the Atlantic,
J. Raphael-Leff and R. J. Perelberg (eds.) *Female Experience: Three Generations of*
British Psychoanalysts on Work and Women (London: Routledge, 1997) looks at
women's experience.

Chapter 10

The Oedipus complex I

Michael Feldman

In a lecture he gave during the First World War, Freud described an episode which took place on the German front somewhere in Poland. When his medical colleagues realised that one of their fellow officers was interested in psychoanalysis, they invited him to share his knowledge with them. For a while the medical officers, his colleagues and his superiors, would meet in the evenings to hear about these new ideas:

> All went well for a while; but when he spoke to his audience about the Oedipus complex, one of his superiors rose to his feet in indignation. He declared that he did not believe it, that it was a vile act on the part of the lecturer to speak of such things to them, honest men, fathers of families fighting for their country, and he forbad the lectures to continue. The analyst got himself transferred to another part of the front.
>
> (Freud 1917)

In 1897 Freud had written to Fliess that 'we can understand the riveting power of Oedipus Rex . . . the Greek legend seizes on a compulsion which everyone recognises because he feels its existence within himself' (1897). And yet, paradoxically, Sophocles does not portray Oedipus as having a compulsion within himself to murder his father and marry his mother. On the contrary, when his parents learned of the oracle's awful prophecy they cast out their newborn son to die. Oedipus survived, of course, and was raised by the rulers of Corinth, whom he believed to be his real parents. When in turn he discovered Apollo's prophecy concerning his fate, he fled Corinth in fear and misery. On his journey he encountered an elderly man and his entourage at the crossroads, and finding himself rudely pushed aside and struck, Oedipus retaliated and killed the man and most of his followers. As you may recall, he proceeded to rescue Thebes by solving the riddle of the Sphinx, and was offered the crown of the city and the recently widowed queen as his wife. They lived happily for a dozen years or more, and had four children, until, in a later crisis, Apollo declared that there was someone who had been responsible for the old king's death, polluting the city, and he had to be driven out or killed. Oedipus then embarked on a quest to discover the truth about the king's murderer. He struggled to overcome both his own resistances (Tiresias, who knew the truth, but refused to spell it out, angrily accused him of being 'blind to that which dwells within yourself'), and the queen's attempts to reassure him, where she said:

> Nor need this mother-marrying frighten you;
> Many a man has dreamt as much. Such things
> Must be forgotten, if life is to be endured.
>   (Sophocles 1947: 52)

Thus Sophocles does not describe a man aware of impulses or wishes to kill his father, and marry his mother, but someone helplessly caught in the inevitable unfolding of a dreadful prophecy. It is not difficult to see why Freud saw this magnificent play as a dramatic representation not of the dictates of the gods, but of instinctual impulses present in all of us, which may disturb and frighten us and against which we may employ many of the defences represented in the play.

As Freud himself remarks, the strong attachment of a little boy to his mother, say between the ages of 3 and 5, is not at all remarkable. He may make it quite plain that he would like to have her all to himself, that he regards the presence of his father as a nuisance, he resents father showing any affection towards mother and may be pleased and excited when father is away. He may express his feelings and his wishes in words or actions. He may declare his intention to marry his mother, or behave in ways which seem an overt expression of his sexual interest in her. While we may, like the parents, regard these as touching and amusing manifestations of interest and affection, far removed from the intensity of Sophocles' play, what Freud was able to recognise and tolerate, which the German medical officer was not, was the nature of the underlying, mainly unconscious Oedipal drama.

In a highly schematic form, Freud's theory postulated that the child's object choice was originally the mother, whom he wanted exclusively for himself, seeing her as capable of gratifying both his instinctual needs and his needs for love. Between the ages of 3 and 5, at the height of what Freud termed the 'Phallic' phase, when there is an intense focussing on the phallus, its sensations and functions, the child becomes acutely aware of finding himself in a triangular situation. His rivalry with father for mother's love and attention, and the jealousy and hatred which is aroused in him, leads to his wish to get rid of his father. He then becomes threatened by his father's powerful capacity for retaliation, which might take the form of an attack on the child's own sexuality. While Freud originally developed his theory in relation to the development of a boy, he postulated that there was a symmetry between the courses pursued by the two sexes, with the girl developing a corresponding jealous, erotised relation to the father, and a wish to get rid of the mother. He abandoned this view, however, recognising that the path of the girl's sexual development was different in many respects. He also recognised very early that the child's love and attachment to the parent of the same sex is often very important, as is the contribution of the parents' conscious or unconscious attitude and responses to the child's Oedipal wishes. He began to explore the role of siblings, and the way in which some of the dramas of love, sexuality, jealousy and hatred may be enacted with them. He suggested that, faced with these difficult and frightening conflicts, the child represses his or her sexuality by the age of about 5, entering the so-called 'latency phase', which lasts until puberty. Now, instead of the threats being experienced as coming from a punitive or vengeful parent, an internal agency, which he termed the 'Super-ego' took over these prohibiting parental functions.

I hope it will be apparent, even in this very brief and inadequate sketch, that Freud's elaboration of the Oedipus complex became the basis for his understanding of the individual's pattern of object relations, and hence the basis of the structure of the personality. While Freud places the main emphasis on the manifestations and the consequences of the desires, guilt and persecutory anxieties inherent in the Oedipal situation, there is a further aspect of Sophocles's original play which I should like to draw attention to. When the awful truth of the situation has become revealed and we are faced with the horror of Oedipus's self-blinding, he declares: 'Incestuous sin! Breeding where I was bred! Father, brother, and son; bride, wife and mother; Confounded in one monstrous matrimony!' (Sophocles 1947: 64).

What I think Sophocles draws attention to here is the confusion inherent in the Oedipal situation; the breakdown in the delineation between the generations, and between the different roles. While there may be powerful impulses in the child towards the crossing of such boundaries, one of the functions for which they rely on the parents is to be able to recognise and tolerate the frustration, pain and jealousy which the existence of such boundaries may give rise to. What we have increasingly come to recognise is that if, by contrast, the adults actively contribute towards the breakdown of such boundaries (as we see in various forms of abuse), the resulting confusion often has serious consequences for the individual's development.

Klein and Oedipus

Basing her ideas partly on observations made during play therapy with young children, Klein extended our understanding of object relations, focussing in particular on the early, pre-genital phases of development. Her theories are rich and complex, but one aspect which I would like to take up is the notion that we have, from very early on, the propensity to structure the world in terms of triangular relationships. She argued that the infant's need to preserve a satisfactory relationship with the breast, and later the mother who feeds and cares for him, leads him to split off and project into a 'third area' those elements in his world which he finds hateful and persecuting, which cause him anxiety and pain. The operation of these defence mechanisms thus tends to create a very early prototype of the Oedipal situation, with one object (say, the mother's breast or the mother) being loved and desired, and the other object in the triangular situation (say, the father's penis or the father) being hated and feared as a threat to his possession of the mother's breast, or the mother as a whole.

In the elaboration of her theory she also drew attention to the child's preoccupation with the relationship which the parents had with each other. The child's view of this relationship is always coloured to a greater or lesser extent by the phantasies which he projects into it. While a good and loving relationship between the parents is usually a source of security and support, it also provokes intense jealousy and envy, with some of the aggressive and violent wishes directed either towards one parent, or towards the couple. Conversely, if the relationship is experienced as a bad or destructive one, the child may feel this is desirable as it gives him greater access to one parent or the other, but it is likely to make the child feel insecure and troubled by anxiety and guilt.

In an early paper Klein (1924) describes her work with a 6-year-old girl, Erna, who suffered from a variety of disabling symptoms. She had difficulty sleeping at night, often being frightened of robbers, and she showed a number of repetitive forms of behaviour – banging her head on the pillow, rocking, compulsive thumb-sucking and compulsive masturbation. She behaved in a very domineering way towards her mother, giving her no freedom of move-ment. Sometimes she would behave like a very good, over-affectionate child, at other times she was aggressive and hateful. Erna also showed a very severe inhibition in her capacity to learn.

Klein describes how in the sessions, the child would often play with bricks, apparently trying to divide them equally between herself and the analyst, but always managing to keep more for herself. She asked the analyst to build with her bricks, only to prove that her own building was always much more beauti-ful than the analyst's, or she would contrive to knock the analyst's building down, apparently by accident. Sometimes she would get a male doll to be the judge, and he always decided that her house was much better than the analyst's.

On another occasion, Erna used one of the male dolls as a teacher who was supposed to give his girl pupil violin lessons. However, he threw down the book or the violin and began to dance with his pupil. The two then kissed and embraced, and at this point Erna asked the analyst if she would allow a marriage between teacher and pupil. Another time in her play, a male and female teacher – represented by dolls – were giving the children lessons in manners, teaching them how to bow and curtsy. At first the children were obedient and polite (just as Erna herself always tried to behave nicely), then suddenly they attacked the teachers, trampled them underfoot, killed them and roasted them. The children had now become devils, gloating over the torments of their victims. But all at once the male and female teachers were in heaven, and the former devils had turned into angels, who had no knowledge of ever having been devils. God the father, the former teacher, began kissing and embracing the woman, the angels worshipped them, and all was well again. In this example, the child uses the toys, or the analyst herself to represent the important figures in her life, and to enact some of the dramas and conflicts which preoccupy and torment her. She demonstrates her rivalry with the mother in the play with bricks, and the toy man, representing the father, judges her building to be the best (Klein 1924).

The nature of her Oedipal wishes towards the father become more explicit when the violin teacher abandons the lessons and they begin to dance, kiss and embrace, but one can infer that the question to the analyst about a teacher and pupil marrying might also refer to the child's wishes and phantasies towards the analyst herself. It is clear, however, that the child is unable to lose her awareness of the parental couple, and although for a while she accepts the lessons in manners, the underlying jealousy and murderousness briefly erupt when the children turn into devils (as Erna herself was prone to do). I thought there was then a fascinating description of the way in which her anxiety and guilt about this attack was dealt with. Erna becomes angelic, restores the parents to a state of heavenly (and presumably asexual) bliss, and she retains no connection in her mind with what had gone on before.

In Klein's description of her work with her 10-year-old patient Richard during the war, which she published as the *Narrative of a Child Analysis* (1945), she reports on some sessions which followed her absence on a visit to London (1945: 374–5). Richard seemed depressed and withdrawn, and there was some evidence that during her absence he had been frightened of all the bad and dangerous things that might have happened to Mrs Klein during the bombing, and the thunderstorms which had occurred. He also described a conversation he had had with his mother during the analyst's absence, in which he had expressed considerable anxieties about what he believed took place between men and women, and the whole business of having babies which seemed very frightening and dangerous.

In his play at this time, he was very preoccupied with warships and battles and would repeatedly play with a set of toy ships – one representing each of his parents, the others having varying roles. For example, he made a destroyer, which he called 'Vampire' bump into the battleship 'Rodney' which always represented his mother. When he became aware of the analyst observing him, he seemed to become uneasy and quickly rearranged the fleet. When asked who the 'Vampire' stood for, he reluctantly acknowledged it was himself. Klein makes the point that the bumping of one ship against another had repeatedly, in the analysis, turned out to be his way of representing sexual intercourse. She suggests that when the patient became too clearly aware of his genital desires towards his mother, and their oral-sadistic nature (the name 'Vampire'), he displayed a sudden inhibition of play, corresponding with the process of psychic repression.

Immediately after bumping the 'Vampire' into 'Rodney', Richard put the battleships 'Rodney' and 'Nelson' (which always represented his mother and father) side by side, and then arranged a row of ships representing his brother, himself and his dog; arranged, as he said, in order of age. Klein comments:

> Here the fleet game was expressing his wish to restore harmony and peace in the family, by allowing his parents to come together and by giving way to his father's and brother's authority. This implied the need to restrain jealousy and hatred, for only then, he felt, could he avoid the fight with his father for the possession of his mother. In that way he warded off his castration fear and moreover preserved the good father and good brother. Above all, he also saved his mother from being injured in the fight between his father and himself. Thus Richard was not only dominated by the need to defend himself against the fear of being attacked by his rivals, his father and brother, but also by concern for his good objects.
>
> (Klein 1945: 378)

However, peace and harmony in the family could only be achieved, jealousy and hatred could only be restrained, and the loved object preserved if Richard repressed his Oedipal wishes. At times this repression led to the partial regression to an idealised mother–baby relationship, in which he would of course be free from aggression, and in particular free from oral-sadistic impulses, and involved in a loving relationship with an ideal mother, with ideal breasts which never frustrated him. All her bad and frustrating qualities were split off and projected elsewhere – sometimes onto the bad analyst.

Some time later Richard produced a drawing in which there were a lot of baby fishes, the battleship 'Rodney' on the surface, and a submarine which he called 'Sunfish' below, with its periscope sticking up into 'Rodney', which you will recall always represented mother. At the bottom of the sea there was a starfish (which usually represented a baby, but which he said was a grown-up person) apparently contentedly nestling amongst the plants there, while a plane patrolled in the sky above. To summarise Mrs Klein's inferences and conclusions from her work with Richard over this and other similar drawings, it seemed as if his Oedipal wishes including his genital desires for the mother were now represented more openly. He had achieved this in a variety of ways: one was to make his father into a baby, giving him a safe nestling position within the nurturing plants. Richard had not represented himself as a baby fish, but more openly as the submarine with the erect periscope sticking into the mother ship. However, his attempt to solve his Oedipal conflicts by taking his father's place and offering father the infantile role was only partially successful, and father's presence as an observing and threatening figure is of course represented by the patrolling plane (p. 378).

Klein and her co-workers have thus expanded our understanding of the Oedipus complex by developing the concept of the child's inner world, inhabited by figures derived from early experiences, whose qualities and functions are influenced by projections and distortions. She showed how, in the child's phantasy, these figures relate to the child, and interact with one another in complex ways, some of these relationships constituting early versions of the Oedipus complex. She confirmed and elaborated Freud's understanding of the way in which the nature and relationships of these internal figures remain alive in the person's mind, and influence his current relationships, including the way he experiences and uses the therapist in the clinical situation.

Two clinical examples

I recently had a consultation interview with a woman in her early thirties who complained of depression and occasional suicidal feelings. She told me that her childhood had been very happy until she was 10 or 11, when everything seemed to go wrong. Her father gave up a good job in which he had been for many years, the family moved, and her parents bought a small tobacconist shop which they ran together. She became aware of persistent arguments between her parents, which frightened and distressed her, which she couldn't understand, and didn't dare ask about. She remembers that she and her brother and sister would sometimes find their parents' bedroom door closed, and they knew they must not disturb them. She said this always meant her parents were having a serious discussion or an argument, and in her narrative it seemed to carry no other significance for her. She remembers a couple of occasions when her father was upset and crying, and he later told her that he was depressed and suicidal at that time. It was only his concern for his three children which stopped him killing himself.

She would come home from school, tense and apprehensive, and if her mum and dad were not standing close to each other she would worry about what was going on. If one parent was not in sight, she would be terrified that he or she had left, and would never come back. It was very striking, in the interview, how little she seemed to know or understand about the nature of the problems between her parents. She said she had always been too frightened to ask her mother (to whom she was otherwise close) what she called 'personal questions'. What became clear as the interview proceeded, however, was how guilty she felt about the problems between her parents – as if she had in some way been responsible for the difficulties between them. In fact her father had sometimes been driven to reassure her that it was something between them, and she shouldn't worry.

When the patient was 20 she married, and for a while was very happy and everything was fine. She was very keen to have a baby, and after some discussion her husband agreed. Around the time she conceived, she noticed some changes in him, which she couldn't understand, and when she was three months pregnant she discovered he had started an affair with a woman 12 years older than herself, and shortly afterwards he left to live with the other woman. She felt devastated and decided, apparently without much conflict, to seek a termination. She told me in the interview that what she had never told anyone before was that she believed that if she had an abortion perhaps he would come back, and they could be as they had been before. Although she has no contact with her husband, she has recurrent dreams of remarrying him, and then trying to get away from him. In the interview, I noticed that there was something very appealing, even seductive, in the patient's manner of confiding to me something she had never told anyone else.

A number of points struck me about this patient's history. She saw herself as close and special to each parent in turn. There was, I suspect, an underlying phantasy of forming an Oedipal alliance with each parent and being the cause of the problems between them. The parental bedroom could never be allowed to be a place in which any good sexual activity took place, but was exclusively the scene of terrible fights. Her sense of responsibility and guilt led to a constant feeling of anxiety lest her wishes would be realised, that mother would leave and she would actually find herself in possession of father. There was undoubtedly also a wish to make things better, to bring the parents together in a good way, and to recreate the idyllic family she remembered from her early childhood, thus avoiding or denying both her own Oedipal wishes and phantasies and the actual difficulties between her parents.

She hoped to find in her own husband a safer alternative to father, and for a while seems to have had the experience of being part of this good – perhaps somewhat idealised – couple that she dreamt about. Her wish for a baby was an extension of this, thus recreating a new version of the family who provided love and warmth for the little girl. Her husband's departure came as a terrible shock, and she couldn't face the prospect of repeating, with her child, the pain and unhappiness she had endured. She also reported the phantasy which confirmed, I thought, her view that it was the foetus or the child which had actually come between the parents, and if the child was disposed of (as in the Oedipus myth) the couple could remain happily together.

The last issue I want to draw attention to is the patient's apparent inability to question, to think, to understand what was going on between her parents, or indeed in her own marriage. Following the work of Klein and Bion, we have become increasingly interested in the link between the child's phantasy of the nature of the parental couple and the parental sexuality on the one hand, and the child's capacity to use her own mind on the other. Curiosity, the acquisition of knowledge, and the activity of thinking depend on the phantasy of things coming together in our minds. If our phantasy regarding the nature of the parental couple is that when they come together it is a violent and dangerous business, then the activity of putting things together in our minds will also be problematic. The inhibition of this otherwise intelligent woman's capacity for thought, observation and understanding was very striking.

In my second example, I want to refer to material from the analysis of a woman in which I think it is possible to see how aspects of the patient's Oedipal phantasies and wishes are recreated in the analytical situation, and determine the nature and quality of the transference and countertransference. There are some similarities between this patient's view of the Oedipal couple as involved in something fraught and dangerous, and that of the patient I saw for consultation. This patient's mode of functioning was, however, strongly influenced by her need to provide constant reassurance against her fears of being rejected or attacked.

The patient's parents had separated when she was very young, and her childhood was dominated by a painful and difficult relationship with her mother, a very disturbed woman. Her mother criticised and denigrated the absent father, blaming him for everything, always putting herself completely in the right. My patient was under tremendous pressure to accept her mother's view, and if she ever questioned it there would be a violent outburst. She gradually came to realise how disturbed the mother actually was and the elaborate web of lies and distortions with which she had grown up, but she was always too frightened to challenge.

At the same time, she entertained secret phantasies of her father returning to rescue her, like a knight on a white charger. It was important for her to imagine that he would see that she had done everything very well. She was an excellent pupil at school, and looked after the house much better than her mother did (like the man in Erna's play, who always judged her brick building to be the best). Father could hardly fail to take her side, and recognise how bad, cruel and neglectful her mother was, and take her away with him. The alternative scenario, which she hardly dared think about, was that mother and father would 'gang up' against her, see her as aggressive, nasty and dirty, and get rid of her.

In one session the patient brought up familiar difficulties in the relationship with her partner, where she often felt painfully rejected. She was quite defensive about her contribution to any of the problems and found it difficult to acknowledge her own hostility and resentment. As the session proceeded, she became less defensive and a more complex, real picture of their interaction began to emerge. She seemed to feel something important had been addressed and felt some relief.

She arrived a few minutes late for the next session and carefully explained how she had been delayed by things which were totally beyond her control.

She then said that something had happened the previous day, which she felt tempted to push away, but then thought she ought to talk about it, especially as there was nothing else she could think of to say. She told me about all the things she had done, emphasising how well she had managed. She had been able to remain very patient and calm with all the people she had had to deal with. Her partner had had a meeting to attend in the evening, and as he was very short of time, she had prepared a nice snack for him to eat in the car. She had been very patient and understanding, and hadn't raised any objections to his going out, even though she had seen very little of him lately. There was a sing-song tone to her voice, and I had a fairly good idea that the story would turn out in a familiar way, with my patient let down, hurt and disappointed.

When her partner returned from his meeting, he was very tired and just sat in front of the television, watching the news. She said she didn't mind, although she had heard it herself an hour before. While sitting there, he dozed off, which I knew often irritated her. Then his friend Peter telephoned, and he spoke to Peter for about half an hour. It wasn't anything urgent or connected with his work (which she could have understood), they were just chatting. She suddenly felt absolutely furious. He was too tired to bother with her, but had the energy to speak to his friend. It wasn't that she was making any great demands on him, or anything like that, she just wanted a bit of attention.

This all sounded terribly reasonable and compelling. There was a tone in her voice which pulled me into agreeing completely with her, being unequivocally 'on her side'. I was struck by the extent to which it had been necessary for her to build up a case, emphasising how good and tolerant she had been all evening. She made a point of acknowledging that she had been able to deal with the difficulties in this way because of the help she had received in the previous session, and spelled out that she had accepted the idea that her underlying anger and resentment might have an effect on her partner, which was one reason why she had tried to be so good and patient.

I tried to take up the way she needed to place herself beyond reproach, and to demarcate so clearly that it was her partner who behaved inconsiderately, and unappreciatively. Although she referred to the previous session as having been helpful, and the way she had been able to recognise her contribution to the difficulties between her and her partner, in this session I thought she was actually trying to repudiate what she saw as my doubts about her. She tried to demonstrate to me how her partner treated her in a hurtful and rejecting way, even when her own conduct was beyond reproach. There was a considerable pressure on me to agree with this point of view, to admit (at least to myself) that I was wrong to have any doubts about her, and to join her in an unreserved condemnation of her partner. When, instead of simply fitting into this, I pointed out this pressure, what then occurred in the session seemed to be a repetition of the scene of the previous evening. She felt hurt and misunderstood, offended and puzzled by my failure to join her. It was as if I was either siding with her partner against her, or was only interested in attending to what I was interested in (like her partner talking to Peter on the telephone). Both alternatives made her feel rebuffed and excluded, and raised again the possibility that I might dislike her, seeing her as having undesirable qualities.

I have briefly outlined some of the experiences and fantasies which I think preoccupied my patient during her childhood and adolescence. The point I wish to stress is the extent to which she felt driven, like her mother, to maintain a position in which she was totally in the right, and the other person was responsible for all the damage. Like with her mother, this often had a frantic, desperate quality about it, as it served to fend off the alternative view, where she herself would be recognised as being full of angry, destructive, jealous and sexual impulses, which were felt to be extremely threatening. For my patient in particular, if she were identified as 'bad', she would be lost – her mother would violently attack her, and her father would never rescue her. On the contrary, he might form an alliance with her mother against her. Her jealous Oedipal wishes are not completely split off, however, and she has some inklings of the impulses which she is at such pains to repudiate. Indeed, part of the motive for being so good is to prevent any possibility of the couple coming together, whether the couple is the original parental couple, her partner and his friend Peter, or the possibility that I would ally myself with her partner, and she would be excluded.

I thought the patient did have some inkling of the ways in which she subtly attacked and provoked her partner, and her impulse to stop me having my own ideas about the situation which threatened her, even when she appeared to be so appreciative. Any knowledge she had of her jealousy and the rage it gave rise to made her very anxious, both because it might lead me to attack her (like her mother), or I might abandon her in favour of a different alliance. The patient thus found it very difficult to tolerate ambivalence, or conflict within herself, and she became very anxious if she felt I wasn't completely on her side, but trying to judge for myself what was going on. Just as she put pressure on me only to see her as the virtuous girl whom I would be bound to love and support, so she spent a lot of time reassuring herself about her own motives, although she never completely succeed in fending off her doubts and suspicions.

It was thus a constant struggle for her to achieve any freedom to think about some of the painful and unwelcome aspects of herself, since allowing such thoughts and such knowledge to come together in her mind felt very threatening. In the analysis it has been a great relief to her not only to discover that I go on seeing her, and working with her even if I discover bad things about her, but also she can gradually build up a capacity to think about herself in a more three-dimensional way. Thus it is not only the case that in the analysis I don't simply confirm her Oedipal phantasies – either enacting the role of the controlling, demanding and explosive mother, or the seductive and collusive father – but it is as if she can allow a more constructive intercourse to take place within her own mind, letting different ideas come together there, without constantly fearing that that will result in a catastrophe.

Discussion

I hope I have been able to give you some sense of the way in which the concept of the Oedipus complex has evolved within psychoanalysis. Freud's original concern was with the way the child negotiated a particular phase of his development, finding ways of dealing with intense wishes and impulses directed towards each parent. He saw that the way these conflicts were resolved contributed in an important way to the individual's personality, and the pattern of object relations which was laid down.

Subsequent psychoanalytical research has enriched and developed his findings by drawing attention to early or pre-genital aspects of the Oedipus complex, the intense feelings of love and hate, envy and jealousy to which the awareness of triangular situations give rise even in very young children. I hope some of the brief clinical examples will give some indication that beyond the child's desire to possess one parent for himself or herself and to get rid of the other, there are complex patterns of relating to both parents, which are always represented and re-enacted in the clinical situation. These often arise out of the child's (or the adult's) anxieties about the nature of the parental couple, and the mixture of triumph, guilt and concern which the patient may either be confronted with, or may take pains to avoid. Part of the task of the analyst is to understand the nature of the patient's Oedipal phantasies, and to try to free the patient from a sense of entrapment in the repetition of very limited ways of relating which derive from these phantasies. This may involve the patient coming to recognise both parents as more three-dimensional, and their interaction as complex, and such changes in the patient usually go hand in hand with them being able to use their own minds and their resources more creatively.

References

Freud, S. (1897) Letter to Fliess no. 71, October 15, 1897. *Standard Edition*, vol. 1, p. 265, London: Hogarth Press.
—— (1917) *Introductory Lectures, Standard Edition*, vol. 16, p. 330, London: Hogarth Press.
Klein, M. (1924) 'An obsessional neurosis in a six-year-old girl', *The Psycho-Analysis of Children*, vol. 2 *The Writings of Melanie Klein*, London: Hogarth Press, 1975, pp. 36–7.
Klein, M. (1945) 'The Oedipus complex in the light of early anxieties', *International Journal of Psychoanalysis* 26; reprinted in *The Writings of Melanie Klein*, vol. 1, pp. 370–419, London: Hogarth Press, 1975.
Sophocles (1947) *Oedipus Rex*, trans. E.F. Watling, London: Penguin.

Suggestions for further reading

The main sources are probably John Steiner (ed.) *The Oedipus Complex Today: Clinical Implications* (London: Karnac, 1998); and Robin Anderson (ed.) *Clinical Lectures on Klein and Bion* (London: Routledge, 1992).

Chapter 11

The Oedipus complex II

Gregorio Kohon

In spite of its many contradictions, inconsistencies, paradoxes and ambiguities, psychoanalytic theory has a certain definite structure. Within it, one single aspect of the theory cannot be understood without taking into consideration the rest of the metapsychological structure. The Oedipus complex would not make sense unless put in the context of the psychoanalytic understanding of the unconscious. At the same time, the concept of the unconscious cannot make any sense without understanding the meaning given to sexuality in psychoanalysis. The psychoanalytic concepts of sexuality and the dynamics of the unconscious cannot be understood without reference to the Oedipus complex and its corollaries, the castration complex and the concept of penis envy. Yet, castration would not make much sense without its theoretical connection to the primal scene and the phantasies of seduction. The theory is intricate and comprises a multiplicity of meanings, which are all interlocked and interconnected.

At the same time (and to complicate things a bit further), the use of common, already known and frequently employed concepts in everyday language have been transformed and changed by psychoanalytic theory in such a way as to make them unrecognisable. Psychoanalysis should be understood as a theoretically and clinically distinct discipline, with its own specific paradigms. In trying to comprehend psychoanalysis, we are constantly taking the risk of sliding back to more familiar paradigms, which distorts the endeavour. For example, the understanding of the body in psychoanalysis does not follow the same laws that biology does. The body in psychoanalysis is a sexual body, it is organised and structured in a different manner to the 'natural' one, as studied by biology and physiology. The same applies to other concepts, like sexuality, or the distinction between sex and gender; or the debate between nature and culture; or the question of time, etc. With the discovery of the unconscious, Freud produced an epistemological jump, a rupture that turned psychoanalysis into something different from any other psychological theory of the mind.

Psychoanalysis and tragedy

From its beginnings, psychoanalysis was as much a therapeutic method of treating the neuroses as it was a theory of the mind. And as such, it was concerned with the destiny of human beings as tragic subjects. In this respect, psychoanalytic ideas address the same fundamental questions posed by literature and other forms of thought across the centuries:

> how to live in a world in which justice and power, right and might, often seem to have nothing to do with each other? how to deal with the fear that my own aggression and violence will overflow and violate all that I care about? how to confront my own death, and the deaths of those I love? how to act responsibly in the absence of freedom? how to make this inhumane world a more human place, and so comfort myself, and offer comfort to others?
>
> (Alford 1992: ix)

The interest and passion that Freud showed for Greek tragedy and the great myths of literature were motivated not only by a wish to explain or justify his theories. Freud found in Oedipus the representation of universal unconscious incestuous wishes, the interplay of transgression and punishment implied in the actions of a literary character who appeared to be both innocent and guilty, and the impact and significance of the basic laws presiding over our morality in somebody who 'knows and does not know a thing at the same time' (Freud 1893: 117; 2: 117).

The core of Freudian psychoanalytic ideas rests, in fact, upon a double tragic model: not only on Oedipus's unconscious predicament of incest and crime, but also on the repressed symbolic reproduction of this drama in the guilty consciousness of Hamlet. In *The Interpretation of Dreams*, Freud says:

> Shakespeare's *Hamlet* has its roots in the same soil as *Oedipus Rex* . . . In the Oedipus the child's wishful phantasy that underlies it is brought into the open and realised as it would in a dream. In Hamlet it remains repressed . . . we only learn of its existence from its inhibiting consequences . . . Hamlet is able to do anything – except take vengeance on the man who did away with his father and took that father's place with his mother, the man who shows him the repressed wishes of his own childhood realised.
>
> (Freud 1900: 263–4)

As neurotic patients, we are closer to Hamlet than to Oedipus.

When we search for the concept of the Oedipus complex in the psychoanalytic literature, we might become confused by the multiple, at times rather subtle and sophisticated interpretations of the myth. Yet the interpretations are impossible to systematise. Freud himself refused to, or could not give a systematic account of the complex. Nevertheless, while the meaning of Hamlet's drama, as popular as it has been, has remained relatively obscure in the imagination of the general public, Oedipus's tragedy has rather mystifyingly become a commonplace. The simplistic understanding of the Oedipus complex, its distortions and simplifications (including those that have been produced by psychoanalysts themselves), hide its rejection. Freud commented in a footnote to *The Interpretation of Dreams*:

> None of the findings of psychoanalytic research has provoked such embittered denials, such fierce opposition – or such amusing contortions – on the part of critics as this indication of the childhood impulses towards incest which persist in the unconscious.
>
> (Freud 1900: 263)

Freud believed that the Oedipus complex defined psychoanalysis. No psychoanalytic theory could be accepted as such unless, according to him, it admitted the universality of this complex, and the importance of the incest theme. The Oedipal drama represents for him the fate of us all (Freud 1900: 262). In this, Freud followed the classics: in making the Chorus describe Oedipus as the paradigm of the human condition, Sophocles gave the same recognition to Oedipus. Aristotle too, in his *Poetics*, considered the drama of Oedipus Rex the prime example, the archetype of all tragedies. For Freud, it was perfectly understandable that many people would disagree with his views, but then, he argued, their theories should be called something else, not psychoanalysis. It seems a fair request. In the *New Introductory Lectures on Psychoanalysis*, ironically referring to the theories of his dissident followers, Rank and Jung, he says:

> Suppose, for instance, that an analyst attaches little value to the influence of the patient's personal past and looks for the causation of neuroses exclusively in present-day motives and in expectations of the future . . . We for our part will then say: 'This may be a school of wisdom; but it is no longer analysis.'
>
> (Freud 1933a: 143)

In psychoanalysis, the Oedipus complex plays a central role in the structuring of the personality of each individual. The vicissitudes of its resolution will define the sexual orientation of the person. The concept helps us to understand and to explain the psychopathological presentations of the self as well as the variations and changes of the individual's identification processes.

Oedipus Rex was written around 320bc. After 23 centuries, we are still deeply struck by the themes of love, hate, guilt, incest, desire and death which are explored in Sophocles's play. The Oedipus myth is, in many ways, a relatively simple story. At one level of interpretation, it describes an incestuous sexual love for the parent of the opposite sex and a murderous impulse towards the rival, the parent of the same sex. This is what Freud described as the positive form of the Oedipus complex. In its negative form, we find the reverse picture: love for the parent of the same sex, and murderous hatred of the opposite one. In fact, these two different forms do not exclude each other; they always co-exist in every individual, complementing and supplementing each other, surviving in a dynamic tension, in an ever-changing, permanent conflict. In any case, in presenting us with this distinction Freud was simplifying things a bit too much: the love of a child (whether male or female) towards his or her mother cannot be simply put side by side with the love for the father; the two forms of love fulfil a different structuring function in the development of the subject. As we will later see, there is no actual symmetry which would allow us to make this comparison possible.

Universal phantasies

In *The Interpretation of Dreams*, Freud commented:

> Like Oedipus, we live in ignorance of these wishes, repugnant to morality, which has been forced upon us by Nature, and after their revelation we may all of us well seek to close our eyes to the scenes of our childhood. There is an unmistakable indication that the legend of Oedipus sprang from some primaeval dream-material.
>
> (Freud 1900: 263)

In this view, Freud speaks of a myth that transcends the individual history of a person (Laplanche and Pontalis 1967: 283). He suggests that there is, in the unconscious of each and every individual, the same complex of instinctual impulses dominated by the Oedipal drama. It tells the universal story of how each of us resolves the unavoidable challenge of how to become a man or a woman. In psychoanalysis, the Oedipus complex is there from the beginning of life, giving expression in an imaginary form to our instinctual sexual life. It is what makes the sexuality of human beings human.

It is a notion very closely connected to another difficult Freudian concept: primal phantasies, patterns – if you wish – which structure the imaginative life of the subject. These are scenarios which provide a form of representation to the enigmas of childhood: Where do I come from? How are babies made? Am I a boy or a girl? The structures cannot be reduced, or explained just by the individual's lived experience, and yet:

It is against the backdrop of these given scenarios that the individual's own story develops, a story marked by psychic and bodily inscriptions that are both uniquely personal and socially shared.

(Kohon 1999: 67)

The themes present in primal phantasies are limited. In the first place, there is the phantasy of a *primal scene*, which describes the sexual intercourse between the parents. This, of course, could have been actually observed by the child, but it seems to have been more frequently inferred on the basis of certain details picked up by him or her. In any case, it is not a question of 'empirical evidence' which would demonstrate the existence of the event. It has to be understood that Freud came to the conclusion of its existence through the analysis of adults, through the material provided by his patients in the actual psychoanalytic situation. It was something arrived at through interpretation and speculation. Phantasised or perceived, the relevant aspect of this primal scene is that it is always imagined by the child as an aggressive act on the part of the father, who is pictured as having anal intercourse with the mother in the context of a sado-masochistic relationship. The scene itself is both frightening and exciting for the child, and provides the background to castration anxieties.

Another primal phantasy is constituted by the phantasy of *seduction*, which describes the imaginary scene in which a child has been passively subjected to the sexual advances or manipulations of an adult. This concept has been greatly misunderstood. Freud did not deny the actual existence of sexual abuse in childhood, nor ever doubted that it could play a significant part in the creation of the neuroses. The sexual abuse of children, as any other form of violence in childhood, is a serious, traumatic event. But Freud was rather shocked to discover that some of the accounts offered by his patients had been imagined or phantasised. Therefore, he had to admit that an infantile sexual trauma was not always the cause of hysteria.

Finally, another central primal phantasy worth mentioning here is that of *castration*, which is produced 'in response to the child's puzzlement over the anatomical difference between the sexes (presence or absence of the penis): the child attributes this difference to the fact of the girl's penis having been cut off' (Laplanche and Pontalis 1967: 56). The phantasies of castration play an important part in the scenario of the Oedipus complex: the threat of castration will put an end to the boy's attachment to the mother, while penis envy will motivate the girl to look for something other than the mother. We will come back to these controversial issues later.

As Laplanche and Pontalis point out, all these unconscious, primal phantasies have something in common; they are all related to the question of origins, played out in the realm of sexuality. In the primal scene, it is the origin of the subject that is represented. In seduction phantasies, it is the origin or emergence of sexuality. In the phantasy of castration, it is the origin of the distinction between the sexes (p. 332).

Klein and Oedipus

For Melanie Klein primal phantasies were also very important. In her case, she believed that one could see, through the child's play, the presence of multiple identifications with each of the parents from very early on. In this context, she believed that there were pregenital phantasies connected with the primal scene. This primal scene, she suggested, was understood by the child (who was ignorant of the facts) in terms of his own oral and anal impulses and needs. She said:

> Intercourse comes to mean to the child a performance in which eating, cooking, exchange of faeces and sadistic acts of every kind (beating, cutting up, and so on) play the principal part.
>
> (Klein 1927: 175–6)

While Freud had also understood the primal scene in terms of an attack by the father against the mother (which, as we saw, took the form of a sadistic anal intercourse), Melanie Klein kept the idea of a sadistic attack, but changed it in a radical way. First of all, the parents were seen as part-objects; the early Oedipal parents were not people, they were individual organs: the penis in the vagina, the nipple in the breast. The mother's breast engages with the father's penis, the father's penis inhabits the mother's vagina. The parents became, in her concept of an 'early' Oedipus complex, a combined parental figure. The central characteristic of this combined parental figure at this early stage was, for her, that of a fearful couple locked in violent intercourse that would destroy each other and the infant (Klein: 1932):

> [The] combined parents (or their organs) destroy each other in a world disaster for the infant that leaves nothing for him; at the same time the figure turns on him because of his own omnipotent phantasies against the parents and subjects him to the same destructive forces that he believes they wreak upon each other.
>
> (Hinshelwood 1989: 60)

To this terrifying world one has to add the phantasised babies who (the child believes, according to Melanie Klein) live in the mother's creative body, arousing in the infant intense aggressive feelings and phantasies. In Melanie Klein's view, there were at least two important consequences for the infant: (a) the sadistic phantasies provoked great anxieties, fear for the parents, fear of a retaliation, and a sense of remorse; (b) in the early stages, the 'positive' and the 'inverted' Oedipus complexes are combined, co-existing at one and the same time. This creates intense mixed and ambivalent feelings towards each parent (Hinshelwood 1989: 58–9).

Castration anxiety and penis envy according to Melanie Klein became different concepts to those expounded by Freud. In terms of the castration complex, for Melanie Klein the fear of castration was reinforced in the boy by the phantasised attacks on the mother's body, in order to destroy the father's penis. In the case of penis envy, it was connected in the girl with her attacks on the mother; she wished to destroy, not only the father's penis contained in the mother's body, but the babies the mother was creating. As a consequence of the theoretical modifications introduced by Klein, the anxieties which she described were then of a different sort to those described by Freud. As Hinshelwood says: 'Klein in the 1920s had described a new anxiety – that of violently invading mother's body, and the fear of a comparable retaliation on the child's own body' (p. 62).

Furthermore, the very nature of the complex is essentially changed. In the words of Hanna Segal:

> Klein considered that the Oedipus complex starts in the first year of life and is fundamentally affected by the child's relation to the breast. *It is the frustration at the breast, and crucially the weaning, that makes the infant turn to the father's penis and become aware of the triangular situation.*
>
> (Steiner, 1989: 2; italics added)

We can see how, in changing the understanding of psychoanalytic concepts, we inevitably then change the theory and its structure; it becomes a different metapsychology. In replacing castration by the process of weaning as the decisive moment of the structuring of subjectivity, Klein radically changed the Freudian concept of the Oedipus complex. In her account, the father's penis is an alternative to the mother's breast. The theoretical changes are inevitably reflected in the clinical practice of psychoanalysis. For many Kleinian analysts:

> If weaning is the fundamental moment in the relationship with the primary object, it follows then that separation should be considered as central to the task of interpretation. This would explain the disproportionate emphasis given to the effect of weekends and holidays.
>
> (Kohon 1999: 13)

In addition, if these changes introduced in the metapsychology of psycho-analysis are not well kept in mind, they can become the locus of multiple misunderstandings, errors, misapprehensions, and confusion amongst psycho-analytic colleagues, let alone amongst those outside the psychoanalytic field.

Oedipus and language

More recently, Jean Laplanche offered an alternative view of primitive unconscious phantasies. He described a primitive situation, which he calls the *fundamental anthropological situation* of the human infant. He argues that, whatever the individual circumstances of the child, it is not possible for the baby to survive without encountering an adult world. This encounter takes place between an adult and the newborn child in a relationship in which, together with the necessary care provided by the adult, there is an unconscious implantation of enigmatic messages in the unconscious body-ego of the infant. These messages are traumatic for the child because they are derived from the unconscious sexuality of the adult in what then becomes inevitably a situation of seduction (Laplanche 1999).

The adult world is a world full of meanings, containing linguistic, proto-linguistic and para-linguistic messages that a child might not understand but to which he or she has to respond. For better or worse, there is a 'confusion of tongues' (Ferenczi 1933: 156–67). The relationship established between the infant and the adult takes place in two different registers at one and the same time. At one level, there is a loving and reciprocal relationship; at another, the relationship is implicitly sexual, where the two partners are not equal. The primal situation of seduction describes a fundamental scenario in which 'an adult proffers to a child verbal, non-verbal and even behavioural signifiers which are pregnant with unconscious sexual significations' (Laplanche 1987: 126).

For example, the breast offered to the child by the mother is not only an object that satisfies a need, it also contains a double message, explicit and implicit. The mother gives the breast to the child while she is also having positive, or (at worst) negative sexual unconscious feelings. If the feelings are positive, she communicates pleasure; if they are negative, she may communicate disgust. This cannot be ignored by the infant, who will have to respond in some way, even if the message signified is a mystery to him. Laplanche has, in this way, argued against the Freudian notion of a pre-given reality, mysteriously and genetically inherited, as suggested by the concept of primal phantasies. The response of the child consists of the attribution of meaning to a specific message coming from the adult. Therefore, the phantasy conveyed by the primal scene becomes, in Laplanche's view, an attempt to translate the enigma for the child of his or her parents' sexuality.

Let us try to develop further some of the ideas described above. Given the fact that human beings are born prematurely, the baby only survives because there is a physical and psychological environment that will protect him, look after him, feed him, and in general terms help him to survive and develop for a relatively long time. Freud described the human baby as being born in a state of helplessness. The baby is completely dependent on other people for the satisfaction of his most basic needs. In 'Inhibitions, symptoms and anxiety' (1926) Freud used the concept of helplessness as the prototype of all traumatic situations.

This extreme situation, of having to have his or her biological needs satisfied if the baby is to survive, applies to both sexes. They both depend completely on a mother, their first love object, with whom they cannot communicate through language. In the context of the infant's initial dependency, it is specifically the mother's breast which plays a decisive fundamental role in the development of the mental, physical and emotional life of the child. The breast is the infant's first object of desire; the physical relationship with mother (nursing, touching, cuddles and caressing) necessarily includes sexual and erotic feelings. It provides the necessary milk for the baby's survival but at the same time, in doing so, it will also come to represent the lost union with the mother which the baby once had inside her body. It should be noted that one of the most important aspects of the relationship with the breast is the ongoing process of comings and goings, of the presence and absence of the mother. One could argue that, with each absence, the desire for her presence is established more clearly.

The need for nourishment provides the first experience of satisfaction, one that will determine all future experiences of satisfaction. The baby is hungry and he screams. The timely intervention of the mother provides relief. Freud says:

> An essential component of this experience of satisfaction is a particular perception (that of nourishment, in our example) the mnemic image of which remains associated thenceforward with the memory trace of the excitation produced by the need.
>
> (Freud 1900: 565)

What does this mean? First, there is an original situation of satisfaction of a biological need; the baby is hungry and he gets the milk provided by the breast. Second, there is a mnemic image of this experience, a particular perception which remains linked to a memory trace of the excitation produced by the need. Every time the need emerges (hunger) this will be accompanied by the mnemic image, the memory of the original perception of the breast. In psychoanalysis, we call this a wish. Perhaps the best example is thumb sucking: that which was once present (the breast) is now hallucinated and replaced by something else. At this precise moment, when this hallucination appears, we find ourselves in the realm of the unconscious. It is here that psychology turns into psychoanalysis.

Need then is different from wish. Need derives from a state of internal tension (hunger), and achieves satisfaction through the specific action which is offered by the adequate object (breast, milk). From then on, wishes will always be associated to memory traces. In the unconscious, wishes will be fulfilled through the hallucinatory experiences which have become the signs of the satisfaction. In one example taken from literature, this hallucinatory experience and its dynamic interplay with reality is expressed thus:

> I touch your mouth, I touch the edge of your mouth with my finger, I am drawing it as if it were something my hand was sketching, as if for the first time your mouth opened a little, and all I have to do is close my eyes to erase it and start all over again, every time I can make the mouth I want appear, the mouth which my hand chooses and sketches on your face, and which by some chance that I do not seek to understand coincides exactly with your mouth which smiles beneath the one my hand is sketching on you.
>
> (Cortázar 1963: 32)

The search for a love-object in the real world is a symbolic venture, entirely governed by a relationship to signs. Wishes are related to the real objects only through the mediation of the phantasies that form part of them. Wish fulfillment could be said to be an illusion: the wish appears to the human imagination to have been realised. The tendency of the primary process is towards reinvesting the ideas attached to the original experiences of satisfaction (primitive hallucination) by establishing a perceptual identity.

It is not difficult to see that all this constitutes a mythical, retroactive structure, which is the effect of a symbolisation of a past which never really was. This is also clearly reflected in literature as well as in language. Alberto Manguel makes Robert Louis Stevenson say:

> The word 'nostalgia' . . . had been invented in the seventeenth century by an Alsatian student in a medical thesis, to describe the malady that afflicted Swiss soldiers when far from their native mountains. For (Stevenson) it was the contrary: nostalgia was the pain of missing places that he had never seen before.
>
> (Manguel 2002: 40)

Equivalent forms of understanding nostalgia have specific, untranslatable words in other languages, one example among others being the word *saudade* in Brazilian Portuguese. The fact that these words cannot be properly translated into other languages might justify the claim that language, after all, refers to something that knowledge cannot properly apprehend (Kertész 1997: 116).

There is another important consequence of the total dependence of the human infant on its environment: 'the state of helplessness implies the mother's omnipotence' (Laplanche and Pontalis 1967: 190). This first object of love, what is known as the pre-Oedipal mother, is an omnipotent mother, who could do anything and who possesses everything. How could she not, if she is the one who saves the baby from total destruction and allows him to survive? This omnipotent, pre-Oedipal mother does not need anybody else. The baby's fixation to the primary relationship with her, in the initial phase of exclusive and equally intense lasting attachment, will be at the source or at the origin of psychotic states and of the perversions.

In time, the mother's breast will become the mother as a whole person. She was believed to have it all but soon the love object will be discovered to be not perfect after all; mother is not omnipotent. In Freudian language, mother was believed to have a phallus. Now she is seen *not* to have everything. She needs something else for her completeness; she demands some kind of satisfaction from the baby; she wants to be loved, and cared for. The form that this question takes in the unconscious is, 'Do I have that which mother needs? Do I have what it takes to satisfy mother?' Both boys and girls are forced to recognise that *no* is the answer to this question. I have previously put forward this idea:

> It is the realisation that boys and girls do not and cannot have what it takes to satisfy mother fully which creates the logical moment in the structure of the unconscious that allows the subject to separate from her. It is as if the boy has to acknowledge that 'he hasn't got that which mother needs (for procreating) and desires (for her sexual satisfaction); and even if he were to pretend that he's got it, it is too small, too inefficient, and it can be cut off (in other words, it's only a penis and not a phallus); so he'd better give mother up, he'll renounce his phallic narcissistic identification, acknowledge that which he does have, and use it as best as he can somewhere else, with somebody else at the appropriate time'. There is a similar (although not the same) challenge for the girl: 'she is not (and she hasn't got) that which mother needs and desires; she'll renounce her phallic narcissism, accept what she does have, and look for somebody to give her satisfaction, the baby that she wants (or might not want)'. This relinquishing of the primary object, of course, is never completely achieved. On the one hand, from the point of view of the mother, she will never stop hoping for something beyond the baby, which might take the form of an implicit demand addressed to all children, boys and girls, for the rest of their lives: 'Why don't you do as I wish? Why aren't you as I wish you to be? Why don't you do as I tell you?' On the other hand, from the point of view of the subject, he or she will never sufficiently forego the identification with the imaginary object, the phallus (or with a primary object that is believed to possess it). But if the subject does not face this necessary disappointment, then narcissism, omnipotence and envy will prevail in the subject's love life.

It is impossible not to take a position in relation to the desire of the mother, not to decide who (what sexual being) we are for her. First, we desperately need to believe that we are the object of her desire, and then we have to go through the disillusion and the painful realisation that we are not it. This moving away from the primary object is overdetermined, not free, but this does not necessarily mean that it is prescriptive of heterosexuality ... The resolution of the oedipal conflict is never dictated by social norms alone, nor can it be exclusively determined by biological forces. The psychoanalytic explanation of the differentiation of the sexes through the resolution of the phallic position in the context of the oedipal conflict seems to be the only theory that describes this predicament mainly in terms of an unconscious process.

(Kohon 1999: 8–10)

From a psychoanalytic point of view, it is not possible to appeal to biology to explain the difference between the sexes. As I have previously argued:

There is in the unconscious a danger and a threat for the man, and a desire and envy for the woman. There is not (as it is at times assumed) an over-valued penis and an under-valued vagina. A penis, just as much as a vagina, does not secure or guarantee anything for the subject in becoming a sexual human being (Masotta: 1976). If nothing else, the idea of bisexuality in psychoanalysis denotes precisely the uncertainty of the process and the struggle through which all human beings become either a woman or a man.

(Kohon 1999: 10)

It is not a question of an actual penis or a real vagina – the concern has nothing to do with anatomical reality. It is only the presence or the absence of *that which the infant imagines mother wanting* (see also Kohon 1986: 362–80).

The father and not-I

What is the place of the father in all this? The father is there to reveal the desire of the mother, a desire not exhausted by her wish to have a baby. This is the condition – a father who is desired by the mother, and, one should add, a mother who wants to be, and accepts being, desired by a father – which will liberate the child from the illusion that he or she is the sole object of his or her mother's wishes. The mother, after all, desires somebody else. Children are forced to confront, sooner or later, the fact that their mother's desires extend beyond them.

Described as the father of the individual prehistory (Freud), the imaginary father (Lacan), the non-mother (Le Guen), the absence of the mother, the stranger, or the phallus, this place has been aptly named as *not I* (Kristeva 1983). The imaginary father would thus be the indication that the mother is not complete but that she wants: 'Who? What? The question has no answer other than the one that uncovers narcissistic emptiness: "At any rate, not I" ' (Kristeva 1983; translated for this edition).

Not I denotes a recognition of the subject's radical separation from the original object, the giving up of an omnipotent dream of a blessed harmony with the world.

If there is a father (imaginary or real) who fulfils this function in the mind of the mother, the child will have to accept that he or she cannot be what the mother wants. The child will be able to recognise himself or herself as a son or a daughter, as a testimony and a consequence of the parents' intercourse, not as the cause of such an intercourse.

All this, in the last resort, is inevitably condensed and extremely reductive. By necessity, an 'introduction' would tend to simplify, misrepresent, perhaps thus even distort the complexity of psychoanalytic theory. The question concerning the father is certainly one of the most difficult to summarise. In Freud, there is a very specific and clear theoretical movement from the original conceptualisation of the father according to the interpretation of the *Oedipus Rex*, to the myth of the terrifying and perverse father of *Totem and Taboo*, not to mention the later vision of the father in *Moses and Monotheism*. Nevertheless, in the context of this chapter, what we need to emphasise is the importance and relevance of the paternal function as a structuring figure: how his word is (or should be) present in the mother's discourse as a third agency. The father, as this third party, is not merely a rival to be defeated and killed, but an irrevocable law, a principle which mediates and establishes difference: difference between mother and child, between boys and girls, between incest and exogamy, between biological origins and identity. The paternal function, in psychoanalysis, is not a sociological role but a symbolic principle.

The most important aspect of this triangular structure is that it forces the child into a specific, definite place within the family. The structure regulates desire, introducing a repetitive process of substitution of symbolic objects. There is a radical asymmetry between being caught in the imaginary relationship with the mother (which is narcissistic and specular) and the symbolic participation in a triangular structure with access to language, the acknowledgment of sexual difference, the need for recognition by the other and the difference between generations, and the acceptance of death.

Many critics of Freud have insisted that, in focusing his attention on the character of Oedipus, he neglected or ignored the other elements in Sophocles's play. For example, it has been claimed that the murder of Laius by Oedipus is only one aspect of the different dramas taking place in the Oedipus cycle. What about the abduction of Chrysippus, some critics protested, and the homosexual seduction which is the source of the original curse? What about the consequent important 'original' crime of the father wanting to get rid of the son, the filicidal wishes of Laius against Oedipus? And what about Jocasta's complicity? According to some authors, this would explain, if not justify, Oedipus's crime as a true act of self-defence.

We should remind ourselves once and again that Freud was talking about the unconscious mind of the child, not about the real events that take place in the life of an individual. Freud's genius resided in seeing Sophocles' play in terms of a dramatisation of unconscious wishes. In fact, it can be argued that this was Sophocles's own originality: he also ignored the previous 'history' of the characters and did not offer any 'explanation'. That which is critically 'explained' in the play (by a considerable number of authors and commentators) comes from other sources, not from the play itself (Rudnytsky 1987: 255). Sophocles himself had made a creative choice: the play is not about the culpability of Laius but about the tragedy of Oedipus in his search for his origins.

Many of the criticisms perennially addressed to Freud originate from a basic misunderstanding: the unconscious and its laws are ignored, and the primary process is denied. Another important psychoanalytic concept, primary process, describes a type of mental functioning completely different to the thought processes traditionally understood by psychology. It has its own mechanisms and its own laws; for example, it functions within a different concept of time; in fact, there is no time. The model of the primary process would be the dream, where past and present are mixed. The criticisms then are based on phenomena which belong to the secondary process, in other words to the conscious part of our minds. Some of these attacks are not so much anti-Freudian but – as Juliet Mitchell clearly showed – pre-Freudian (1974: 9), they predate the discovery of the unconscious.

We are expected here to make a very special effort of imagination in order to understand that the Oedipus complex is not the actual history of a family constellation; it is not the account of the conscious desires involved in a social situation. Furthermore, it does not originate in the mindful acceptance of incestuous wishes, or murderous phantasies. The Oedipus complex is the 'nucleus of neuroses' because it shows the repression of all these wishes and phantasies. These things can only be deduced, interpreted, speculated upon. The specificity of psychoanalysis as a theory of the mind consists in its attempt to describe unconscious psychic reality. We infer and construe the Oedipal infantile sexual organisation from what we hear from adults in the consulting room. It is a process that works retroactively, from the present to the past.

The question forced upon each subject by the Oedipus drama is not only the triangular tragedy of rivalry, jealousy, and love but the misrecognition (*méconnaissance*) of the subject's own history: Oedipus is the son of Jocasta and Laius but he does not know it. Or, perhaps, he does not want to know it. According to Freud, one can be afflicted by a 'blindness of the seeing eye'. From this point of view, we could say that the Oedipal drama describes 'the strange state of mind [as I have quoted above] in which one knows and does not know a thing at the same time' (Freud 1893: 117; see also Steiner 1993).

As in the world of law, not knowing does not make human beings less responsible. This is what inevitably turns every single human destiny *tragic*.

'Tragedy means, above all else,' Alford argues, 'that people are responsible without being free' (1992: 115). We might become more insightful through psychoanalysis, but this would not make us necessarily any wiser.

References

Alford, C.F. (1992) *The Psychoanalytic Theory of Greek Tragedy*, New Haven, CT/London: Yale University Press.

Cortázar, J. (1963) *Hopscotch*. London: Harvill Press.

Ferenzci, S. (1933) 'Confusion of tongues between adults and the child', in *Final Contributions to the Problems & Methods of Psycho-Analysis*, London: Hogarth Press. Reprinted London: Karnac, 1980.

Freud, S. with Breuer, J. (1893–1895) *Studies on Hysteria, Standard Edition*, vol. 2, London: Hogarth Press.

Freud, S. (1900) *The Interpretation of Dreams, Standard Edition*, vols 4–5, London: Hogarth Press.

—— (1926) 'Inhibitions, symptoms and anxiety', *Standard Edition*, vol. 20, pp. 75–175, London: Hogarth Press.

—— (1933) *New Introductory Lectures on Psychoanalysis, Standard Edition*, vol. 22, London: Hogarth Press.

Hinshelwood, R.D. (1989) *A Dictionary of Kleinian Thought*, London: Free Association Books.

Kertész, I. (1997) *Yo, otro – Crónica del Cambio*, Barcelona: Acantilado, 2002.

Klein, M. (1927) 'Criminal tendencies in normal children', *British Journal of Medical Psychology* 7: 177–92. Reprinted in *The Writings of Melanie Klein*, vol. III, *Love, Guilt and Reparation, and Other Works*, London: Karnac, 1993.

—— (1932) *The Psychoanalysis of Children*, London: Hogarth Press. Reprinted in *The Writings of Melanie Klein*, vol. II, *The Psychoanalysis of Children*, London: Karnac, 1998.

Kohon, G. (ed.) (1986) *The British School of Psychoanalysis – The Independent Tradition*, London: Free Association Books.

—— (1999) *No Lost Certainties to be Recovered*, London: Karnac.

Kristeva, J. (1983) *Histoires d'Amour*, Paris: Denoel. (*Tales of Love*, New York: Columbia University Press, 1987).

Laplanche, J. (1987) *New Foundations in Psychoanalysis*, Oxford: Blackwell.

—— (1999) *Essays on Otherness*, John Fletcher (ed.), London: Routledge.

Laplanche, J. and Pontalis, J.-B. (1967) *The Language of Psychoanalysis*, London: Hogarth Press, 1973.

Manguel, A. (2002) *Stevenson under the Palm Trees*, Edinburgh: Canongate.

Mitchell, J. (1974) *Psychoanalysis and Feminism*, London: Allen Lane.

Rudnytsky, P.L. (1987) *Freud and Oedipus*, New York: Columbia University Press.

Steiner, J. (ed.) (1989) *The Oedipus Complex – Clinical Implications*, London: Karnac.

—— (1993) *Psychic Retreats – Pathological Organizations in Psychotic, Neurotic and Borderline Patients*, London/New York: Routledge.

Part 4

Patient and analyst

By this time, it will be evident to the reader that the attention of the contemporary psychoanalyst has shifted from the attempt to see the patient 'objectively' to the acceptance that the interaction between analyst and patient is the main source of information, both about the patient and the therapeutic effect of analysis. As Freud went on working, he saw ever more clearly how elusive and complex the concept of 'memory' is. The idea that memory is laid down in layers, which are in theory recoverable, was replaced by the recognition that memories are also constructed, and continuously reconstructed, as we attempt to evoke them in the present. There is no evidence that Freud or Proust ever read each other, but the similarities between their ideas are striking. The taste of the madeleine or the sense of the unevenness of the Venetian flagstones, which re-evoked a world which had been forgotten or discarded, enabled Marcel to reconsider his present in the light of his adult, changed understanding of his past.

Similarly, Freud believed that experiences which may not have been understood by the child at the time are stored in the memory and may be re-evoked in a different form when a recent experience recalls them to us. Their significance is only now understood, and they can act as a kind of depth charge, shattering our view of the past. The German term for this, *Nachträglichkeit*, was translated into French as '*après-coup*', and rather less adequately into English as 'deferred action'. Psychoanalytic treatment is concerned with the recovery and understanding of the unconscious memories and phantasies which populate our minds. The main means of their recovery is to look at how they are re-evoked between analyst and patient in the session, in 'the transference'.

In Chapter 12 on the development of the concepts of transference and countertransference, Margret Tonnesmann takes us back to Freud's gradual and somewhat reluctant discovery of the universal existence of transference. She shows how the concept changed as psychoanalytic theory changed, and the significance of the difference between psychoanalysis in Vienna, and developments in Budapest and Berlin, and how these contributed to Klein's rather different view of transference, not as a repetition but as part of ongoing psychic reality.

Freud recognized the existence of countertransference, the analyst's response to his patient, but only to disapprove of it. The metaphors he used, 'evenly-hovering attention', 'the skilful surgeon', 'the well-polished mirror', suggest that the analyst should master his personal reactions, keep them out of the work and, if necessary undergo further analysis for himself. Melanie Klein was also inclined to believe that claiming the analyst's response was due to his countertransference could be used to justify poor practice. There is a nice story of a student who ended his account of a session by saying to her, 'And so, you see, the patient put her confusion into me.' 'No, dear,' said Mrs Klein, ' *You* are confused.' However, over time, it has become clearer that using our countertransference in an attempt to think about what is happening in the session is a unique source of information, even if it can easily be misinterpreted. The difference between Klein and those analysts who became interested in countertransference as a form of communication was resolved by the near-universal adoption in British psychoanalysis of Wilfred Bion's view (1963) that the analyst's countertransference resembled that of a mother to her infant. The analyst's task, like that of the mother, was to receive distress, contain and process it, and give it back only when the patient/child was capable of receiving it.

Many analysts from the Independent group have been interested in the pre- or non-verbal aspects of communication, and have been less concerned to interpret the patient's communications as solely produced from their inner world, rather than as having arisen in the matrix between themselves and their objects. As Tonnesmann describes, they are therefore more accepting of regression, seeing it not solely as a defence but as the patient's attempt to gain or understand something which had really been lacking in infancy. Balint and Winnicott were probably the most widely known exponents of these views, and more recently Christopher Bollas (1987, 1993) has described this method of working in a popular and evocative series of books.

In Chapter 13, Priscilla Roth describes and illustrates a different way of understanding the same phenomenon via the idea of projective identification; a defence mechanism that was first described by Klein in 1946 (Klein 1946). Roth describes very clearly how this defence of (in phantasy) putting oneself, or parts of oneself, into one's object takes many forms. The concept has been one of Klein's most influential, giving rise to extensive further elaboration both in the UK and in North and South America. She clarifies the universal application of this mechanism; how the motivation behind its use can be loving or inquisitive, not only hostile; how central it is in all communication from babyhood onwards; and how it underpins the analyst's emotional understanding of his or her patient through countertransference. She does this by means of a detailed clinical example, in this case of a patient who was frightened of a picture that she had of Roth as a powerful and cold person, and dealt with this by herself becoming such a person in the interview. Although this was a very uncomfortable experience for both of them, it enabled Roth to understand with emotional conviction, and not merely intellectually, what the patient was feeling. Projective identification in ordinary mental life is a rapidly reversible process which is the basis for all understanding between people, but in pathology it becomes stuck, and it is harder for disconfirming reality to reverse it.

In Chapter 14, David Riley carries on the discussion of what is actually said in the analytic session by contrasting two ideal types of psychoanalysis: that which follows an agreed upon and exemplary technique, and that which is based upon the needs of the patient. They are associated with different psychoanalytic traditions but, as Riley points out, what analysts of any persuasion actually do in their consulting rooms is likely to vary and is hard to discover. The exemplary technique in contemporary British psychoanalysis is correct verbal interpretation of the transference, which James Strachey (1934) in a uniquely influential paper, described as the only *mutative* intervention. But there are some influential qualifiers, primarily Wilfred Bion, who suggested that the need to interpret may be due to the analyst's need to alleviate his own anxiety rather than to the needs of his patient. Most analysts have wrestled with the problem of how to deal with patients for whom words do not mean very much, either at times, or all the time.

Riley argues that the second approach, a greater responsiveness to the specific patient, is more open, not in the sense of open minded, which we must all hope to be, but more pluralist, more accepting of contradiction and paradox, and more rooted in the interaction between mother and baby, analyst and patient, than in the analyst's capacity to discern what is going on in the patient. He makes a distinction between theories that see pathology as the product of real traumatic events, or a reaction to helplessness, on the one hand, and on the other, more drive-based theories in which the child, and later the adult, is struggling to externalize pressures which originate from within, although mitigated or exacerbated by the environment. It could be argued that the first theories underestimate the role of instinct and the unconscious phantasy it generates, and the second the importance of the environment to which the child reacts. Again, theorists of the different schools typically differ on the question of aggression and regression.

In an ideal world we all, of course, hope to be both rigorous and open minded, disciplined but free. Yet we all have to find our own way of being psychoanalysts. It is tempting to fetishize difference and paradox; to exalt unusual patients and ways of dealing with them, which may reflect the narcissism of both patient and analyst. Conversely, if we follow agreed upon practice too slavishly we may become rigid and the patient may conclude that we cannot really hear them, or become compliant. However, most of us have had the experience with some patients of having tried all the techniques in our repertoire to little avail. How far it is effective or legitimate to modify the parameters of treatment is a perennial question (see the discussion by Kohon 1986).

One of the costs of the group structure in the British Society has been that theories are too often seen as the 'possessions' of different groups. What Freud often described as 'the narcissism of minor differences' (Freud 1918) comes into play, and makes it more difficult to see to what extent British analysts have influenced each other across groups, and therefore seem to outsiders to share beliefs and techniques. By focusing on the differences, it makes it hard to acknowledge either that there are other really different perspectives in the psychoanalytic world, particularly perhaps in France or the USA, and that the practice of defining British psychoanalysts by group has reified the distinctions which do exist. Victoria Hamilton, in a pioneering work, *The Analyst's Preconscious* (1996) interviewed a number of English analysts, together with many more from the USA, about their views of various aspects of technique. She has been able to show that there are differences, both between analysts and between groups, but not always where we would expect them to be. Paradoxically, it is probably when analysts are working outside their consulting rooms that they are more likely to learn about and possibly adopt some of the views and techniques of their colleagues from other groups.

References

Bion, W. (1963) *Elements of Psychoanalysis*, London: Heinemann.

Bollas, C. (1987) *The Shadow of the Object: Psychoanalysis of the Unthought Known*, London: Free Association Books

—— (1993) *Being a Character: Psychoanalysis and Self Experience*, London: Routledge.

Freud, S. (1918) 'The taboo of virginity', *Standard Edition*, vol. 11, p. 199, London: Hogarth Press. (Also in 'Group psychology' and 'Civilization and its discontents'.)

Hamilton, V. (1996) *The Analyst's Preconscious*, New Jersey: Analytic Press.

Klein, M. (1946) 'Notes on some schizoid mechanisms', *International Journal of Psychoanalysis* 27: 99–110. Revised version in M. Klein, P. Heimann, S. Isaacs and J. Riviere, *Developments in Psycho-Analysis*, London: Hogarth Press, 1952, pp. 292–320. Reprinted in *The Writings of Melanie Klein*, vol. 3, pp. 1–24, London: Hogarth Press, 1975, and Virago Press, 1997.

Kohon, G. (1986) *The British School of Psychoanalysis: The Independent Tradition*, London: Free Association Books.

Strachey, J. (1934) 'The nature of the therapeutic action of psychoanalysis', *International Journal of Psychoanalysis* 15: 127–59.

Chapter 12

Transference and countertransference

An historical approach

Margret Tonnesmann

In 1905 Freud stated:

> Transferences are new editions or facsimiles of the impulses and phantasies which are aroused and made conscious during the progress of the analysis; but they have this peculiarity, which is characteristic for their species, that they replace some earlier person by the person of the physician. To put it in another way: a whole series of psychological experiences are revived, not as belonging to the past, but as applying to the person of the physician at the present moment.
>
> (Freud 1905)

Freud then differentiated between those new editions that are, so to speak, reprints and those that are revised editions. The latter are sometimes ingeniously constructed and often take clever advantage of some real peculiarities in the physician's person or circumstances and attach themselves to that.

Sixty-two years later, Laplanche and Pontalis pointed out in *The Language of Psychoanalysis* (1973) that it is difficult to propose a single definition of transference, as different authors have extended the concept so that all the phenomena that constitute the patient's relationship with the analyst may be included. The result is that the concept is loaded with each analyst's particular views on the treatment. This trend has been maintained up to the present time. In this chapter, I will trace the history of the development of the concept of transference, and also that of countertransference which was introduced into psychoanalytic theory later on.

Before Freud opened his practice as a physician and neurologist in Vienna in 1886, he had won a travelling fellowship and went to Paris to study Charcot's famous experiments with patients suffering from conversion hysteria. Charcot had a daily ward round during which he demonstrated that under hypnosis patients would lose their somatic symptoms when he gave them orders to do so. On waking up they had regained their somatic symptoms and also could not remember what had happened to them during their hypnotic state. Freud was most impressed that somatic symptoms could be influenced by words. Later he went to Nancy where the French psychiatrist Bernheim had shown that he could persuade his patients to remember post-hypnotically what had happened to them when they were under hypnosis. However, he often had to bully his patients to submit to him. Freud noticed that the patients' memories had not been lost; they were merely not easily available to conscious recall.

In Vienna, Freud's older colleague and friend, the physician Joseph Breuer, had treated a young woman Anna O with hypnosis. She suffered from hysterical symptoms, and under hypnosis related her symptoms to events from the time when she had nursed her dying father and had often had to suppress her emotions. Under hypnosis she could remember event after event, and she did so with great emotional intensity, after which her symptom disappeared. Breuer (Freud and Breuer 1893–95) concluded from this treatment that hysterical symptoms are the symbolic conscious manifestations of events when emotions had to be suppressed. The treatment became known as cathartic therapy. The treatment of Anna O ended abruptly when one day she staged a phantom pregnancy and declared that she was giving birth to Breuer's baby. Freud understood this much later as an instance of transference in which Anna O had activated an repressed early Oedipal wish for a baby from her father.

Freud (Freud and Breuer 1893–95) conceived of hysterical symptoms differently. He saw them as manifestations of repressed conflictual wishes, and argued that people would remain healthier if they had more courage to face their objectionable wishes and wants. Instead they succeeded in pushing them out of their conscious minds. However, they only partially succeeded as the wishes remained active in the unconscious part of the mind and found their way back in the form of the symbolic manifestation of hysterical symptoms. Hence, he conceived of hysteria as a defence.

At first Freud treated patients who suffered from hysteria with hypnosis, but found that some patients could not be hypnotised. He disliked the method and introduced what is known as the pressure technique. That meant that patients lay on the couch and were advised to concentrate and remember the circumstances of the onset of their symptoms. Whenever a patient showed resistance, because they had come too near their repressed memories, he told them that they would remember when he put his hand on their forehead. He utilised here what he had observed in Nancy when he visited Bernheim. However, as some patients remained defiant, Freud devised what is now the standard psychoanalytic treatment setting, in which the patient was allowed to talk freely to an analyst who remained out of sight. This was a revolutionary step at the end of the century before last. He gave up the doctor's authoritative role and offered his patients a working alliance with divided roles. The patient was told to free associate and say whatever goes through his mind. To act as though 'you were a traveller sitting next to a window in a railway carriage and describing to someone inside the carriage the changing views which you see outside' (Freud 1913: 135). Freud told his patients that various thoughts would occur to them which they would like to put aside on the grounds of various criticisms or objections. This or that may appear to them to be irrelevant, unimportant or nonsensical but 'Never leave anything out because, for some reason or other, it is unpleasant to tell it' (Freud 1913: 135).

This is the *fundamental rule* for every patient undergoing analytic therapy, and has remained the cornerstone of psychoanalytic treatment to the present day. The analyst contributes to the analytic setting by listening with what Freud called *free hovering attention*. It is the counterpart to the patient's free associating. The analyst has to make use of everything the patient says in order to recognise the concealed unconscious material in the patient's free associations without substituting a censorship of his own. Freud put it into a formula:

> He must turn his own unconscious like a receptive organ towards the transmitting unconscious of the patient. He must adjust himself to the patient as a telephone receiver is adjusted to the transmitting telephone. Just as the receiver converts back into sound-waves the electric oscillations in the telephone line which were set up by sound waves, so the doctor's unconscious is able, from the derivatives of the unconscious which are communicated to him, to reconstruct that unconscious, which has determined the patient's free associations.
>
> (Freud 1912e: 115–16)

Hence 'the analyst may not tolerate resistances in himself which hold back from his consciousness what has been perceived by his unconscious' (ibid.). Freud described the *art of interpreting*, by which he means the translation of the analyst's unconscious understanding into verbal thought.

The discovery of transference

It was within this analytic treatment setting that patients at times resisted further association and told Freud that nothing was coming into their minds any more. When he insisted that there must have been something on their minds, to his astonishment they reluctantly told him that they had had thoughts about him. Such thoughts were sometimes either an acute grievance against him that he thought was relatively easy to get out of the way, or sometimes they had had a forbidden erotic wish they felt embarrassed about, or they experienced Freud as if he were a forbidding parental figure from their childhoods who was arousing castration anxieties. At first he was annoyed about these interruptions as they held up the analytic work. But then he saw the advantage of such incidents, as inevitably such material always brought the repressed nearer to the patient's conscious awareness.

Transference therefore was seen on the one hand as the expression of resistance to maintain the defences against the recall of objectionable material, and it was also seen as a great help to understanding the repressed unconscious.

It was only later when Freud had studied dreams that he could conceptualise transference. Just as in dreams the dreamer has to use day residues from his recent memories to experience unconscious wishes as fulfilled during a dream, he has to use the analyst as the object of such wishes to reactivate them in the *here and now* experiences of the session. It is a displacement of unconscious material onto the analyst in a new edition, but the analyst does not fulfil such wishes: he interprets them instead. Hence it is said that psychoanalytic therapy takes place in abstinence.

Freud (1912b) pointed out that transference is a common phenomenon: psychoanalytic therapy only makes a special use of it. Patients tend in general to relate to doctors with an affectionate transference, using a parental imago. Sometimes one can observe in hospitals how such relationships escalate into frank erotic wishes. In psychoanalytic therapy the unobjectionable affectionate transference relationship is not interpreted, but used as a vehicle to contain the patient over stormy times within the relationship to the analyst and to enhance some basic trust. However, the repressed, forbidden and defended against transferences should be interpreted as they occur during sessions. They are repetitions from childhood with their ambivalent positive and negative currents.

When the analyst first points out these unconscious repetitions the patient has a conscious knowledge of what he has been told. But it does not change the repressed unconscious complex. Only when there is a repetition in a new edition of the repressed original ambivalent conflicts or traumata, with all the emotional involvement belonging to them, will the patient experience the old situation anew. But the patient wants to experience satisfaction in the present and he may be convinced that he is in love with the analyst, or certainly that the analyst is in love with him. Then a struggle develops between the analyst who wants the patient to understand that these feelings belong to an old experience that is now revived in the transference which he wants the patient to remember, but the patient wants to have satisfaction and to act out this new edition. That is what we call transference neurosis. It always takes time to work through such highly charged situations.

However, the patient does not repeat only the repressed loving but forbidden wishes: he also repeats the repressed narcissistic traumata with their hostile feelings towards the object. Freud (1905) had experienced this early on in his career when a young patient, whom he called Dora, terminated the treatment prematurely. With hindsight he could see how he had missed the girl's hostile feelings for him, as she had substituted him for a friend of her father's who had treated her badly in the past. She was now taking revenge, using Freud as the substitute object for her hostile feelings. Often such hostile currents are defended against by conscious positive feelings towards the analyst.

When Freud introduced his second model of the mind with the id, ego and super-ego structures (1923) and the revision of the concept of anxiety (1926), ego defence mechanisms were assumed to be unconscious in quality too. Transference was now conceived of as an ego-resistance, as the patient relates to the analyst with typical defences and so is avoiding anxieties that the threatening repressed id content might arouse. Moreover, the analyst is also at times experienced as the patient's super-ego, and the tensions between super-ego and ego within the patient are battled out with the analyst in the transference, when the patient may experience the analyst as a powerful, critical father. Only when the ego defences are sufficiently loosened can the transference neurosis emerge. It was now assumed that only those patients whose ego was strong enough to form a therapeutic alliance with the analyst were suitable for psychoanalytic treatment. It meant that the ego had to therapeutically split into an observing part that, identified with the analyst, could observe the other acting part of his ego. When after some analytic work the ego defences have been sufficiently weakened, the transference neurosis will spontaneously develop. There is always a part of the ego that retains a working alliance with the analyst. This has become known as the *classical analysis* approach to psychoanalytic therapy. In particular those analysts who are primarily influenced by theories of ego psychology and its developments use it in their clinical practice.

Countertransference

Freud understood countertransference as the analyst's transference to the patient. He maintained that the analyst should be a well-polished mirror to the patient and nothing more (or less). In 1910 he wrote that countertransference arises in the analyst as a result of the patient's influence on his unconscious feelings. But he has to recognise this countertransference in himself and overcome it. In 1909[1] Freud replied by letter to C.G. Jung's 'confession' that he had been unable to resist the strong transference seduction of a young Russian patient, Sabine Spielrein, a medical student who suffered from hysterical symptoms.[2] Freud wrote to Jung that he had been in a similar situation himself several times, but had had a 'narrow escape'. He felt that it was probably the hardship of his work, and having been older when starting his clinical work, that had saved him. It gave him a hard skin and he felt that he could master the countertransference which one is put into every time. One learns to displace one's own affects and place them expediently. It is a blessing in disguise (Spielrein 1986). In 1915 Freud wrote a paper on 'Transference love' in which he advised younger analysts not to misinterpret the patient's transference love as genuine love feelings for themselves. At that time Freud was probably concerned specifically with the analyst's ability to master erotic countertransference feelings.

In later publications Freud did not refer to countertransference again, but he had been interested from early on in how, under conditions of free association – freely hovering attention – non-sensory thought perception from the patient's unconscious to the analyst's unconscious could occur. In this context he investigated telepathic phenomena and wrote three papers (1922, 1933, 1941) about it. But he remained sceptical about the occult, and he was unable to conceptualise the phenomena of non-sensory perceptions as they occur during analytic therapy. Freud's description of the analyst's free hovering attention seems not dissimilar to what some analysts have later termed countertransference, namely the analyst's emotional response to the patient's communications.

As early as 1926, Helene Deutsch discussed the metapsychology of countertransference. She compared it to telepathy: the reception of mental processes by one person from another by means other than sensory perception, as Freud had described. Listening to the patient, the analyst unconsciously receives the patient's strongly emotionally coloured, unconsciously determined free associations. What may also play a part are the patient's emotional motor-verbal expressions that are available to the analyst's perception. Only as long as the analyst's unconscious is *concordant* with the unconscious thoughts of the patient can he experience them in his free hovering attention as inner states in his mind.

Deutsch (1926) reasoned that the revival of memory traces in the analyst that are concordant with the patient's material allow his identification with the patient. Maybe it is important to remind ourselves that at that time only patients who suffered from psycho-neurotic symptoms or character disorders were regarded as suitable for psychoanalytic therapy. Hence analyst and patient shared the experience of the Oedipal stage of development with its readiness to be unconsciously reactivated.

However, in a *complementary* attitude, the analyst also has to distance himself from his inner experience in order to understand what transference role he plays in the patient's material. This may require some intellectual work and sublimation, as the patient may have assigned to the analyst a transference role totally at variance with the analyst's own self-image. Both the concordant and the complementary attitude constitute the analyst's countertransference.

Disturbance of the countertransference can arise when the concordant, unconscious identification has been blocked either by the analyst's repression or when the identification with the patient's unconscious transference object is too frightening or too satisfying. Deutsch mentioned that typically it is difficult for students to make transference interpretations. She gave the example of how the analyst's unrecognised unconscious desire can influence the patient's unconscious. When her patient told her of the forthcoming marriage of his cousin she recognised that she knew the bride. The patient reported more and more details in session after session, until she became aware of how her unconscious curiosity had influenced the patient's material.

Once she had become conscious of it, the patient stopped talking about the cousin's marriage. This was an example of the effects of the analyst's transference to the patient.

Freud maintained that psychoanalytic therapy was only applicable to those patients who suffered from transference neuroses; that is only those who could use the analyst in a new edition as the object of their revived repressed Oedipal wishes and conflicts. With the introduction of the structural model of the mind, transference could also be understood as the repetition of the patient's typical defences against the threat of recurrent unconscious impulses. So in Vienna, ego psychological research was at the centre of the development of psychoanalytic theory.

Other approaches

Under the leadership of Sandor Ferenczi, analysts in Budapest became interested in applying psychoanalytic therapy to more disturbed patients. He tried out various methods to help his patients to repeat and so master in a transference relationship early pre-Oedipal traumata which he saw as the events that had led to severe pathology in adult life (Ferenczi 1930).

In Berlin, Karl Abraham, a psychiatrist and a psychoanalyst, made important contributions to the psychoanalytic understanding of psychotic phenomena and symptoms. He studied the fate of the object of the instinctual impulse in psychic reality, and he also drew attention to the often concealed hostile impulses in such disturbed patients (Abraham 1924).

When Melanie Klein came to London after Abraham's death in 1926, she had studied first with Ferenczi in Budapest and then with Abraham in Berlin. She had already observed in her kindergarten in Berlin how small children play out and verbalise phantasies that signify instinctual impulses and their built-in conflicts with objects (Klein 1946, 1952a, 1952c). Klein developed an object-relations theory of early development that was informed by unconscious phantasies of emotionally intense involvement with objects. A succession of typical conflict situations builds up the internal structure of an ego-object world. In particular, early destructive impulses cause the infant great anxieties and are defended against by an already functioning primitive ego, so that dangerous bits of the ego and primitive persecutory part-objects are projected first onto the breast and later onto mother. Breast and mother then become identified with these bad, dangerous projected objects.

Accordingly, transference is understood as the analyst being experienced by the patient as the object of his unconscious phantasies. Transference, then, is not a repetition of past events but a constantly dynamically alive part of an intra-psychic ego-object world. Klein speaks of movement between two positions, the more primitive ego–part-object position and a more mature ego–whole-object position that in time builds up the inner world. Both positions remain dynamically active right throughout the individual's life.

As in the Kleinian model unconscious phantasies underlie all mental activity, the patient's free associations are conceived of as communications to the analyst as if he were the object of their unconscious phantasies. Hence they are transference manifestations and the analyst's interventions are all transference interpretations in the *here and now*. Klein remained committed to instinct theory and she therefore assumed that the infant is born with a constitutional set of strong impulses. The loving and caring mother strives to give her infant the best conditions for healthy development from its innate capacities. It is assumed that conflicts which stem from the early intra-psychic ego-object world must to a varying degree underlie all pathology. Hence the working through of these conflicts in the transference remains the same whether the patient is severely disturbed, or is suffering from psycho-neurotic symptoms or character pathology. Paula Heimann (1956) put it succinctly when she said that the main question for the analyst is always *who is speaking, to whom, about what, and why now*? Paula Heimann (1950) was one of the first analysts to show the utility of countertransference. She defined it as the emotional response of the analyst to the patient's communications, and therefore one of his most important tools. But the analyst has to sustain his feelings, and use them as indications to bring about a better understanding of his patient instead of acting on them. Melanie Klein was most critical of this idea. She never accepted countertransference, and once remarked that an analyst who suffers from countertransference feelings should have more analysis (personal communication: T. Hayley). However, Heimann's paper opened the floodgates, and over the next few years a lively discussion developed as to whether countertransference was a legitimate and informative emotional response to the patient's communications, or whether it was solely based on the analyst's transference to the patient.

In time Kleinian analysts also came to accept countertransference as an important tool. The main impetus came from Bion (1962) who conceived of projective identification as an interpersonal phenomenon that affected the analyst's mind. He came to psychoanalysis as an experienced group analyst, and he had already published important research on the psychodynamics of groups. He maintained that the analyst has to contain the patient's projective identifications into him, and then do some mental work to understand the patient's unconscious communications and give them meaning in his interpretations. He based this on his conceptualisation of the early mother–infant relationship. The infant projects his distress, which the mother contains and remains in a state of reverie, in which she understands her infant's non-verbal communications, gives them meaning through her ministrations and so reduces her infant's pains and anxieties. The infant can then re-introject the detoxified experience, and in time develops good internal objects. From these basic assumptions Bion developed a theory of the development of thinking which he also applied to his understanding of the transference–countertransference relationship in the therapeutic situation. Pathology is bound to arise when the mother is unable to contain her infant's distress. He or she maintains his communications with his objects via massive projective identifications, and no good internal objects can develop. Bion showed how this happens in transference–countertransference manifestations as they develop in the treatment of schizophrenic patients. Most post-Kleinian analysts use some of Bion's concepts in their clinical work.

Transference and infancy

A further approach to an object-relations theory of infant development, and with it a different understanding of the transference, has been put forward by psychoanalysts who emphasise that it is the post-partum nursing environment that facilitates the development of a self and the early ego. Michael Balint, Donald Winnicott, Marion Milner, Margaret Little, Masud Khan, then later Paula Heimann and other analysts took this view. They were all members of what is known as the Independent Group of the British Psycho-analytical Society. From the early 1940s onwards, these analysts looked at early non-verbal emotional development and identified the early traumata that may lead to severe pathology in later life. During the early stages of development such traumata are largely normal, and they only become pathogenic when they are quantitatively or qualitatively greater than any particular infant can cope with. They may be due to a failure of proper mothering, but they can also be caused by constitutional factors, or unfortunate life events that affect the mother or infant, such as somatic illness or separation.

Clinical material from borderline patients has shown time and again how they had experienced privation during their earliest non-verbal stages of development. Winnicott maintained that infant observation alone would not have allowed him to draw conclusions about the impact of the pre-verbal period. He said that he learned more about infant development from the adult borderline patients whom he analysed during the war than he had from babies.

Melanie Klein had introduced the concepts of the paranoid-schizoid position as operative from the beginning of life, and viewed the ego as capable of using primitive defence mechanisms from the word go. Winnicott (1945) argued that there is no ego operative from birth, and the infant's earliest development is not motivated by instinctual conflicts but by the nursing mother's facilitation within the mother–infant matrix. He believed that at the beginning the infant lives in an omnipotent primary narcissistic state.

Michael Balint assumed there to be a pre-object stage; a harmonious mix-up with environmental substances from which primitive objects and spaces between objects emerge. The infant then lives for a time in a state of passive primary love, during which he takes his mother's care for granted. Balint saw this as a period of adaptation during which the intra-uterine existence of total provision for the embryo's needs is prolonged. Whereas Independent analysts emphasised that the infant's emotional development is essential for the health of the individual, or responsible for his ill-health if the infant has suffered privation and traumata, none of them challenged the importance of the Oedipal stage of development or tried to reconceptualise it. Balint (1968) assumes a basic fault area of the mind that develops at the beginning of life, in which the infant is involved exclusively in two-person relating. Out of this area develops the Oedipal constellation with its triangular object relationships.

Winnicott assumed that the baby begins in a state of absolute dependence. During this primary narcissistic stage he does not know this. Relative dependence develops when the infant has begun to experience mother as a separate object and then becomes aware of his dependence on her. Winnicott reasoned that the Oedipal stage could only be reached when the child has successfully mastered the pre-Oedipal stages of development. The triangular object relationships are now motivated by instinctual impulses. Winnicott emphasised that the sexual impulses with their phantasy elaborations are now experienced as part of the interpersonal relationships with the parents. He felt that Freud had already fully described this process.

It is these concepts of early emotional development, with the fateful and lasting deficiencies which can arise when the infant has experienced considerable privation and deprivation, that lend transference and countertransference a new dimension. Paula Heimann (1966) argued that the analytic setting represents the early emotional relationship between the pre-verbal nursing mother–infant couple. If the patient relates to the analyst on the Oedipal level, that is if he is engaged in an interpersonal verbal relationship with the analyst, the setting is the backcloth, and becomes a surround that is taken for granted and not specifically referred to. The actual analytic work then takes place in the centre, where patient and analyst are engaged in the renewal of unconscious old unresolved conflicts in the *here and now* of the analytic situation. Whether the analyst makes a transference interpretation or an extra-transference comment, there is always a transference–countertransference relationship of an early pre-verbal kind active right through the analytic treatment. It is maintained by the patient's emotionally charged relating and the analyst's affective responses to the patient's communications. At times during therapy the verbal interpersonal relating breaks down, and some disturbance in the analyst–patient relationship becomes apparent. The surround now becomes more important, and the communications have ceased to be of an interpersonal verbal kind. Instead analyst and patient are engaged in an emotionally highly charged encounter. The analyst becomes aware that his countertransference is disturbed, and he will pay it attention, aiming at gaining some understanding of the patient's state of mind. It means that the patient has regressed to an early pre-verbal trauma.

To take an example from my clinical work with a 40-year-old professional man: After a long period of analysis I started to find it difficult to hear what the patient was saying, and I noticed that my patient did not hear me properly either. He became quite angry, and after a while I remarked on our difficulty in hearing each other. The patient was startled, and said that he had had a nearly deaf mother from birth onwards. This allowed us both to return to the interpersonal verbal relating we had been used to. In the analysis of a psychoneurotic patient such incidents are usually short-lived. What I want to stress here is that at such moments it is not an interpretation but a recognition of the non-verbal transference relationship which brings it to the patient's awareness. Regression is usually seen in psychoanalysis as a defence against unbearable conflicts and anxieties. In cases such as this, regression is used by the patient in the service of the ego and therefore needs recognition rather than an interpretation.

Regression

However, if patients suffer from narcissistic disorders and have been severely traumatised during early development, they may need a prolonged period of regression in the service of the ego during their therapy. When pre-verbal traumata have become operative again during therapy, our countertransference then remains our only guide. The analyst is required to emotionally respond to the patient as the facilitating early environment failed to do adequately enough. Both Balint (1968) and Winnicott (1949, 1955, 1956, 1960, 1963) discussed the treatment of such patients, based on their particular conceptions of infant development.

They agreed that severely disturbed patients who have suffered emotional privation within the mother–infant matrix will regress during therapy. The transference–countertransference relationship changes into an emotional encounter in the *here and now* of the analytic session. Such regression is to be conceived of not as a defensive move but as a sign of the patient's hope that somehow analysis will put right what has been wrong for a long time. Balint called it a benign regression for recognition, and compared it with malignant regression, which is when acting-out patients demand satisfaction for their instinctual cravings. Winnicott called it regression aiming at progression. As the patient has regressed to non-verbal emotional self-experiences, interpretations have become inappropriate and instead the analyst is guided by his countertransferential emotional response to recognise the patient's vulnerable emotional state. The underlying theoretical assumption is that early traumata of sensory and emotional pain have been registered, but are not available to recall. Christopher Bollas (1987) has called them the *unthought known*. Winnicott spoke of the experience *being* the memory. Such periods of regression begin when the analyst and patient cannot communicate verbally any longer, as the patient does not feel understood by the analyst's interventions. In other cases the analyst may have made a mistake, or the patient suddenly regards the analyst's normal behaviour pattern as neglectful unfriendliness towards him.

For example, once I had to tell a patient that due to an unforeseen emergency I would have to leave the room during the session to open the entrance door. On my return to the consulting room I apologised. The patient went into a rage and accused me of being most insensitive towards her own needs. It was not important that I had to leave the room for a moment – such things can happen – but that I apologised and so interrupted the session due to my own need to apologise was most objectionable! I had indeed intruded into her and during the years of analysis that followed this event I learned a lot about her psychotic mother's handling of her. By expressing her rage she could make sense of such an experience in the *here and now* and so integrate it.

What is far more controversial (not all of those analysts who are informed by the theory of a facilitating environment for the development of self and an early ego would agree with it) is the analytic management of the deeply regressed patient. It involves an active response from the analyst to acknowledge what Balint has called the patient's *arglose*, that is childlike demands to hold the analyst's hand, for example. This is not, as it has often been critically called, the same as a corrective emotional experience. The latter is a term coined by Alexander (1950) which advocates that the analyst actively adopt a role that explicitly differs from the behaviour of the patient's parents in early childhood. The aim of this technical procedure is to counteract the patient's tendency to regress to an early developmental stage and become unduly dependent on the analyst. It also claims to avoid an unwanted prolongation of treatment. As Zetzel (1956) has pointed out, the corrective emotional experience assumes positive therapeutic results without relying on insight and recall. It therefore operates outside the transference–countertransference in contradistinction to Balint, Winnicott and others who work through the regression to early traumata within the transference–countertransference relationship by responding to the patient's need in the *here and now*. The technical handling of regression to early pre-Oedipal stages of development and with it the repetition of early traumata in the transference remains problematic. Transference is a phenomenon of the repetition compulsion. It can be an attempt to master traumatic experiences, or it can be a defensive attempt to return to earlier states of satisfaction and/or gratification.

In Freud's later theories repetition compulsion is a product of the death instinct. Kleinian analysts and those of similar orientation view the patient's severe regression as transference expressions of destructive impulses, often culminating in negative therapeutic reactions. Other analysts view the patient's early transference regressions as a need to return to problems that have remained unsolved. But there are also analysts who think that patients who are likely to regress to early states of development are unsuitable for treatment by psychoanalysis. They maintain that the repetition compulsion of such early destructive forces cannot be worked through within the matrix of transference–countertransference in a psychoanalytic treatment setting. They usually recommend supportive therapy which aims at strengthening the

patients' ego defences. They are likely to be patients who suffer from borderline conditions or frank psychotic disorders.

Conclusion

I have tried to trace the developments of the concepts of transference and
countertransference as they have evolved in psychoanalytic theory. Freud
discovered transference in the clinical situation. At first he saw it as an obstacle to the analytic task of making the unconscious conscious, but then he
understood transference to be an important tool: patients who suffered from
psycho-neurotic disorders repeated in their transference neuroses their old
repressed conflicts in a new edition.

With the advance of object-relations theory, concepts of pre-Oedipal
development were developed, and transference became understood as the
patient relating to the analyst as the object of his or her unconscious phantasies in an interplay of projection and introjection. It had been Abraham in
Berlin who first studied the intra-psychic fate of the object of the instinctual
impulse in patients suffering from psychoses. Melanie Klein observed that
young children are often preoccupied in their play activities with unconscious
phantasies which can be understood as elaborations of primitive instinctual
impulses. The enlarged understanding of transference based on our new
understanding of early development now allows us to analyse severely disturbed patients. Ferenczi in Budapest stressed that patients suffering from
narcissistic disorders have suffered early traumata and privation. He tried in
various experiments to adjust analytic technique so that his patients were
allowed to regress, and so repeat the early traumata in the analytic situation.
At the end of his life he said that all his experiments failed but that he had
learned a lot from them. Both Abraham and Ferenczi died early, leaving their
work unfinished.

Both these theoretical orientations led to transference becoming understood as an interpersonal encounter in which both analyst and patient
are intersubjectively involved. That not only gave transference a new dimension, but it also shifted the emphasis towards the analyst's countertransference as an integral part of the analytic relationship. I have tried to show
that it is the different theoretical assumptions about the early mother–infant
matrix that have led to a different technical handling of the transference–
countertransference relationship within the object-relations school of
psychoanalysis.

Notes

1 English translation by the author.
2 Jung's disagreement with Freud's theories seems to have come to the fore later.
   They led him to leave the psychoanalytic movement in 1913 after there had been

difficulties for some time over his fulfilment of his duties as president of the International Psychoanalytic Association. Theoretically, what was particularly at issue was the concept of the libido; Freud conceived of it as the energy of the sexual drives, whereas Jung understood it as psychic energy per se. Freud modified and changed his drive theory several times but insisted that the concept of the duality of the drives remained a basic assumption of psychoanalytic theory.

References

Abraham, K. (1924) 'A short study of the development of the libido, viewed in the light of mental disorders', in *Selected Papers on Psycho-Analysis*, London: Hogarth Press, 1965, pp. 418–99.

Alexander, F. (1950) 'Analysis of the therapeutic factors in psycho-analytic treatment', *Psychoanalytic Quarterly* 19: 482–500.

Balint, M. (1968) *The Basic Fault*, London: Tavistock.

Bion, W.R. (1962) *Learning from Experience*, London: Heinemann.

—— (1967) *Second Thoughts*, London: Maresfield, 1984.

Bollas, C. (1987) *The Shadow of the Object*: *Psychoanalysis of the Unthought Known*, London: Free Association Books.

Deutsch, H. (1926) 'Okkulte Vorgaenge waehrend der Psychoanalyse', *Imago* 12.

Ferenczi, S. (1930) 'The principles of relaxation and neurocatharsis', *International Journal of Psychoanalysis* 11: 428–43.

Freud, S. (1905) 'Fragment of an analysis of a case of hysteria', *Standard Edition*, vol. 7, pp. 3–123, London: Hogarth Press.

—— (1910) 'The future prospects of psycho-analytic therapy', *Standard Edition*, vol. 11, London: Hogarth Press.

—— (1912b) 'The dynamics of transference', *Standard Edition*, vol. 12, London: Hogarth Press.

—— (1912e) 'Recommendations to physicians practising psychoanalysis', *Standard Edition*, vol. 12, London: Hogarth Press.

—— (1913) 'On beginning the treatment', *Standard Edition*, vol. 12, London: Hogarth Press.

—— (1915) 'Observations on transference love', *Standard Edition*, vol. 12, London: Hogarth Press.

—— (1922) 'Dreams and telepathy', *Standard Edition*, vol. 18, London: Hogarth Press.

—— (1923) *The Ego and the Id, Standard Edition*, vol. 19, London: Hogarth Press.

—— (1926) 'Inhibitions, symptoms and anxiety', *Standard Edition*, vol. 20, pp. 75–175, London: Hogarth Press.

—— (1933) *New Introductory Lectures on Psycho-analysis*: Chapter 30, 'Dreams and occultism', *Standard Edition*, vol. 22, London: Hogarth Press.

—— (1941) 'Psychoanalysis and telepathy', *Standard Edition*, vol. 18, London: Hogarth Press.

Freud, S. and Breuer, J. (1893–1895) *Studies on Hysteria, Standard Edition*, vol. 2, London: Hogarth Press.

Heimann, P. (1950) 'On counter-transference', *International Journal of Psychoanalysis* 31: 81–4.

—— (1956) 'Dynamics of transference interpretations', *International Journal of Psychoanalysis* 37: 303–10.

—— (1966) 'Comments on the psychoanalytic concept of work', in *About Children and Children-no-Longer*, London and New York: Tavistock/Routledge, 1989, pp. 191–205.

Klein, M. (1946) 'Notes on some schizoid mechanisms', *International Journal of Psychoanalysis* 27: 99–110.

—— (1952a) 'The origins of transference', *International Journal of Psychoanalysis* 33: 433–8.

—— (1952c) 'Some theoretical conclusions regarding the emotional life of the infant', in M. Klein, P. Heimann, S. Isaacs and J. Riviere *New Developments in Psychoanalysis*, London: Hogarth Press.

Laplanche, J. and Pontalis, J.B. (1973) *The Language of Psychoanalysis*, London: Hogarth Press.

Spielrein, S. (1986) 'Sabine Spielrein in dem Briefwechsel zwischen Sigmund Freud und Carl Gustav Jung (1906–1912)', in A. Carotenuto (ed.) *Tagebuch einer heimlichen Symetrie*, Freiburg: Traute Hensch.

Winnicott, D. (1945) 'Primitive emotional development', *International Journal of Psychoanalysis* 26: 137–43.

—— (1949) 'Hate in the countertransference', *International Journal of Psychoanalysis* 30: 69–74.

—— (1955) 'Metapsychological and clinical aspects of regression within the psychoanalytical set-up', *International Journal of Psychoanalysis* 36: 16–26.

—— (1956) 'On transference', *International Journal of Psychoanalysis* 37: 386–8.

—— (1960) 'Countertransference', *British Journal of Medical Psychology* 33: 17–21.

—— (1963) 'Dependence in infant-care, in child-care and in the psycho-analytic setting', *International Journal of Psychoanalysis* 44: 339–44.

Zetzel, E. (1956) 'Current concepts of transference', *International Journal of Psychoanalysis* 37: 369–75.

Suggestions for further reading

Further discussion of the subject matter of this paper from a Kleinian object-relations theoretical orientation can be found in R.D. Hinshelwood, *A Dictionary of Kleinian Thought* (London: Free Association Books, 1991, 2nd edn). In particular, the sections 'A. Main Entries: 1. Technique' and 'B. General Entries: Transference, Countertransference' are relevant here.

An approach to the same area from an Independent object-relations theoretical orientation can be found in E. Rayner, *The Independent Mind in British Psychoanalysis* (London: Free Association Books, 1990). In particular Chapters 8–10: 'The Psychoanalytic Process – For the Patient', 'The Psychoanalytic Process – The Analyst's Contribution', and 'The Psychoanalytic Process – The Dialogue of Patient and Analyst', are relevant here.

Chapter 13

Projective identification

Priscilla Roth

I think it is a good idea to start out by acknowledging that projective identification is an extremely difficult concept to get hold of. The original definition, in 1946, came from Melanie Klein when she noted:

> Together with . . . harmful excrements, expelled in hatred, split off parts of the ego are also projected onto the mother or, as I would rather call it, into the mother . . . This leads to a particular form of identification which establishes the prototype of an aggressive object-relation. I suggest for these processes the term 'projective identification'.
>
> (Klein 1946: 8)

The most basic descriptions describe how projective identification involves putting parts of oneself into an object, so that the object becomes identified with these unwanted aspects of the self. I expect that readers with some clinical experience will be able to point to things that have happened in their consulting rooms with patients or clients which seem to feel as if they might be explained by calling them 'projective identification'. What this frequently means is that as clinicians we feel something weird has gone on; we have felt not ourselves during some period of time with a patient, and we attribute our confusion to this rather all-embracing term 'projective identification'. So we say that the patient or client 'put his sleepiness into us', or his boredom, or his confusion – because it seems to explain why we feel sleepy or bored or confused. And of course we may be right, but we may not be. In this chapter I hope to clarify as much about this difficult concept as I can, to give some taste of how psychoanalysts might use it to help understand highly complicated phenomena, and to describe what some of the dangers and pitfalls are. I will not list here who said what about the concept except very briefly to state that while it was originally described by Klein in 1946, in 'Notes on some schizoid mechanisms', she did not develop it much. Its real development came later, by such authors as Bion (1957, 1959) and Rosenfeld (1949, 1952). Joseph Sandler (1988) has also written extensively on this concept, and clarified it for psychoanalysts working outside the Kleinian theoretical framework. Of all of Klein's discoveries, projective identification is the one which has won most widespread acceptance, although of course there are disagreements about exactly what the mechanics of the phenomenon are.

If we go back to the original definition of projective identification, we can see that there are various questions to be asked. The first might be 'Why would someone, say a patient, need to put some part of himself into someone else, say an analyst?' Before I begin to answer this, I want to make it clear that we are talking about a phantasy – a patient has an unconscious phantasy that he has put a part of himself into his analyst. Or, to put it another way: a patient attributes some aspect of his picture of himself, say his greed, to his picture of his analyst. The picture he has of his analyst is altered to include some unwanted aspect of himself. So if we now go back to our question 'Why would someone need to attribute some unwanted quality of his own to his analyst?', we are ready to answer: for one or more of several possible reasons. He may find this aspect of himself intolerable because it is hateful to him. It would fill him with unbearable shame or guilt to have to acknowledge that such impulses or qualities are actually part of him. Thus in order not to be overwhelmed with anxiety or shame or guilt, he must project these aspects into someone else in order to be rid of them himself.

At this point I would like to describe something that happened to me some years ago. A senior colleague phoned and asked me if I would see a 32-year-old woman for a consultation with a view to taking her into analysis. The colleague had had an interview with Miss B and reported to me that Miss B wanted analysis because she had trouble with relationships. She came, I was told, from a very disturbed background in which violence had played a strong part, with one sister who had broken down and another who had committed suicide. My colleague had some anxieties about her and felt that she might be quite ill underneath what she described as an overly co-operative and conciliatory facade.

Miss B phoned me for an appointment and I offered her a time some five days later. She agreed, and then asked me what parking would be like near my consulting room. I told her that the area had recently been rezoned for resident parking, so that parking was sometimes difficult. I said that she should give herself time; that she might very well not be able to park just in front, but that within a couple of blocks she would be able to find a place. 'But allow a bit of time,' I said. 'What do your other patients do?' she asked. I said that they sometimes have difficulty, but that if she gave herself an extra ten minutes she should find a place.

On the day of the appointment she arrived nearly 15 minutes late. I opened the door to find a tall, slim, handsome woman, stylishly dressed, and I extended my hand and introduced myself. I found I was interrupted by her asking in a very loud, very disdainful voice, 'Is this 23 X Street?' I said it was and asked her to come in. We walked towards the stairs and, noticing the coat rack, she asked in an imperious tone if this was where she should hang her coat and leave her umbrella. I said, 'That's fine.' She noticed a magazine on the floor by the umbrella stand and with a great deal of obvious disgust picked it up with two fingers and placed it on the umbrella stand. She gave the impression of being haughty, imperious, arrogant and disdainful. I said that my room was all the way at the top of the stairs, so I would lead her up. As we began to go up, she asked in a very loud voice, 'Do you work in a group, or is this your own home?' Hoping to delay the conversation until we got to the room, I answered truthfully, 'Neither,' and continued up the stairs. I was aware even as I said it that I was being somewhat short with her and that this was only partly because I didn't want to speak in the corridor; it was partly because I was slightly taken aback by her manner.

In the room I motioned to her to sit down in the chair opposite mine, and then I settled into my chair. After a brief moment I said that I didn't know much about her except that my colleague had told me that she is interested in psychoanalysis. 'Perhaps you could tell me about yourself,' I said.

She responded with rage. She said, furiously, that she had absolutely no idea who I was, or what this place was, but that it was entirely unaccommodating and unwelcoming. Why on earth should she talk to me? She never had trouble talking to doctors, not even on the first meeting, but she really didn't see any reason why she should tell someone who makes her so entirely uncomfortable anything at all of a personal nature. She comes from a family with quite a difficult history, she said, but she is certainly not prepared to discuss that with someone about whom she knows nothing and who she feels is so completely unsympathetic.

I was flabbergasted. I said I understood how difficult it was to begin to talk to a perfect stranger in a strange set-up. She interrupted: No, it is not that. She had no difficulty with Mrs X, the person she saw for a consultation, but this is something else. Perhaps she is particularly sensitive and courteous, she said. She is always a concerned hostess, wanting to make people comfortable in her home, very concerned that they feel comfortable and – gesturing towards my slightly opened window – she would never, *never* invite anyone to sit down in a room with a window wide open, without enquiring whether they had a cold or were cold. 'And,' she went on, 'what is that nonsense you were speaking about parking difficulties? What on earth was that supposed to be about when I found a parking space two steps, literally two steps from your front door?'

I said I wondered if it felt that I was being cold to her too. She laughed coldly. 'Well, you certainly don't know anything about making conversation, do you? You certainly have no wish to smooth things along.' All of this was delivered in a most haughty, contemptuous voice so that I felt that I was a very inept little girl in the company of the cruellest of headmistresses, icy and judgemental. I certainly felt she was older, more in charge, better educated and better bred than I was. I had a fleeting memory of Miss C, the last psychotic patient I had had in analysis. I tried to talk with Miss B about how difficult it is to come to someplace new, but I knew I was not going to make any impact whatsoever on her demeanour. Indeed I was struck by how little I believed in what I was saying. She said, 'You are very kind. I am certain that your patients all think very highly of you, but I am afraid there is absolutely no point in my continuing to sit here, and so if you would be kind enough to render me your account, I would like to settle your bill immediately.'

After a few further futile attempts to say something that might change the atmosphere between us, I said I was sorry she insisted on leaving, but that she had only been here for a few moments and there would not be a bill. She said, 'I am afraid that will not do. I insist on settling with you.' I again said there was no charge. She said, 'Then if you insist, I shall have to sit here for the hour.' She looked at her watch. I asked was she going to sit here just in order to get the bill? She said yes. I said that I would give her my bill, and I did so. 'Thank you,' she said, then got up, took out her chequebook and pen and sat down at my desk amid my papers, to write out her cheque. 'To whom do I write out the cheque?' 'Priscilla Roth,' I answered. 'Is that Dr or . . .' 'Mrs,' I answered, somewhat apologetically I think. She wrote out the cheque to 'Priscilla Roth', handed it to me saying, 'I am sorry to have taken your time from your other patients. I take it I see myself out.' I said, 'Yes' and, as she went through the door, 'Goodbye.'

At the time I felt very shaken. I felt as though I had been run over by a steam train. And I had to acknowledge to myself that I had failed miserably to make any contact with this young woman. Indeed, there was nothing about me or my behaviour that seemed to justify my thinking of myself as a psychoanalyst. I felt entirely without skills, insight or analytic capacities. Afterwards, when I thought about it, I thought I could understand a little more about what had happened and I wished that I had been able to think more clearly at the time. I think that at some point between her meeting with my colleague and her arrival in my consulting room, the patient became anxious, or threatened with anxiety. I am not sure when it began – possibly as soon as I said that parking might be a problem, possibly when she was driving around looking for a parking place, or when she found a meter (I don't know how!) near the consulting room. But by the time she arrived at the front door she was not anxious. She was cold and arrogant and displeased, not at all overly sweet and conciliatory as I had been led to believe. I think that in the few minutes in the hall I made things very much worse. By not making 'social conversation' and by answering her question curtly ('neither') I probably threatened her with further anxiety. By the time she got to the room she had become the iciest, most anxiety producing, forbidding, least friendly and receptive person I had ever been with. She had entirely projected whatever anxiety she might have been threatened with into me, and I reacted by feeling tremendously anxious and entirely unable to process what was going on in order to be able to help her with it.

Miss B's state of mind in the consultation was a result of her anxieties and perhaps my exacerbation of them – my not being sensitive enough in the beginning to how paranoid and persecuted she could get. But what would be a fairly minor failure with someone else was a huge failure with this particular woman. For Miss B, my curtness became something monstrously cold, forbidding and unreachable. And it was then as if she herself actually *became* something like a powerfully cruel, punitive, contemptuous mother and I became like a terribly anxious, seriously frightened child.

There are, I believe, two aspects of projective identification which we can see in this story. The first is to do with what I think happened in Miss B. I think that faced with a situation that threatened to terrify her, she identified herself with a picture of a powerful, cruel figure, and she, as it were, took on and took over the characteristics of this object. She *became* powerful, cold and cruel. And, at the same time, I think she immediately and violently projected into me the part of herself that was threatened with feeling terrified. Why do I say violently? Because I think in this instance I was *forced* to feel terrified and small and helpless. (This doesn't mean I blame Miss B, which I don't, or that I don't wish I had been better able to withstand and understand it at the time, which I do. But it does mean that with a ruthless disregard for how I might feel about it, she was forcing into me feelings which she could not tolerate having.)

Another thing which I hope this rather dramatic example demonstrates, is why it is not enough to refer to such a process as 'reversal', or 'role reversal'. It seems pretty clear that with Miss B the process involved a complicated series of identifications, introjections, projections, more identifications: a desperate attempt to deal with very threatening feelings by manipulating internal and external objects. So, what we have been looking at is one answer to the question 'Why would someone want to do that?' And the answer in this case is in order to get rid of intolerable feelings, to evacuate them.

While we have got this example of Miss B in our minds, we can address another question about projective identification: Does it have to work to be projective identification? We can see that with the example of Miss B and me the projective identification 'worked'; that is, I was affected and my feelings and behaviour altered by the processes that were going on between us. So we could say that in this example events did not take place only in phantasy; I was affected by her projections and actually became for a while frightened, incompetent and, from her point of view, contemptible. I was in this case pushed to acquire certain characteristics which (however much they might or might not fit with characteristics of my own) derived from her mental landscape.

But it is certainly not necessary that the object become so affected to feel that there is projective identification going on. Sometimes as an analyst I am aware that the patient is speaking to me in a particularly careful voice, explaining his situation terribly patiently and painstakingly. I begin to realize that I am being spoken to as though I am an idiot, or a very slow dim-witted child, by someone who seems to feel very patronizing indeed; but I can see this quite clearly, without actually feeling like an idiot. I can interpret, then, that the patient seems to have become a version of a parent or an analyst who in her mind feels quite superior to her rather slow-witted child, but who is trying very hard to be patient.

In such a case the patient has introjected a somewhat smug, patronizing version of me, and has projected into me his own vulnerability, anxiety, and confusion, but for one reason or another I can be aware of what is being projected without actually being affected by it. In fact, I think it is probably not correct to say I am not affected by it. I think in fact I am very subtly aware of feeling momentarily a bit inferior, a little bit slow to catch on, but it is at a tolerable level, so that I pick it up almost unconsciously, and I can process it without difficulty. By process it, I mean I can realize what the patient wants, is indeed gently nudging me to feel, and what this, together with what I can observe about his behaviour, tells me about the state of his object relationships at that moment.

Now, to go back to our first question, why else might someone project aspects of himself into someone else, besides wishing to evacuate intolerable feelings? A second common reason is in order to control the other person. Certainly Miss B had a firmer control over me than I had over her. I was unable to make use of what I had felt to be my qualities. Instead I was in a sense taken over by her. I was disarmed of anything she might be afraid would be dangerous. Sometimes control is for a different reason, not only coming from a wish to disarm. Someone can wish to control another person by taking over, as it were, the other person's qualities, by being peculiarly like the object, in order to avoid whatever feelings of envy, or competitiveness or dependency might ensue if the object were felt to have desirable qualities of its own. I have a patient who is ostensibly very appreciative of me, brings lots of nice material, is eager to praise me when she feels I have made a good interpretation, and eager to tell me when she hears good things about me. But I get a peculiar sense that I am being run by her, as though I am largely under her control, and her pleasure in me is me as 'her' analyst, in a very concrete way. I find it very difficult to get myself into a position where I can surprise or shock her. When I do, being able to shock her immediately becomes part of what she always knew was so good about me. At the same time, I have noticed that she has begun to dress more and more as I do, and to pick up and use my turns of phrase in a way that feels like a takeover. What I hope I am conveying is that this woman is using projective identification primarily in order to defend against feelings of envy, of rivalry and of actual dependence on me as an external object. It is as if she has created a situation in her mind where I am a kind of pseudopodial extension of her – and it is only as such that I can be admired.

There is a point I want to stress about projective identification in relation to my discussion of this patient and also of Miss B, the woman who came for the single consultation. It is that as we listen to the description of these people and their behaviour, it is easy to see it as foolish, a little laughable, a kind of pretending to be something that they are not. But there are two things that are important to emphasize. The first is that we all use this mechanism some-times; for instance, as grown men and women we find ourselves speaking in our mother's or father's voice. The second is that when projective identifica-tion is used massively and much of the time, it is because it appears to be the best possible solution for what are experienced as uncontainable psycho-logical pressures. The alternative to such states feels as if it would be over-whelming anxiety, genuinely threatening a mental breakdown. It is to avoid what would feel like psychological catastrophe that people resort to massive use of projective identification in order to maintain some mental equilibrium. It is not a state of mind entered into lightly; it feels life-saving.

The problem is, of course, that there are prices to be paid for such massive shifts of bits of the personality – for moving around the molecules of reality. In the first place, projective identification seriously diminishes the personal-ity; it deprives the subject of real qualities and capabilities, and leaves him a mental shadow of what could be himself. When someone evacuates qualities like greed, or rage, or fear he also evacuates the part of his mind that is aware of such feelings, and his capacity to think and to know about himself is greatly weakened.

Second, projective identification is a process, not an event – and as a pro-cess it has consequences, which lead to further consequences, and so on. When we project anger into another person, we then (by definition) expect that person to be angry with us, and we behave towards the person as if he is an angry, threatening persecutor. The person is felt to be threatening both because he contains our anger, and because he is felt to want to get rid of it back into us. It is very much as if there is an actual quantity of bad, horrible stuff, bad feeling, which will be located either in the subject or the object, each trying to get rid of it into the other, neither being able to bear having it. Caught up in this vicious cycle, the subject may feel the need to attack his object further, or to withdraw in order to protect himself. This is one reason why it is difficult to deal with someone in the state of mind that Miss B was in when she came for her consultation with me. Having projected fear and anx-iety into me, I then became very dangerous to her, because I was felt to want to get rid of this by shoving it back into her. I think she was afraid I would want to bring her down, both in revenge for what she had done to me, and to bring myself back up. So even had I been more aware of what was going on, it would be difficult to know how to speak to her without threatening her more than she could bear.

What is projective identification for?

I am going to return again to the question about what projective identifica-tion is for, and discuss two other reasons why someone might need to put parts of himself into another person. The first is very much in contrast to evacuating felt-to-be bad bits of the self – it is when someone projects felt-to-be good and valuable bits of himself into an object. This happens when these qualities are not thought to be safe inside the personality and thus have to be located in an object for safekeeping. I had a patient some years ago who continually saw herself as stupid and incapable of thought but who saw me as very clever and able to think well. Interestingly, I found I could think well in her presence and about her. We began to be able to see that when she had a thought or an idea it would immediately be attacked inside her mind: 'This is probably stupid,' she would say, or 'I think what I just said is completely boring', or sometimes, more worryingly, she would just get muddled and not be able to formulate what she was thinking at all. Under these circumstances, she felt much safer simply conveying the contents of her mind, and allowing me to have the capacity to think about them and to put them into some kind of order, because she felt I could stand up to her attacks – 'What nonsense!' – better than she could. At the beginning of her analysis I think she actually needed me to do this: to take in, hold on to, unconsciously respond to, sift through, metabolize and think about all the stuff that she produced – to put my mind to it. But while she was doing this she was evacuating her own thinking capacities and projecting them into me. And of course the analytic task became to enable her gradually to take these capacities back, so that we could watch together how they were attacked inside her, and to help her to withstand these attacks and go on thinking with her own mind.

This leads me to another purpose of projective identification and that is to communicate states of mind. This is very important because what analysts have begun to realize is that whether it is *primarily* in order to communicate, or is primarily designed to evacuate bad feelings, projective identification always happens between people. It is always at least minimally object related and therefore, if properly understood, it always is a form of communication. In fact, projective identification always does communicate something terribly important about the state of mind, the pressures and solutions, the internal objects and the anxieties of the person employing it. I was sorry, in the end, to know that Miss B would not come back, because once I could think about what had gone on between us I felt I knew quite a bit about her most terrible fears. I felt she had communicated this very well indeed, and I would have very much liked the opportunity to try to help her think about them.

You will have noticed that I have not yet written about the relationship between these processes I have been describing and the psychological development of the infant and child. An understanding of this depends on an understanding of Melanie Klein's formulations of infant development: the paranoid-schizoid and depressive positions. Chapters 2 and 3 in this book discuss these developmental positions in detail. Here I want only to stress that when Klein wrote about bad experiences being split off and projected – that is, felt as coming from outside the infant's self – from within the paranoid-schizoid position, she was speaking primarily of the infant's over-whelming fear of annihilation. It is this fear of annihilation, of falling to pieces, which the young infant has to project into his object, to get rid of it from within his own psyche. The object – the mother – is then felt dangerously to contain his fear, and his knowledge of it: dangerously because she will, in his mind, want to push it back into him. But also the infant is constantly introjecting his object, and now introjects an object distorted by this projec-tion, so that he is now felt to have a destructive internal object attacking him from inside. Following the work of Bion, Kleinian analysts feel that the earli-est forms of projective identification were used not only for evacuation and control, and to avoid recognition of separateness and envy, but normally and essentially as forms of communication. Bion's work on the mother's function as a container of her infant's anxieties focused on the process by which the infant makes use of his mother's mind to hold and deal with his desperate feelings until such time as his own mind is able to contain and deal with internal and external events. And of course Bion's work led to an ongoing examination of the consequences for an infant and child of having a mother who is herself unable to contain and work through the child's projections. To go back one last time to Miss B, my assumption about her is that the terror she felt threatened with feeling would have made her feel so weak, so vulnerable, so fragmented and in bits, so unable to have a coherent self, that she had no recourse but to force such a state of mind into me. I assume, further, that she had very little experience as a small baby of a mother who could have under-stood her terror, who might have held and comforted her, thereby enabling her to take inside and identify with a mother who could bear terrible fear. (Of course I am entirely speculating at this point. My only evidence, apart from the experience itself of being with her, is the fact that one of her sisters had a severe mental breakdown, and another committed suicide.)

This leads me to my last point. I referred earlier to the pitfalls for the analyst of trying to understand and deal with the concept of projective iden-tification, and they are serious. It is of course always very difficult to be sure that what we as analysts are experiencing as coming from the patient is actu-ally coming from the patient and not our own neurotic response to something the patient has stirred up. Years ago I had a student psychotherapist come to me for supervision. One day he told me that the previous week he had simply forgotten his patient's session, had just not shown up. I said 'Oh dear,' and commiserated with him and he then told me that when the patient had arrived for her following appointment, he had told her that she had somehow made him forget the session. 'Projective identification,' he said to me, wisely. I was, needless to say, appalled.

How do we disentangle what comes from the patient and what from us? There is no simple answer, but any attempt to answer it must include our own long, thorough personal analysis, which helps us to be aware of our own anxieties and weak spots and tendencies to project, and supervisions and consultations with senior colleagues; and, above all, a constant vigilance that comes from an interest in knowing about ourselves and our own peculiar responses and defences as much as those of our patients.

References

Bion, W.R. (1957) 'Differentiation of the psychotic from the non-psychotic personalities', *International Journal of Psychoanalysis*, 38: 266–75. Reprinted in *Second Thoughts* London: Heinemann, 1967; and also in E.B. Spillius (ed.) *Melanie Klein Today*, vol. 1, London: Routledge, 1988.

—— (1959) 'Attacks on linking', *International Journal of Psychoanalysis* 40: 308–15. Reprinted in *Second Thoughts*, London: Heinemann, 1967; and also in E.B. Spillius (ed.) *Melanie Klein Today*, vol. 1, London: Routledge, 1988.

Klein, M. (1946) 'Notes on some schizoid mechanisms', *International Journal of Psychoanalysis*, 27: 99–110. Reprinted in *Melanie Klein: Envy and Gratitude and Other Works 1946–1963*, London: Vintage, 1997, pp. 1–24.

Rosenfeld, H.A. (1949) 'Remarks on the relation of male homosexuality to paranoia', *International Journal of Psychoanalysis*, 30: 36–47. Reprinted in *Psychotic States*, London: Hogarth Press, 1965.

—— (1952) 'Notes on the psychoanalysis of the superego conflict in an acute schizophrenic patient', *International Journal of Psychoanalysis* 33: 11–31. Reprinted in *Psychotic States*, London: Hogarth Press, 1965.

Sandler, J. (1988) *Projection, Identification, Projective Identification*, London: Karnac.

Suggestions for further reading

The classic papers describing processes of projective identification in severely disturbed patients are W.R. Bion, (1957) 'Differentiation of the psychotic from the non-psychotic personalities', *International Journal of Psychoanalysis* 38: 266–75; reprinted in *Second Thoughts* (London: Heinemann, 1967); and also in E.B. Spillius (ed.) *Melanie Klein Today*, vol. 1 (London: Routledge, 1988); and his (1959) paper, 'Attacks on linking', *International Journal of Psychoanalysis* 40: 308–15; reprinted in *Second Thoughts* (London: Heinemann, 1967); and also in E.B. Spillius (ed.) *Melanie Klein Today*, vol. 1 (London: Routledge, 1988).

There are two papers by Herbert Rosenfeld: H.A. Rosenfeld (1949) 'Remarks on the relation of male homosexuality to paranoia', *International Journal of Psychoanalysis* 30: 36–47, reprinted in *Psychotic States* (London: Hogarth Press, 1965); and (1952) 'Notes on the psychoanalysis of the superego conflict in an acute schizophrenic patient', *International Journal of Psychoanalysis* 33: 11–31; reprinted in *Psychotic States* (London: Hogarth Press, 1965). For a clarifying explanation of the concept, including an instructive discussion of some of Rosenfeld's clinical material, see R.D. Hinshelwood, *Clinical Klein* (London: Free Association Books, 1994).

For a well-written and scholarly discussion of the history of the concept of projective identification, and a differentiation of its various uses, see D. Bell, 'Projective identification', in *Kleinian Theory: A Contemporary Perspective*, C. Bronstein (ed.) (London: Whurr, 2001). Some of Klein's most noted followers have further developed the concept of projective identification. For interesting clinical illustrations, see especially: B. Joseph, 'Projective identification: some clinical aspects', in M. Feldman and E. Bott Spillius (eds) *Equilibrium and Psychic Change: Selected Papers of Betty Joseph* (London: Routledge, 1989); H. Segal, 'A note on schizoid mechanisms under-lying phobia formation', in *The Work of Hanna Segal. A Kleinian Approach to Clinical Practice* (New York and London: Jason Aronson, 1981); I. Sodré, 'Who's who? Notes on pathological identification', in E. Hargreaves and A. Varchevker (eds) *In Pursuit of Psychic Change* (London: Brunner-Routledge, 2004); J. Steiner, *Psychic Retreats* (London: Routledge, 1993 especially Chapters 1–5).

Chapter 14

Two approaches to interpretation and the relationship between them

David Riley

Ever since Freud's papers on technique (1914), psychoanalysts have necess-arily been concerned to describe what they do, how they do it and why. This chapter is a contribution to aspects of this ongoing debate. Whilst rooted in the author's experience of being brought up in the British Society, the issues raised will be familiar to analysts all over the world.

During the Controversial Discussions in the British Society (see Tonnesmann, Chapter 12 in this volume) one of the main discussants on technique was Ella Sharpe, who wrote:

> Technique is only a vital method when it is employed by people who have found as individuals it is the only method that suits them . . . technique can be taught . . . but that is a very different thing from the *finding* of a technique that is suited to the individuality of the practitioner.
>
> (King and Steiner 1991: 639–47, emphasis added)

Many authors since Freud have contributed to this issue of analytic style: for example, Annie Reich (1960) on 'characterological countertransference'; Kit Bollas on 'personal idiom' (Bollas 1989); and John Klauber (1986), much of whose writing could be described as an exploration of this issue.

My contention is that one dimension of analytic style is a divergence between one in which the analyst believes he is conducting an analysis more or less as he would wish, albeit with the expected ups and downs, and a contrasting attitude in which emphasis is placed more upon the capacity of the analyst to facilitate a process in which analysis evolves out of the interaction between analyst and patient; this may at times include what Winnicott called the 'area of play' (1974). For example, does the analyst give primacy to the fact of his interpretations and their effects or is there a preference for the patient to find meaning as the analysis unfolds? The first analyst can be seen at work when he writes: 'I showed the patient that he was doing x with y consequences for him and for me.' The second is a more difficult beast to apprehend: he is likely to be less active and more unobtrusive in his presence in the room and much more likely to try to widen the scope of the patient's associations and his own responses to those associations.

Now, in practice, this distinction quickly breaks down because most analysts will recognize themselves in both summary descriptions. Nevertheless, the distinction is drawn in order to open up an inquiry into what I contend is felt by most of us at some time as a tension in our everyday experience of being with our patients. For the time being let us refer to the first approach as A and the second as B. On a lighter note, A and B are readily recognizable in the old joke about two sorts of analysis: the analyst who wouldn't notice if his patient died and the patient who wouldn't notice if his analyst died!

Having introduced my theme it must be immediately acknowledged that few of us know what other analysts are like in their consulting rooms, and a great deal of what we think or say is therefore influenced by fantasy. There is presumably good and bad analysis in all our work, and what I describe here would probably be regarded by most colleagues, regardless of clinical or theoretical orientation, as 'good enough' analysis since, as John Klauber once wrote: 'There are quite a few warts in most analyses' (1971: 28–9).

To return to A and B, we can say that A's position is derived from the *asymmetry* of the classical psychoanalytical situation as devised by Freud and elaborated by many others, but especially in Britain by Klein. Position B is a later development, though many seeds were sown in the earliest days of psychoanalysis by Ferenczi. What Ferenczi initiated and later authors developed was an emphasis on the mutuality of the analytic pair, and especially to underline that important features of analysis derive from the interaction between analyst and patient. Let us call this *interdependence*.

You will be aware that analyst A works with a central conviction that the sole mutative factor in psychoanalysis is correct verbal interpretation of the transference. This position was described in detail by Strachey (1934) in a paper which has been amongst the most influential papers on technique ever written. By contrast, analyst B, whilst accepting the ever-present awareness of transference in the mind of the analyst, does not accept that A's position is a complete account. (Stewart (1990) has provided a wider view of what is mutative in psychoanalysis.) For example, Klauber drew attention to the question with which Strachey ends his paper – the analyst's difficulty in making interpretations – and argued that a major function of interpretation is to regulate the inevitable psychic tension which occurs between analyst and patient. A similar theme was taken up by Bion who described the analyst's need to interpret in order to deny the anxiety aroused in him by the fact that the situation is unknown to him and correspondingly dangerous.

Note here the similarity between Klauber and Bion, each tackling the issue of the analyst's personal need to interpret and thus in agreement about the existence of a serious problem. They share a consistency of viewpoint, yet differences arise when each describes the underlying anxiety. For Klauber, the psychoanalytic situation inevitably provokes a kind of 'tease' because infantile sexual gratification is implicitly promised but usually frustrated. By contrast Bion draws attention to the more primitive anxieties which can be aroused by the analyst's claim to knowledge, perhaps best captured in his statement that 'when in the presence of arrogance we are at the scene of a psychic catastrophe' (Bion 1967: 87). That is to say, when the analyst is aware of arrogance in the patient, he becomes identified with that emotion since 'to pursue the truth at no matter what cost is felt to be synonymous with a claim to a capacity for containing the discarded, split-off aspects of other personalities while retaining a balanced outlook' (Bion 1967: 88–9). Therefore, not only may arrogance in the patient be a defence against pain that is believed to be unbearable, but it is also an ongoing problem for the analyst. I take it that this is because he cannot know in advance the consequences of his interpretations and so cannot know what facing the truth will mean. This is particularly so for the patient but also, on account of the patient's reactions, for the analyst himself. If the analyst does fail to retain his balance, as is not uncommon, enactment will occur, and the resulting traumatizing situation comes to resemble, or be a repetition of, the original psychic disaster.

Each of these authors identifies the problem of how the analyst meets his own personal needs as these are inevitably aroused by the activity of analysing, and in so doing take us beyond Freud's recommendation of detachment (the image underlying his concept of neutrality). Yet each writes from a recognizably distinct tradition: Klauber from within what Eric Rayner (1991) has termed the 'Independent line of thought', and Bion, usually regarded as Kleinian, yet in one of his most influential contributions, the notion of container-contained, giving significantly greater emphasis to the influence of the environment than Klein herself had done at that time.

I am suggesting that one method of apprehending the two approaches which are here arbitrarily described as A and B is by providing a condensed account of some key conceptual developments since Freud, so that from these comparisons we can draw out the tensions I am wanting to describe. (We can find evidence for these differences in Freud's own work. His recommendations on analysing the transference were sometimes honoured more in the breach than in the observance. We read, for example, how he fed his patients, lent them money or told them jokes. See Lipton 1977 and Gill 1982, for an extensive account.) It is commonly observed that sometimes there is more consistency across psychoanalytic groupings than within them. This being so, it is inevitable that any attempt to describe particular contributions will steer an uneasy course between historical and political ideal constructs on the one hand, and on the other real differences which should not be evaded.

Many psychoanalytic institutions have suffered over the years painful, sometimes divisive conflicts arising from theoretical differences and the British Society is no exception; yet compromise has always been possible and splitting into disparate societies avoided. For example, amongst Independent analysts there are some generally accepted Independent contributions which sit beside essentially classical Freudian and Kleinian concepts.

These contributions are most marked in our understanding of earliest child development and, specifically, the effect of environmental provision and trauma. The essential notion of unconscious states which 'store' early inter-active experience was *added to* the classical Freudian theory of repression and defences, it did not supplant them. The classical Freudian model is based on intra-psychic conflict, perhaps especially when those conflicts have reached the complexity and maturity of the Oedipal situation. Later, Klein described the pre-Oedipal stages of development but did so in terms of essentially intra-psychic states.

The lines of thought in which Independents have been particularly inter-ested are those disorders of the self that are rooted in the infant's early experience in the world. These concepts are different from the much more internally coherent and unified theories of development (and technique too, perhaps) of the Kleinian approach on the one hand; and the emphasis in the Contemporary Freudian group on a particular meta-psychology and its con-tinuing evolution on the other. Yet, within the Independent tradition there are both examples of rigorously unified theory, for example, Fairbairn on object relations (1952), and the work of individual practitioners such as Winnicott, which is a series of acute and uniquely original observations rather than an organized theoretical system. By emphasizing lines of thought rather than unified theory, and by including such methodological differences as those between Fairbairn and Winnicott, a further defining characteristic begins to emerge: that is, an attitude to knowledge which is essentially an *open* system rather than the desire for a *closed* one.

Please note here an important distinction. 'Open system' refers *not* to the mind of the analyst; most analysts would like to be seen as open-minded. Rather the term applies to the kind of data collection and theory building that each individual analyst is drawn towards. Some prefer the effort to con-struct an internally coherent account within which clinical experience can be located. Others prefer a looser, even internally contradictory narrative, per-haps where certainty is more postponed and the clinical experience therefore rests more awkwardly within the analyst's available internal schema. Clearly there are strengths and weaknesses in such a position but, most importantly, it can be seen that Independent thought is centrally rooted in a *struggle for identity* rather than unified theory building. I believe that this struggle for identity on the part of the analyst mirrors the emphasis in much Independent writing on the patient's struggle to secure a viable self. This aim was felici-tously expressed by Ella Sharpe (1930, see Whelan 2000), who described a desirable outcome of analysis as being the patient's conviction of a right to exist.

Eric Rayner (1991: 8) has described how many of the original British analysts had come from Protestant religious backgrounds, were marked by

English empiricism and 'disliked romantic ideologies that *could* be tainted by fanaticism'. Rayner argued that the philosophical roots of this group of people can be traced back to the political liberalism of the late seventeenth century. This tradition is characterized by respecting ideas for their use and truth value no matter where they come from.

Influence of Fairbairn

In summary then, it could be said that Independents are characterized not so much by adherence to a particular theoretical system but rather by an attitude to knowledge which finds expression in a reluctance to espouse a closed system of thought. Many ideas which are accepted by Independents and, in some cases, elaborated by them, have developed out of a creative interplay between the ideas of Freud on the one hand and Klein on the other. For example, Anna Freud's notion of developmental lines is accepted by many Independents, as is Klein's account of denial, splitting, projection and introjection as significant defences that contribute to cleavages in the personality; a complex of defences usually referred to as projective identification. However, it was Ronald Fairbairn (1952) who, with a theoretical challenge to Freud on the one hand and a keen interest in Klein's notion of internal objects on the other, first defined the concept of a schizoid position, i.e. the very early splitting of the ego and the consequent psychic structures.

In trying to explain this state he emphasized the failure of environmental provision. Essentially the infant feels that his love is bad and has destroyed his mother's love. This preceded what at that time Klein called the paranoid and depressive positions, in which guilt over aggression is central so that 'hate is bad'. For Fairbairn, it was the corresponding failure of the mother to convince her baby that he is loved for himself which resulted in the fateful splitting into good and bad selves and their corresponding good and bad objects, which constitute the core of the psychic structure. By contrast, Klein had emphasized anxiety as arising from the death instinct in the individual, a situation which can be *mitigated* by the environment. Here the emphasis is very much on the primacy of destructive phantasies as derivatives of instinct, rather than the Independent stress on phantasy as the *outcome of the interplay between* instinctual derivatives on one side and environmental influence on the other.

From this highly condensed overview, two inferences may be drawn. First, the philosophical: Independents emphasize that psychic reality is more a *contingent* state, i.e. it is a product of a continuously evolving interaction. This is in contrast to more determinist theories that rely heavily on the drives as the underpinning of psychic structure. Bowlby called such theories a 'boiling tea kettle' explanation, i.e. cure lies in the reduction of instinctual tension. This was especially so for Freud but also for Klein. By contrast, *contingency* leads, as in Fairbairn's account, to a systems theory of mismatch reduction.

The analogy here would be with your central heating system which clicks back on when the temperature drops below a certain point. So, in the relationship between subject and object, motivational systems are aroused when particular needs, including those for a relationship with the object, are insufficiently met. This is an interpersonal, as well as intra-psychic, account.

These theories differ in their *assumed motivational systems.* Fairbairn emphasized motives that are environmentally dependent from the outset. The best known advocate of the significance of environmental factors was Winnicott, who famously wrote that 'when you set out to study a baby, what you find is a baby and a mother' (1952: 99). Fairbairn emphasized the loss of intimacy with mother as a basic trauma and, in doing so, heralded a shift in psychoanalysis to thinking of dependency as fundamental; or, put in another way, that the basic anxiety situation is the *helplessness* of the infant. The shifting of dependency and its vicissitudes into central aetiological signifi-cance – which contrasted at the time with Freud's emphasis on infantile sexuality and Klein's innate destructiveness – was to be worked out in more detail by Winnicott and later by Bion and currently, for example, Judith Mitrani, a Californian analyst much influenced by Frances Tustin (2001).

To summarize so far: Independents are characterized more by an attitude to knowledge than by adherence to a particular theory or account of devel-opment. In addition, the evolution of their ideas depended upon an historical situation in which they played a mediating role. Within this historical context, they explicitly shifted the basis of development away from innate instincts to also thinking about the role of motives such as dependency and intimacy within a response-potential framework.

Freud and Ferenczi

Having given an overview of the Independent position, what about specific writers? One of the main contributors to the debate was Michael Balint, a Hungarian analyst who had been influenced by Ferenczi, another Hungarian, and one of Freud's closest early collaborators. The disputes between Freud and Ferenczi contained many, if not even all, of the major differences within psychoanalysis that continue to this day, and not only within the British Society. I will discuss some of the differences between Freud and Ferenczi by drawing on two of Ferenczi's major papers (1913, 1933). I want to show both the beginnings of significant strands in Independent thinking, and also to demonstrate that some of our fundamental theoretical differences have been present from the start.

One of Freud's most influential papers was 'Formulations on the two principles of mental functioning' (1911) in which he describes the transition between being ruled by the pleasure principle – what is wished – to the reality principle – what is real, even if it is unpleasant. He also believed that such a shift was impossible unless it took into account the care which the baby received from its mother. Ferenczi, in 'Stages in the development of the sense of reality' (1913) developed the significance of the idea of environmental provision. He disagreed openly with Freud about the incidence of actual sexual and emotional abuse, which he thought common (Ferenczi 1933) and reinstated *trauma* as a central pathogen. Freud had come to regard the vicissitudes of infantile sexuality and, later, the death instinct as more significant for the individual's health or pathology. Although Freud's first model of the mind (Sandler *et al.* 1997) depended entirely on the effects of early trauma – 'hysterics suffer mainly from reminiscences' – he discarded this view in favour of the ubiquitous effects of fantasy, especially those that comprise the Oedipus complex. In his third and last model, the environment is reinstated in a more limited way, as when he described the effects of the loss of love by the object. However, this model still proposed that psychic structure was the outcome of internal adaptation.

Ferenczi is perhaps best known for his experiments with technique, including mutual analysis and the analyst's selective disclosure or confession of hatred and errors to his patient. Having made the first attempts to deal with and use countertransference pressures on the analyst, he also introduced *regression* as a potential therapeutic tool. His most prescient contribution was to the interpersonal, as well as intra-psychic, nature of defences. He described (Ferenczi 1933) how abused children would accept and defend their abusers, a defence which Anna Freud would later describe as 'identification with the aggressor'. He showed how this was not only a defence against intolerable sexual and aggressive impulses but also a means of internalizing a bad object in order to modify it. Unfortunately for the child the consequence of this 'precocious maturity' is severe splitting of the ego. Ferenczi also described another interpersonal defence: the reversal of roles between child and parent. He wrote that the 'fear of a mad adult . . . turns the child into a psychiatrist' (1933: 165). Later, Fairbairn explained the common observation that abused children defend their parents by the idea of the 'moral defence'. It is easier for the child to believe that he is guilty – since then he may be able to change the situation – rather than that the parent is bad because the powerful parent is beyond the child's control, and then his situation is truly hopeless (1952).

Ferenczi's description of the reversal of roles between parent and child is nowadays a commonplace clinical observation in both children and adults. Indeed recent attachment research (Hesse and Main 2000) has found that the 'disorganized/disoriented attachment' category includes a significant number of children who are role-inverting, shown by punitive and inappropriately care-giving/solicitous behaviour towards the parent.

Marjorie Brierley was one of the main analysts to develop Ferenczi's ideas. She argued that affects had been neglected in favour of instincts, but that this did not accord with clinical experience: 'affect . . . is the Ariadne's thread . . . that connects the analyst to the transference' (1937: 257). She described how at the beginning the object is indistinguishable from the affect. The infant is aware of feelings which are bodily experiences. They are the main objects of his subjective experience, i.e. the object *is* the affect. The French analyst André Green observed that 'for writers of the English school it is not a question of pushing affect back towards biology but rather of setting it [affect] in a frame of primitive sensibility, the vestiges of which must be sought by the analyst through the transference/countertransference' (1977: 144).

To return to our historical sequence, Brierley was arguing for an increased clinical emphasis on affect. Charles Rycroft (1958) took this further. Based on the work of Suzanne Langer (1942), he described how human behaviour derives not only from instinctual needs but also from the wish to communicate. Affects in particular have an *effect* on the listener; the psychoanalytic situation is no exception.

At about this time John Bowlby was beginning to develop his work on attachment, having also been influenced by Langer and by Charles Darwin on the survival value of feelings and their communication. He went on to write his influential trilogy *Attachment* (1969), *Separation* (1973) and *Loss* (1980) on maternal separation and its role in delinquency and depression which has had a major influence worldwide on social and health policy. Yet today he occupies an uncertain place within psychoanalysis. This is partly because of the level of explanation, i.e. the biological, which he used. Many clinicians find it difficult to 'marry' his findings with the psychoanalytic focus on the ways in which internal reality is transformed in complex ways.

Brierley's emphasis on the affective attunement of the analyst, often through non-verbal communication, paved the way for Paula Heimann (1950) on countertransference. Her paper has had a major influence on analysts' attitudes to the feelings they had about their analysands. Until this point, countertransference had generally been regarded as an obstacle. Freud wrote of it as something to be neutralized, or as requiring more analysis for the analyst. Heimann showed that 'the analyst's emotional response to his patient within the analytic situation represents one of the most important tools for his work' (1950: 81).

Balint (1952) and others were also beginning to argue for the primacy of the intersubjective emotional field, following Ferenczi's move towards a two-body psychology. Alice Balint (1939) described what Michael Balint would later term primary love. Remember that for Freud object relatedness developed out of the stage of primary narcissism. Alice Balint described the existence of a fundamental object relation from the start of life, in which the infant's love assumes that the mother is expected to meet his needs with no consideration for her own interests. This may look like ruthless aggression but beneath it is a strange kind of love.

Michael Balint went on to describe this basic anxiety situation in a different way from Klein. He emphasized infantile omnipotence – and by implication the centrality of the baby's dependence on the caregiver – together with two ways of reacting to the loss of omnipotence, which had not been described before. He gave these defences the somewhat unwieldy names of philobatism and ocnophilia (1968). The latter refers to a defensive style in which the individual feels anxious when in open spaces and prefers to cling to an object for safety. Inevitably he will experience his objects as subservient or failing to satisfy his needs. For example, we all know the inevitable consequence when such a novice skier approaches the only tree on the slope! By contrast, the philobat trusts his own skills and gets anxious when approaching objects; in everyday life, entrepreneurs, adventurers and other risk takers are often like this. Of course, these are extremes, and in practice most of us are a mixture of the two. The distinction emphasizes the subjective experience of space as a significant dimension in psychic life. The theme was to be taken up by later Independents, particularly Winnicott, but also by Masud Khan in his contributions to the understanding of sexual perversions.

Balint emphasized that these two kinds of character defences are a reaction to environmental failure. They are responses aimed at restoring certain aspects of the state of primary love between self and environment while denying others. Technically these concepts seem useful, especially when the analyst senses a pull towards regression in the patient's material, or, as Balint would have emphasized, the patient's mood. Whilst many analysts regard regression as resistance, he believed that regression could be either malignant – demanding never ending gratification – or benign – aimed at restoring a derailed development. The distinction has been a helpful one, especially with certain kinds of patients whose pre-verbal experiences have to be managed. With benign regression, he believed what he termed a 'new beginning' could take place, so that signs of a wish for regression in analysis should not automatically be regarded as resistance.

To recap our story so far. Human development in classical psychoanalysis is governed by instinctual strivings and their vicissitudes. Freud's theory was informed by the biological thinking of his time: particular patterns and sequences, such as the oral, anal, phallic, genital, facilitate or inhibit human growth. Several important aspects of Freud's model were to be challenged by later Independent writers. First, for Freud, the object is sought for in order to satisfy an instinct. Second, the adaptation to reality is painfully learned by renouncing pleasure. Although Freud recognized the importance of the environment, he believed that development takes place through a series of *internal* adaptations – this is a *one body psychology*. Klein's emphasis was even more specific in that she focused on unconscious phantasies as representatives of the instinctual strivings and their objects in an intra-psychic system.

The Independents were reacting to what they believed to be the insufficient significance given to the environment in psychoanalytic thinking; they emphasized the interaction between self and environment in creating the psyche. For them unconscious phantasy is contingent upon the interplay between the self (or instincts) and the environment. This contrasted sharply with Klein's view of phantasy as the direct derivative of instinct, where the environment can be *mitigating* – via love – but it is not primary. Because of this emphasis, Independents are sometimes accused of downgrading the significance of internal psychic structures and phantasy.

Fairbairn (1952), who worked mostly in Edinburgh, openly challenged major parts of classical theory. Essentially, he reversed Freud's basic model from 'tension discharge' to one of 'balance within a whole system'. For Fairbairn, the relationship to the object is primary and libidinal/aggressive strivings are the means of achieving it: 'libido is the signpost to the object' summarizes not only Fairbairn's reformulation but much of what is now called British object relations theory. Some regard this as a paradigm shift in psychoanalytic theory building. It assumes that self and object are differentiable from the outset, dissenting from Freud's assumption of primary narcissism; object relations are central, and should move from infantile to mature dependence. In the later years of his clinical practice, Fairbairn modified his analytic technique by often sitting facing his patients (John Padel, personal communication). This has been commented on by former patients such as Professor Malcolm Millar, who described how Fairbairn would sometimes recognize the real relationship between them when they worked in the same hospital by making a comment about work as he was leaving the session (personal communication). For Fairbairn, 'analysis is about the real situations that people have lived through' (Padel 1972) and therefore he saw reconstruction as particularly valuable. Today we take it for granted that some defences and anxieties are rooted in the patient's dependence on the analyst and the analytic setting. It is often overlooked that Fairbairn was the first to discuss this systematically.

Of course there are problems, some of them serious, with aspects of Fairbairn's theory. I shall describe two. The first, aggression, is a source of dispute not only about Fairbairn, but within and between many different psychoanalytic positions. Fairbairn rejected aggression as a drive – many analysts would disagree. However, he did not underestimate the importance of aggression. He thought that there is always a *capacity for* aggression, but not necessarily a *'need to discharge'*. He is here implicitly shifting the meaning of drives towards 'response potential' and in so doing seems more in line with contemporary biological and ethological thinking that there is a pre-wired readiness to respond, given appropriate stimulation at the right time.

A second criticism of Fairbairn's theory is that he did not acknowledge the positive effects of maternal failure. This aspect was to be addressed by Winnicott who described how (as he might have said 'as any mother knows') *disillusionment* is critical for the infant's development provided it is in manageable doses. By including maternal failure as a central factor in both healthy development or pathology, Winnicott corrected a major difficulty with Fairbairn's account, namely the implicit idealization of maternal care.

Influence of Winnicott

Winnicott's position within the Independent line of thought can hardly be overestimated. For example, he thought that psychoanalysts had written a great deal about psychic or internal reality and adaptation to external reality but had neglected what he termed a third or transitional area. This is neither intra-psychic nor shared external reality but a developmental stage – based on his close study of the infant's first possession – in which the infant is in between being merged with the mother on the one hand and, on the other, able to relate to a separate person who is outside himself. That earliest merged state could also be called the area of illusion (the illusion that the infant has created the breast, or the satisfying part-object), and without that being established there cannot really be disillusion, and without disillusion there cannot be weaning: 'the mere termination of breast feeding is not a weaning' (Winnicott 1974: 15). In this account, the transitional area represents the infant's creative use of illusion and can be observed in any child who is 'lost' in play.

In Winnicott's description of the infant's creating the breast, an hallucination which is also a creative gesture, there is an echo of Ferenczi, who 50 years earlier had described a stage of 'hallucinatory magic omnipotence'. Winnicott also described what happens when this goes wrong – impingements on the infant, which in good-enough mothering can be coped with, but when insufficiently contained lead to dissociation and splits in the personality, or what he termed false-self organizations, often marked by compliance.

Note that there are differences between the two. For Ferenczi, ego development followed from a process of adaptation to increasing levels of frustration; the awareness of separateness painfully ensues from the frustration of omnipotent wishes. This is the classical, originally Freudian, model. I suggest that this view is recognizable as an aspect of the model which underpins the position of our analyst A who 'conducts an analysis'. But for Winnicott, once ego-relatedness is possible the breast is experienced as a *subjective object*, i.e. one created by the infant which can be joyfully destroyed. However, the good-enough mother will understand the importance of surviving the infant's aggression without retaliation. This ushers in a crucial developmental step: the infant's discovery that the destroyed object has survived, which releases the object from his omnipotent control (Winnicott 1969). For Winnicott it is not the absence of gratification which leads to the recognition of shared reality, as it is in the classical view: it is the survival of the object that has been destroyed. At this stage the *external object* exists and can be trusted. It can be *used*. Next, libido and aggression become fused, the self becomes responsible and it is only now that we can speak of hate and, therefore, of concern. (Note here the contrast between Winnicott and Klein. For the latter, concern or reparative guilt is a consequence of the infant taking responsibility for the damage to the object, whereas for Winnicott concern follows on from the infant's discovery of the object's survival.)

I suggest that Winnicott's account underpins the position of our analyst B. It is the patient's discovery of the analyst's survival of the patient's aggression which is essential for genuine psychic change, especially in the all important area of reality testing and the recognition of separateness. You will recall that this contrasts with A's position, described as the asymmetry of the classical psychoanalytic situation: heavy reliance on correct verbal interpretation of transference and countertransference. All analysts may – at times must – insist upon certain 'psychic facts of life' (Money-Kyrle 1968): 'fact' here meaning an element of experience which is discrete, not yet further reducible and stable over time. Nevertheless, despite this apparent one-sidedness, every analyst is dependent on his patients in all manner of ways whether he is able to acknowledge this or not, not least to realize his identity as a psychoanalyst.

However, one of the main means by which any analyst enables the patient to recognize the fact of the analyst's survival is the act of interpretation itself or, as Bion put it, 'thinking under fire'. Stated in this way, we see that A and B are equally important and their relationship is synergistic. One cannot exist without an awareness of the existence of the other and so they are each necessary: elements of both asymmetry and of interdependence are characteristic of all psychoanalytic inquiry.

I set out to describe an analysis that is 'good enough' and in doing so I might well be trying to describe what most analysts, regardless of their group affiliation, would try to do. I have both tried to outline defining differences, and at the same time contended that we have at least as much in common as that which separates us. Here we have arrived full circle to the beginning of this chapter.

However, we can take this account a stage further. In certain states of mind, particularly those which are most problematic to analyst and patient alike, where words are hard to come by since the experiences being repeated are largely pre-verbal, interpretation itself becomes a hazardous activity. During these phases, which occur in most analyses at some time, interpretation is readily felt as an impingement and therefore as destructive of the patient's struggle for subjectivity. Yet, at the same time, the analytic process cannot develop without interpretation to facilitate it. Here we have a paradox, which must be borne, perhaps over long periods of time, by both analyst and patient.

Indeed wherever one looks closely at clinical psychoanalysis, paradox looms large. The issues that crop up seem to be universal and fundamental: for example, maintaining the balance between instinctual gratification and its frustration (the classical Freudian view) or the balance between containment and disturbance (a more recent way of thinking). The bearing of paradox then is at the heart of the matter, and you might consider not only that A and

B need each other but also that the tensions between them cannot be resolved and are a fundamental paradox for psychoanalysis. Now, Winnicott observed that the price for resolving paradox may be a heavy one: namely to risk losing one's sanity (1958). For it is the struggle to integrate experience whilst failing to do so which is such an important means of safeguarding our own mind and being. Frank Lloyd Wright believed that the only religion for him was non-conformism because that was the best way to protect the integrity of one's mind. The attitude I am advocating is one which requires the bearing of the paradox: on the one hand, a willingness to accept established authority and, on the other, continuous questioning in order to find one's own authority; when all is said and done, in the consulting room we are alone with our patients.

This 'non-conformism' conveys an attitude to psychoanalytical inquiry which can be found in much of our literature. Currently, for example, Thomas Ogden in America is developing what he terms the concept of the 'analytic third', based partly on Winnicott's 'transitional area'. I believe that sustaining what is essentially a paradox, namely the pull towards asymmetry on the one hand and interdependence on the other, is an ongoing struggle, the bearing of which helps to sustain the analytic endeavour for both analyst and patient

References

Balint, A. (1939) 'Mother love and love for the mother', in M. Balint (ed.) (1952) *Primary Love and Psychoanalytic Technique*, London: Hogarth Press. Reprinted London: Karnac, 1985.

Balint, M. (1952) *Primary Love and Psychoanalytic Technique*, London: Hogarth Press. Reprinted London: Karnac, 1985.

—— (1968) *The Basic Fault*, London: Tavistock.

Bion, W. (1967) 'On arrogance', in W. Bion *Second Thoughts*, New York: Jason Aronson.

Bollas, C. (1989) *Forces of Destiny: Psychoanalysis and Human Idiom*, London: Free Association Books.

Bowlby, J. (1969) *Attachment and Loss. Vol. 1 Attachment*, London: Hogarth Press.

—— (1973) *Attachment and Loss. Vol. 2 Separation*, London: Hogarth Press.

—— (1980) *Attachment and Loss. Vol. 3 Loss*, London: Hogarth Press.

Brierley, M. (1937) 'Affects in theory and practice', *International Journal of Psychoanalysis* 18: 256–63.

Fairbairn, W.R.D. (1952) *Psychoanalytic Studies of the Personality*, London: Tavistock.

Ferenczi, S. (1913) 'Stages in the development of the sense of reality', *First Contributions to Psycho-Analysis*, London: Hogarth Press, 1952.

—— (1933) 'Confusion of tongues between adults and children: The language of tenderness and passion', in *Final Contributions to the Problems and Methods of Psycho-Analysis*, M. Balint (ed.), London: Hogarth Press, 1955.

Freud, S. (1911) 'Formulations on the two principles of mental functioning', *Standard Edition*, vol. 12, pp. 215–26, London: Hogarth Press.
—— (1914) 'Papers on technique', *Standard Edition*, vol. 12, pp. 85–171, London: Hogarth Press.
Gill, M.M. (1982) *Analysis of Transference*, vol. 1, New York: International Universities Press.
Green, A. (1977) 'Conceptions of affect', *International Journal of Psychoanalysis* 58: 129–56.
Heimann, P. (1950) 'On countertransference', *International Journal of Psychoanalysis* 31: 81–4.
Hesse, E. and Main, M. (2000) 'Disorganized infant, child and adult attachment', *Journal of the American Psychoanalytical Association* 48: 1097–1120.
King, P. and Steiner, J. (1991) *The Freud–Klein Controversies 1941–1945*, London: Routledge.
Klauber, J. (1986) *Difficulties in the Psychoanalytic Encounter*, London: Free Association Books.
Kohon, G. (1986) *The British School of Psychoanalysis: The Independent Tradition*, London: Free Association Books.
Langer, S. (1942) *Philosophy in a New Key*, Cambridge, MA: Harvard University Press.
Lipton, S.D. (1997) 'The advantages of Freud's technique as shown in his analysis of the Rat Man', *International Journal of Psychoanalysis* 58: 255–74
Mitrani, J. (2001) *Ordinary People: Extraordinary Protections*, London: Brunner-Routledge.
Money-Kyrle, R. (1968) 'Cognitive development', *International Journal of Psychoanalysis* 49: 691–8.
Ogden, T. (1997) *Reverie and Interpretation*, New York: Aronson.
Padel, J. (1972) 'The contribution of W.R.D. Fairbairn', *Bulletin of the European Psycho-analytical Federation* 2: 13–26.
Rayner, E. (1991) *The Independent Mind in British Psychoanalysis*, London: Free Association Books.
Reich, A. (1960) 'On countertransference', *International Journal of Psychoanalysis* 41: 16–33.
Rycroft, C. (1958) 'An enquiry into the function of words in the psychoanalytic situation', *International Journal of Psychoanalysis* 39: 408–15.
Sandler, J., Holder, A., Dare, C. and Dreher, A.U. (1997) *Freud's Models of the Mind: An Introduction*, London: Karnac.
Stewart, H. (1990) 'Interpretation and other agents for psychic change', *International Journal of Psychoanalysis* 71: 61–70.
Strachey, J. (1934) 'The nature of the therapeutic action of psychoanalysis', *International Journal of Psychoanalysis* 15: 127–59.
Whelan, M. (ed.) (2000) *Mistress of Her Own Thoughts*, London: Rebus Press.
Winnicott, D.W. (1952) 'Anxiety associated with insecurity', *Collected Papers: Through Paediatrics to Psychoanalysis*, London: Hogarth Press, 1975.
—— (1958) 'Transitional objects and transitional phenomena', *Collected Papers: Through Paediatrics to Psychoanalysis*, London: Hogarth Press, 1975.
—— (1968) 'Playing: its theoretical status in the clinical situation', *International Journal of Psychoanalysis* 49: 591–9.

—— (1969) 'The use of an object', *International Journal of Psychoanalysis* 50: 711–6; reprinted in *Playing and Reality*, London: Pelican, 1974.

—— (1974) *Playing and Reality*, London: Pelican.

Suggestions for further reading

The best introduction and background to the history of ideas outlined in this chapter is *The Independent Mind in British Psychoanalysis* by Eric Rayner (London: Free Association Books, 1991), but see also a collection of essays by Gregorio Kohon *The British School of Psychoanalysis: The Independent Tradition* (London: Free Association Books, 1986), which has a useful introductory section by the editor. For an understanding of the theoretical challenge to Freud's model of the mind presented by the British Object Relations School, Chapters 1 to 4 of Ronald Fairbairn's *Psychoanalytic Studies of the Personality* (London: Tavistock, 1952) is recommended. This is a scholarly work and, by way of contrast, readers may find the papers by Winnicott more accessible, since he writes in a way which appeals to everyday experience. In particular the (1958) paper on 'Transitional objects and transitional phenomena' is the basis for the argument in this chapter for an appreciation of the value for psychoanalysis of paradox that remains unresolved: *Collected Papers: Through Paediatrics to Psychoanalysis* (London: Hogarth Press, 1975).

Part 5

Extreme psychic states

The final two chapters deal with violence: the first, by Donald Campbell, with the violence which we commit, in sadism and sexual perversion; and the second, by Caroline Garland, with the effects of traumatic and violent experience on their victims. Human beings seem to be uniquely violent to each other as a species. Freud repeatedly returned in old age, when European civilization was tearing itself apart, to ask in what ways do language and culture foster violence? Extreme acts of torture, violence and terrorism are painful to think about. Again, underlying questions such as whether aggression is innate or reactive, and whether the notion of an aggressive drive implies that of the death instinct, return us to the problem of evil; it is hardly surprising that psychoanalysts are unable to agree about violence (Perelberg 1999).

Many psychoanalysts would accept the idea of a continuum between aggression on the one hand, which can be self-preservative, or used to overcome obstacles (Rizzuto et al. 2004) and violent sadism, culminating in suicide, torture, or murder, on the other. As with sexuality, with which violence is often fused, it is difficult to give mental space to the notion that even extremes of terrorism may be fuelled by poisoned variants of the same phantasies as those of the small child who wants to eat up his mother, or to stay with her forever. Dealing with such patients is peculiarly taxing and painful, even sometimes dangerous, for the analyst, and it is not surprising that many of them are seen in clinics, or as part of research projects which enable analysts to support one another.

Donald Campbell works at the Portman Clinic, a specialist outpatient clinic in London for patients with forensic or sexual difficulties. In Chapter 15 he deals with the links between sadism as a sexual perversion and what he calls self-preservative aggression – showing that what may appear a bizarre or incomprehensible sexual aberration can be understood in the light of the patient's past. Campbell uses the concept of the 'core complex', developed by Mervyn Glasser from the work of the American psychoanalyst Margaret Mahler, in which he described the two opposing states of terror that threaten the infant in relation to its mother: engulfment and abandonment. Glasser's view of the perversions, including sexual sadism, was that they are a way of allowing the infant to preserve a link with the mother whilst at the same time ensuring that it is not engulfed and overwhelmed. As children grow older and their larger maturing bodies make genital sexuality both more real and less threatening, they generally outgrow the need for such solutions, but the chapter describes the case of a young man who continued to use a perverse attempted solution. Campbell does not use Freud's concept of the 'death instinct', which Klein and her followers took up to understand an aspect of perversion as expressing something destructive and hostile towards a parental couple or a mother figure. These different views on aggression – core complex or death instinct – are often seen as alternatives; in fact many perverse states have elements of both constructive defensiveness and destructive aggressiveness.

Caroline Garland works in the trauma unit at the Tavistock Clinic. In Chapter 16 we return to our beginning, as she describes the ways in which the understanding of trauma paralleled the growth of psychoanalysis. Patients who have been traumatized use defences (see Catia Galatariatou, Chapter 1 this volume) in ways that are destructive and self-destructive. Anna Freud (1936) was the first to describe the defence of identification with the aggressor, in which – in order to lessen their feeling of total helplessness – victims accept, even foster, the sadism of guards and tyrants. In therapy a patient may *enact* helplessness by putting pressure on the therapist to feel it instead. However, as Garland shows, if this pressure towards enactment (or, in another variant, for the therapist to become a warm and reassuring figure) can be borne by the analyst and not acted out by her, then what the patient is trying to evacuate from his or her mind can become thought about and does not need to be enacted. She here uses Hanna Segal's (1957) seminal distinction between a symbol proper (where there is an appreciation of the difference between a symbol and what it symbolizes) and a symbolic equation (where this distinction is lost).

In her descriptions of the analyst's difficulty with his or her feelings towards the patient, of the preoccupation of psychoanalysis with psychic meaning and symbolization, and with the way in which we all try to make sense of events by ascribing psychic agency to ourselves, Garland illustrates in relation to trauma questions that are central to all psychoanalytic practice. Why do some people recover their equilibrium after horrifying experiences more readily than others? Why can some children psychically survive childhoods which leave others devastated? In part, a defensive solution like paranoia, or a sexual perversion, even a frank psychotic delusion, may be the best the patient can do to enable them to survive at all. The reality of what happened in the past is less important than how the patient is dealing with the past in the present.

References

Freud, A. (1936) *The Ego and the Mechanisms of Defence*, London: Hogarth Press.

Perelberg, R.J. (1999) *Psychoanalytic Understanding of Violence and Suicide*, London: Routledge.

Rizzuto, A.-M., Meissner, W.W. and Buie, D.H. (2004) *The Dynamics of Human Aggression*, New York: Brunner-Routledge.

Segal, H. (1957) 'Notes on symbol formation', *International Journal of Psychoanalysis*, 38: 391–7. Reprinted in *The Work of Hanna Segal: A Kleinian Approach to Clinical Practice*, New York: Jason Aronson, 1981; reprinted London Free Association Books and Maresfield Library, 1986.

Chapter 15

Perversion – sadism and survival

Don Campbell

Introduction

Psychoanalysis has always been to a greater or lesser extent politically incorrect. Psychoanalytic thinking about perversion has aroused condemnation from the right of the intellectual and political spectrum, and criticism that we have got it all wrong from gay rights activists and feminist writers. I am going to begin with a quote from Freud's paper on 'A Case of Hysteria':

> All psycho-neurotics are persons with strongly marked perverse tendencies, which had been repressed in the course of their development and had become unconscious. Consequently their unconscious *phantasies* show precisely the same content as the documentarily recorded *actions* of perverts ... Psycho-neuroses are, so to speak, *negative* perversions. In neurotics the sexual constitution, under which the effects of heredity are included, operates in combination with any accidental influences in their life, which may disturb the development of normal sexuality. A stream of water which meets with an obstacle in the river-bed is damned up and flows back into old channels which had formerly seemed fated to run dry.
>
> (Freud 1905: 50–51)

Freud emphasises that none of us can stand in judgement in relation to those who suffer from perversions. I assume that everyone is, in one way or another, neurotic and has entertained perverse fantasies. If Freud is right, all of us have a resource in our unconscious fantasies to understand the use we make of sexual fantasies and behaviour, including perverse behaviour.

Returning to the theme of psychoanalysis as politically incorrect, so many of Freud's discoveries have become an acceptable part of the fabric of our culture that you might be surprised to know that if you had wanted to hear Freud give the lectures that were to become the 'Three essays on the theory of sexuality' in 1905, you would have had to cross a picket line because people were outraged at the thought that children had a sex life.

In a short introduction it is impossible to do more than refer briefly to one aspect of the perversions. I have chosen to focus on the subject of sadism because the desire to inflict pain upon the sexual object and to have it inflicted upon oneself is, as Freud maintained in the 'Three essays on the theory of sexuality': 'the most common and the most significant of all the perversions' (p. 157). I will focus particularly on sadism as a solution to primitive anxieties about survival.

The self-preservative function of the ego

Freud viewed the ego's primary function to be the preservation of the self. We share this primary aim with all living creatures. A constitutional predisposition to preserve the species underpins the individual's protective and reproductive behaviour. We can see graphic illustrations of fight/flight mechanisms on wildlife documentaries. Sometimes our excitement and tension in the stalking and the fight, our revulsion in the killing, our fear and awe of the predator, or our sympathy for the victim, make it difficult to remember that animals compete for territory and mates, and kill for food in order to survive. We are witnessing self-preservative aggression.

Human beings experience threats to survival from far more complex sources than the need for food, shelter and sexual reproduction. Sometimes attacks on vulnerable children, or the ill or elderly, or the sheer scale of violence, such as the horrific terrorist attacks on New York City and Washington on September 11 2001, generate such rage, pain and grief that it is difficult to think about the perpetrator's motivation. It may be difficult to understand the attacks on the World Trade Center and the Pentagon as dramatic examples of aggression in response to a perceived threat to survival. At a conscious level, terrorists are fighting for the survival of their ideology, which they believe is threatened by the domination of Judaeo-Christian and capitalist belief systems. The religious beliefs of the terrorists give them a psychic cohesiveness: they define who they are, and give meaning to their lives and, most importantly, to their deaths. This kind of internal world, supported by faith in a reward of eternal life, makes this type of aggression the most dangerous to combat. Viewed from this perspective, the self-preservative nature of the terrorist's violence becomes clearer, but no less horrific or excusable.

By now you may be wondering what aggression has to do with sex. I have begun with current and graphic illustrations of violence, which is motivated by a self-preservative instinct, to illustrate its destructiveness and the complex nature of the psychological ingredients that humans depend upon for their survival. While the mix of beliefs and internal objects is always idiosyncratic, each of us is motivated to maintain a psychic steady state or homeostatic balance between the internal and external world. The ego's task is to negotiate compromise where there is conflict between the inside and outside in order to achieve stability and balance. The ego organises conscious and unconscious fantasies as solutions to competing and fluctuating internal and external demands, which threaten the homeostasis of the internal world (Sandler and Sandler 1992).

Therefore, the 'best' solution negotiated by the ego is that which creates and maintains a feeling of safety and well-being. A neurotic or psychotic state, a symptom, or a character trait, a defence mechanism or a perversion, however maladapted in the outside world, may be the 'best' solution the ego can negotiate given the external circumstances and the ego's internal resources (Sandler and Sandler 1992), which in turn are built upon constitutional and environmental factors. Sexuality and aggression, with their accompanying fantasies and enactments, are our most fundamental resources for the resolution of our problems.

Temptation Island

Disdaining fiction and documentary, reality television provides a stage for the gratifying enactment of sexual fantasies made into an entertainment genre. Some recent British examples include *Big Brother*, *Pop Idol*, *I'm a Celebrity, Get Me Out of Here*, and *Temptation Island*, where attractive young people enact fantasies for a television audience. On *Temptation Island*, four couples are separated and sent to opposite ends of an island, described by the presenter as 'paradise', to test their faithfulness during 12 days in a romantic, alcohol-enhanced setting with 13 semi-clad, single, apparently available members of the opposite sex. Presumably the audience is attracted to the prospect of identifying with fantasies of finding the better partner who is waiting 'out there', exercising sexual charm and potency while breaking up an Oedipal couple or triumphing over a sibling rival, and, most importantly, gratifying the wish to become an instant celebrity. Of course, it becomes painfully obvious that the participants are not really testing their steadfastness to their partner, but trying to find a sexual solution to anxieties about long-term commitment.

In psychoanalysis we can see that current fantasies, developed as solutions to conflicts in the present, are permeated to a greater or lesser extent by primitive fantasies representing solutions to earlier developmental conflicts. For instance, paranoid fantasies in response to no real threat are likely to be based on earlier solutions to anxieties about safety. These archaic fantasies define our character, aims and behaviour.

Self-preservative aggression

I would now like to turn to the subject of earlier developmental conflicts, particularly those that arouse anxieties about survival, and sketch out for you a model for the development of sadism, its role and function. Later I will illustrate these issues with some clinical material.

When I view the ego's primary function as the preservation of the self, I am referring to anything that constitutes a threat to physical or psychological homeostasis. This includes, in this context, narcissistic equilibrium, that is the maintenance of a dynamic balance, a steady state at optimum levels. Bio-physiologists such as Cannon (1939) have shown that the body has an elaborate reflexive reaction pattern that prepares it for fight or flight in the presence of danger. In the psychic sphere, self-preservative aggression is triggered as a fundamental, immediate and substantial response to any threat to the self with the aim of negating this source of danger. All of us as infants and adults are capable of self-preservative aggression. I should point out that I am using the term self-preservative violence to mean a physical response of aggression, while the term self-preservative aggression I use to denote a psychical response to danger. When self-preservative aggression is enacted in relation to an object it becomes self-preservative violence.

If you suddenly found yourself being stalked by a lion in the African bush and unable to run, you would normally react with self-preservative aggression with the aim of getting rid of the lion. Self-preservative aggression has a single-minded, narrow-vision quality like a laser beam, which focuses on the dangerousness of the object rather than the object itself. If the victim's look is experienced as threatening through accusation, it is the eyes that are attacked; if what is being said is intolerable, the mouth is punched, and so on (Glasser 1998: 888). In infants or extreme situations the laser beam quality is lost and violence is directed indiscriminately.

You may be thinking that there are certain forms of violence that are self-preservative but do not appear to be aimed at negating a danger such as 'predatory violence' (Meloy 1988: 25). When we thought about the lion from the prey's point of view, as the lion was stalking us, we could think of the lion's threat as an example of predatory violence. However, when we look at the dynamics of the attack from the lion's point of view, we can see that the lion is motivated not by the prey's edibility, but rather by the danger of its unavailability, the risk of the prey escaping. As Lantos recognises: 'The animal hunting its prey is driven by hunger. Hunger makes it angry, but his anger is not directed against the prey. On the contrary he is pleased when it comes his way. No subjective aggression is felt while chasing, catching, tearing, biting and swallowing it' (1958: 118).

During a moment of self-preservative aggression or violence the object holds no personal significance other than his/her dangerousness: it is carried out in the interest of self-preservation and any other considerations have no relevance. The response of the object in any other respect is of no interest (Glasser 1998: 891).

With this view of the nature and function of self-preservative aggression in mind I turn now to the mother and her infant. Threats to the infant's psyche and/or physical survival (the infant cannot be expected to know the difference between them) normally mobilise self-preservative aggression directed towards the object, which is perceived as dangerous. The threat may be experienced as a direct assault, engulfment, smothering or abandonment to starve. As I had explained earlier, the aim of self-preservative aggression is to negate the threat.

However, when the object that is perceived as threatening to the child's survival is the same object upon which it depends for its survival – the mother – the exercise of self-preservative aggression poses a dilemma for the child. How can the infant survive the unmitigated and unmediated terror of the other? How is the child to survive if it cannot afford to get rid of mother? How can it survive the consequences of its omnipotent violence? Some children fashion an ingenious solution by libidinising their aggression towards the mother. In this way the child changes the aim of aggression from eliminating mother to controlling her in a libidinally gratifying way. Self-preservative aggression is, thereby, converted into sadism.

The role of sadism

In a self-preservative attack where the aim is, by fight or flight, to eliminate the threat to one's survival, the impact upon the object is irrelevant beyond the achievement of this aim. However, in a sadistic attack the relationship to the object must be preserved, not eliminated. By radically altering the relationship to the threatening object to ensure that both self and object survive, sadism now offers the child a second line of defence.

Subtly modulated mild sadomasochism emerges now as a libidinal component of the good enough bond between mother and child. However, when the mother's sadism is not tempered by reparation or extends beyond the child's capacity to recover a nurturing image, or when mother's narcissism makes it impossible for her to be aware of her infant's needs and respond appropriately, the child may rely on more frequent and more intense sadomasochistic exchanges to control a not-good-enough mother.

As an illustration of the shift from self-preservative aggression to sadism, I will tell you about an interaction between an infant and its mother which I observed. As an analytic student I observed a mother and her infant on a weekly basis. During several months the mother's feeding of the infant coincided with my visit and I noticed that mother often teased the baby by pulling her nipple away from her sucking child and moving it just out of reach as the child groped with its mouth to find and latch onto the nipple again. The mother laughed as she did this while her child became frustrated, tense and eventually enraged. On several occasions the child collapsed into cries. It was painful to watch. After watching this for about six weeks, one day when the mother began to tease her baby by moving her nipple away from the child's mouth before it had finished sucking, I noticed the child did not respond by pursuing the nipple or becoming tense and angry. Instead, the child stopped, looked up at the mother and smiled. The mother then returned the nipple to her child's mouth. I thought that smile represented a libidinisation of the aggression that had been mobilised by the frustration the child experienced in the pursuit of the withdrawn nipple. With its feed and survival at stake the child found a way to control the unavailable breast.

The core complex

Glasser (1979, 1992) has identified a complex which he refers to as the *core complex* because it occurs universally in normal development and begins with the infant's wish to merge with an idealised, omnipotently gratifying mother as an early solution to its anxieties of loss engendered by its own moves towards separation and individuation. The success of the merging 'solution' depends upon:

- a good enough mother who is able to respond to her child's needs at the right time with enough comfort, protection and nourishment
- a good enough father who can protect the child from mother's failures and provide an alternative to the exclusive fused relationship with her.

However, the child with a weak and or unavailable father is vulnerable if mother is narcissistically oriented. A narcissistic mother responds to her child on the basis of her own needs, giving too much too soon, or not enough when it is too late. The child may experience this type of mother as engulfing, intruding or smothering, on the one hand, or indifferent, abandoning and unreachable on the other. In either case, the child becomes acutely anxious about its survival. The infant that I observed was, I think, primarily anxious about abandonment and being left to starve. Such primitive anxieties about being able to find the object during the oral phase of development heighten anxieties later as the child moves towards separation and individuation.

Glasser's *core complex* becomes relevant during the child's anal phase and the solution to the core complex affects its future relationships. This crisis in the *core complex* usually reaches a climax during the child's anal phase when it is preoccupied with urinary and faecal productions, and conflicts within itself and its parents over control of these pleasurable functions and admirable creations. It is not surprising that a child might borrow from its solutions to conflicts over control of its body to fashion ingenious but maladaptive solutions, which enable him or her to retain his or her mother (after a fashion) and to survive (at a price). In this way crises in development around proximity to the object, that is anxieties about engulfment on the one hand and abandonment on the other, become negotiated through sadism, which then becomes a solution to anxieties about the revival of these earlier conflicts in later phases of development. Later I will refer to clinical material, which I hope will illustrate the anxieties associated with the *core complex*.

The development of a perversion

When the line of development from self-preservative aggression to the libidinisation of aggression progresses to the intensification of sadism, the psychic groundwork is laid for the development of perverse solutions to neurotic or psychotic conflicts. By extending this line of development to the point where intensified sadism becomes the dominating organiser of libidinal life, we reach the point where perversions become structured. The aim of defence in the perversions (Glover 1956) is to preserve enough reality sense to be able to function, even in a limited way, in the real world. By reducing paranoid dangers, by whatever means, the individual 'gains breathing space' to assess objective reality. However, the cost of this adaptation is the sacrifice of that part of reality which threatens the individual's survival. A perversion may defend against the dangers represented by psychotic anxieties from pre-Oedipal sources, such as internal chaos, fragmentation or disintegration of the ego; or against the neurotic anxieties arising out of unresolved Oedipal conflicts, such as castration, infantile sexuality, or narcissistic wounds. Whatever the source of the danger, the individual's orientation to reality will be affected. Chasseguet-Smirgel points out:

> The bedrock of reality is created by the difference between the sexes and the difference between generations: the inevitable period of time separating a child from his mother (for whom he is an inadequate sexual partner) and from his father (whose potent adult sexual organ he does not possess) . . . The perverse temptation leads one to accept pregenital desire and satisfactions (attainable by the small boy) as being equal to or even superior to genital desires and satisfactions (attainable only by the father). Erosion of the double difference between the sexes and the generations is the pervert's objective.
>
> (Chasseguet-Smirgel 1985: 2)

This dynamic lies behind the perverse patient's attacks on thinking and linking because of the dangers arising out of the internal and external reality of intercourse. Consequently, the dangers against which the perversion defends will inevitability affect the subject's relationship with the object's sexuality and, for the paedophile, its relationship with the generation of children and adolescents.

The vicissitudes of the sadomasochistic interaction between mother and child shape the nature of the conflicts against which a perversion defends. When the mother's sadism fails to defend her against what she experiences as her child's persecution, she is at risk of relying upon self-preservative aggression or its psychic equivalent. The child's well-being is then no longer relevant to the mother. The mother's only concern is negating or eliminating any aspect of the child that poses a threat to *her survival*. At this point the child's self-development is at greatest risk.

Initially, the child responds to what is experienced as an accelerating risk to its survival by intensifying its sadistic control of an increasingly dangerous object – a borderline or psychotic mother. But what recourse does the child have available if its sadism fails to satisfactorily control a psychotic mother? In such cases, the child is likely to abandon its sadomasochistic relationship with the object and regress to reliance upon self-preservative aggression with the aim of eliminating a too painful reality by psychotic withdrawal or the destruction of its objects.

I have found Rycroft's definition to be closest to my own understanding of a borderline personality, that is someone: 'who is on the border between Neurosis and Psychosis, i.e. either one whose psychopathology defies categorisation, or one whose mechanisms are psychotic but whose behaviour does not warrant his being treated as psychotic. The usage arises from the fact that diagnostic systems assume that neurosis and psychosis are mutually exclusive, which clinical observation show they are not' (Rycroft 1968: 14). Given the ambiguity of the term, it could still be argued that one of the differences between the perverse solution in the neurotic and the perverse solution in the borderline is the amount of reality that the perversion has preserved. The perverse solution in the borderline individual preserves less reality than it does in the neurotic.

I would now like to turn to some clinical material in order to illustrate the defensive function of sadistic perversion, with special reference to fantasy.

The case of Mr J

Mr J is a handsome dark-haired 21-year-old with a self-conscious extravert manner. He made a special point of telling me in our first interview that he is actively heterosexual and has had several girlfriends.

Mr J's father is a probation officer whom he respects and loves. He regards his father as clever, easy-going, friendly and caring, but not emotionally close during his childhood and adolescence. Mother is seen as an hysterical extravert who is not really interested in him. I learned that before his parents divorced, his mother had been fascinated by gay clubs and had taken her husband to them.

Mr J saw himself as obedient and pliable until his parents divorced when he was 12 and father left him at home with his mother who treated him like a 'kicking post'. He began truanting and was obnoxious and defiant towards older men and male teachers. However, he was impressed by the flamboyance of the gay nightclub scene, and after leaving school he worked in gay clubs serving customers while wearing a pair of shorts with braces. It was there that he met a wealthy Greek man and eventually moved in with him.

Mr J recalled the night he and his homosexual lover took his mother to a gay club. He particularly remembers his mother smiling approval when he and his lover held hands. Eventually, Mr J acknowledged his bitter disappointment that his mother was not interested in his heterosexual development and was excited by his homosexual attachment.

Two months later he moved out after meeting a new girlfriend, Jane. Mr J became sexually promiscuous with women and had no respect for them, but felt that he had to prove himself as a man, often comparing himself with his current girlfriend's ex-boyfriend. Still later Mr J told me with embarrassment about his first homosexual relationship when he was 18 with an older flatmate, with whom he indulged in mutual masturbation. He had asked if his friend would urinate on him and the friend agreed.

Mr J recalled that it was at about the time of his parents' separation that he became aroused by young girls. He eventually told me that he masturbated to fantasies of 8-year-old girls. This emerged when Sylvia, his current girlfriend had an abortion. This stimulated anxieties about intimacy and fears of being annihilated by women that he defended against through sadistic fantasies involving young girls and 'jamming my cock into their mouths'. He felt strong as he wrapped his arms around their pure clean bodies. He consciously thought of 6-year-olds as adults and had no sense of the generational boundaries or bodily barriers. Mr J thought about children all the time. With shame and guilt he told me that he would spend his spare time hunting young girls in council flats. Pre-pubertal girls found his charm irresistible. He regularly exposed his genitals to young girls in the street and invited others up to his flat on a pretext of playing an exciting game, and then touched their genitals.

It emerged that his fantasy about young girls included mothers who procured daughters for him, wittingly or unwittingly making their children available directly or by failing to keep them safe. He recounted his exploits with little girls to demonstrate my inability to stop him, as his father had failed to stake a claim for his son and provide an alternative to the seductive mother. In the transference it became clear that Mr J wanted to elicit a gratifying collusion with me, his mother in the transference, that is someone who would be voyeuristically excited by his sadistic use of children. At a deeper level Mr J had projected the despair and confusion he felt with his mother onto little girls, seduced them into dependence upon him and then shocked them with a moment of betrayal when he touched their genitals.

Near the end of his therapy Mr J told me that he brought a kitten back to his room, even though his flatmate had told him from the beginning that animals were not allowed in the flat. Mr J then told me that he planned to take the cat to his mother to see if she would look after it for him. The cat represented Mr J's inability to think realistically about caring for another object. However, this incident was also understood as an enactment of Mr J's experience of himself as the lost kitten, which he could not look after, and his wish for his mother to properly care for him.

Unfortunately, Mr J's recognition of an uncared for, unwanted kitten-self became intolerable for him and uncontainable in his therapy. He reversed the experience of being left by his father by abruptly terminating his treatment after a year. In this way he also protected his illusion of adult heterosexuality in the face of unacceptable paedophilic wishes, which were revived in the transference as he began to trust me more.

Mr J's experience of being his mother's 'kicking post' mobilised self-preservative aggression which was libidinised, that is transformed into sadism and directed towards little girls who did not pose the same threat as his mother or girlfriend. In this way Mr J utilised paedophilia to preserve the object and ensure his survival.

Psychoanalysis has been criticised for seeing homosexuality as a perversion in the same way as fetishism, paedophilia, etc. In the case of Mr J, he recalls that his paedophilic interest in little girls, which began at the age of 12 when his parents separated, predated his homosexual activity and functioned to defend against anxieties associated with his mother and heterosexuality. Mr J's shame and guilt about acting upon his fantasies of sex with young girls, who would be unable to threaten or resist him, contributed to a defensive move toward sexual relationships with men. When this homosexual solution to paedophilic fantasies broke down, Mr J engaged in heterosexual relationships with women that gratified paedophilic fantasies and co-existed with sexual abuse of young girls. Freud (1920) distinguished between homosexuality and other sexual aberrations, arguing that homosexuals who come into treatment are not representative of the whole group; many homosexuals are not ill, cannot be 'cured', can relate to others as whole objects, and there is a capacity for love, concern and sublimation. The homosexuals whom I have seen at the Portman Clinic are not typical of the group as a whole; they are violent and perverse, and their sexuality is disturbing either to themselves or other people. The subject is contentious. It is probably more accurate to speak of different kinds of homosexuality, as one would refer to types of heterosexuality, but that would lead us into another chapter. Nor are the categories necessarily fixed: Mr J, for example, can be seen to be retreating from homosexuality into paedophilic activity with young girls. Many people are actively bisexual, or find their sexual orientation changes over time.

Aggression as reactive or instinctual

The view that perversion arises out of the vicissitudes of aggression takes the reader into an area of psychoanalytic theory where there is widespread disagreement. This chapter can do no more than briefly sketch some of the contending theories about the nature of aggression.

Self-preservative aggression has been described in this chapter as a primal reaction pattern triggered by danger. However, many psychoanalysts follow Freud, who viewed aggression as a drive, with a need for the discharge of organically based energy. Freud's instinct theory has never been substantiated (see Glasser 1998, Hartmann et al. 1949), and is currently under scrutiny from believers and non-believers alike. For instance, Michael Feldman (2000), an advocate of the death drive, uses a case study to argue that the aim of the death instinct is not to kill or annihilate the object, but to maintain a link with the object, albeit a tormenting one. According to Feldman, gratification is not derived from a fusion with the life instinct and consequent libidinisation, but is 'an essential element of such a destructive drive' (p. 64).

James Grotstein (2000) thinks that viewing the death drive as antagonistic to the life instinct is misleading. He views the death instinct as another dimension of the life instinct with a protective and adaptive function that allows for 'partial-to-total death of the mind if the mothering person fails to attune, hold, and/or contain her infant's inchoate infinite distress' (p. 477).

At the other end of the psychoanalytic spectrum, David Black (2001), following his analysis of Freud's arguments based on evolution and neuro-anatomy in support of his hypothesis of a death drive, concludes that the death instinct was a detour of historical interest to psychoanalysis, but 'as such, probably merits no future in psychoanalytic thinking' (p. 185). However, paradoxically, the death drive proved to be fruitful for future developments in psychoanalysis. Black draws attention to Freud's notion of the mutual 'binding' of the drives that is particularly germane to my emphasis in this chapter on the libidinisation of aggression, which transforms the gratification that results from aggressive negation of the object to gratification being derived from control of the object. In this way, self-preservative aggression becomes sadism.

Some thoughts about working with perverse individuals

Translating an understanding of perversion into an effective treatment is an extremely difficult and complex process. Psychoanalysis as a treatment discipline relies upon the recognition and understanding of the transference, that is the transfer of wishes, fantasies, and anxieties associated with important people from one's past onto the analyst, and the countertransference, which is the analyst's pre-conscious or unconscious reaction to the impact of the transference. There are two aspects of the transference which are played out in a session:

- the patient's perception of the analyst as a transference figure
- the patient's evocation or provocation of the analyst in order to actualise elements of the transference, that is to bring to life in the session the object the patient expects to find.

The analytic clinician would expect the perverse patient to relate to the therapist with the same defences as those he employs in his or her perversion. When we return to Mr J, the patient in the case example, we can see that he relied upon projection to control unbearable aspects of his inner world by assaulting young girls. Mr J, who was adept at relating to little girls at their level in order to win their confidence, trust and hope, was preoccupied with trying to win my trust and inspire hope in the effectiveness of therapy. Patients like Mr J will be skilled at 'reading' the practitioner's valuation of his own work and can readily 'co-operate' with assessment or therapy, or simulate attitudes and behaviours consciously or unconsciously promoted by caretakers. The individual suffering from a sexual deviation is likely to rely upon compliance, imitation and simulation to protect himself from the intrusion and rejection he expects from the authority figures represented by the diagnostician, therapist or any professional, just as he did with his parents.

Elsewhere (Campbell 1994) I have written that those working with people suffering from a perversion will be familiar with this phenomenon. This is not a self-conscious pretence. Just as the paedophile actually believes that he or she is their child victim's best friend, sensitive babysitter or helpful tutor, he or she actually believes they are good clients who are co-operating by acknowledging their abusive behaviour, etc. These simulations are believable for the professional because the patient believes them himself.

Nevertheless, the true self beneath the compliance will wage a 'guerrilla campaign' against the therapeutic process that, he believes, aims to take him over completely, just as his abuser had once done. The subtle or gross signs of resistance offer the professional a more reliable clue to the whereabouts of the true self, which may be so deeply buried that even the patient has lost contact with it. It is unlikely that the seriously disturbed sexually deviant person will ever find his or her way back to their actual self without the help of a professional.

However, any individual or group treatment or management programme that adopts a macho or an authoritarian role or focuses exclusively on behavioural change without understanding the individual's internal conflicts and anxieties is in danger of being sabotaged by the abuser's capacity to adopt language, concepts and whatever is suggested as 'normative' behaviour, in the same way as the chameleon takes on the colour of its environment as a protection against attack. Since the change is based on simulated attitudes and behaviour, it only *appears* to be change. Momentarily, one will see changes in the abuser's behaviour as the result of this kind of identification with the therapist, probation officer, child care protection worker, etc., but since the underlying anxieties are not affected, the abuser is at risk of returning to abusive behaviour once the external supports have been taken away and old anxieties re-emerge. Put into the language of child abuse, any treatment or management programme that does not take the abuser's internal world into account is very likely to be victimised by the abuser in the same way as the child victims are: that is, by being deceived by the outwardly positive but inwardly fraudulent behaviour of these clients. When professionals discover they have been deceived they should guard against reacting in an abusive way by abandoning their clients or adopting a punitive attitude (Campbell 1994).

Conclusion

Moralising and 'political correctness' have interfered with efforts to understand the perplexing subject of perversion. There is no place for moral judgements and politics in the psychoanalytic study and treatment of perversion. Freud reminds us that we all have within us the roots of perverse development. Perversions occur in both sexes, adults and adolescents, heterosexuals as well as homosexuals. From a psychoanalytic perspective, no one has the right to cast the first stone.

The task of translating an understanding of perversion into effective treatment is extremely difficult and complex. The practitioner will be hampered by the limited state of knowledge of perversion, and by his own unconscious processes and unresolved conflicts. In order to be effective, mental health practitioners and psychoanalysts have to continually scrutinise themselves for prejudice, fears, phobias, or anxieties associated with perverse fantasies or behaviour. Any psychoanalytically oriented treatment is an intersubjective process involving not only the professional, but also the perverse individual who may play a role in his subsequent abuse within the treatment. For instance, a person suffering from a perversion may expect the therapist or social worker or 'the system' to relate to him in an abusive way, based on his experience of the way his mother and father related to him. It is not unusual for such a patient to attempt to provoke the professional into a response of punishment or collusion (such as feeling sorry for an abuser in such a way as to avoid recognition and understanding of his or her maliciousness), in order to confirm the patient's expectation that he will not be taken seriously as a whole person.

References

Black, D. (2001) 'Mapping a detour: why did Freud speak of a Death Drive?' *British Journal of Psychotherapy* 18, 2: 185–98.

Campbell, D. (1994) 'Breaching the shame shield: thoughts on the assessment of adolescent child sexual abusers', *Journal of Child Psychotherapy* 20: 309–26.

Cannon, W. B. (1939) *The Wisdom of the Body*, London: Kegan Paul, Trench, Trubner.

Chasseguet-Smirgel, J. (1976) 'Freud and female sexuality: the consideration of some blind spots in the exploration of the Dark Continent', *International Journal of Psychoanalysis* 57: 275–86.

—— (1985) *Creativity and Perversion*, London: Free Association Books.

Feldman, M. (2000) 'Some views on the manifestation of the death instinct in clinical work', *International Journal of Psychoanalysis* 81: 53–65.

Freud, S. (1905) 'A case of hysteria', *Standard Edition*, vol. 1, p. 309, London: Hogarth Press.

—— (1905) 'Three essays on the theory of sexuality', *Standard Edition*, vol. 7, pp. 136–248, London: Hogarth Press.

—— (1919) 'A child is being beaten', *Standard Edition*, vol. 17, pp. 175–202, London: Hogarth Press.

—— (1920) 'Beyond the pleasure principle', *Standard Edition*, vol. 18, pp. 3–64, London: Hogarth Press.

—— (1927) 'Fetishism', *Standard Edition*, vol. 21, pp. 149–57, London: Hogarth Press.

—— (1938) 'Splitting of the ego in the process of defence', *Standard Edition*, vol. 23, pp. 271–8, London: Hogarth Press.

Glasser, M. (1978) 'The role of the superego in exhibitionism', *International Journal of Psychoanalytic Psychotherapy* 7: 396–403.

—— (1979) 'Some aspects of the role of aggression in the perversions', in I. Rosen (ed.) *Sexual Deviations*, 2nd edn, Oxford: Oxford University Press, pp. 278–305.

—— (1992) 'Problems in the psychoanalysis of certain narcissistic disorders', *International Journal of Psychoanalysis* 73: 493–503.

—— (1998) 'On violence – A preliminary communication', *International Journal of Psychoanalysis* 79: 887–902.

Glover, E. (1956) 'The relation of perversion-formation to the development of reality sense', in E. Glover (ed.) *On the Early Development of the Mind*, London: Imago.

Grotstein, J. (2000) 'Some considerations of "hate" and a reconsideration of the death instinct', *Psychoanalytic Inquiry* 20: 462–80.

Hartmann, H. et al. (1949) 'Notes on the theory of aggression', *Psychoanalytic Study of the Child*, 3: 9–36.

Lantos, B. (1958) 'The two genetic derivations of aggression with reference to sublimation and neutralisation', *International Journal of Psychoanalysis* 39: 116–20.

Limentani, A. (1977) 'The differential diagnosis of homosexuality', *British Journal of Medical Psychology* 50: 209–216.

McDougall, J. (1970) 'Homosexuality in women', in J. Chasseguet-Smirgel (ed.) *Female Sexuality*, London: Karnac.

Meloy, J.R. (1988) *The Psychopathic Mind – Origins, Dynamics and Treatment*, London: Jason Aronson.

Rycroft, C. (1968) *A Critical Dictionary of Psychoanalysis*, London: Nelson.

Sandler, J. and Sandler, A.-M. (1992) 'Psychoanalytic technique and the theory of psychic change', *Bulletin of the Anna Freud Centre* 15: 35–51.

Stoller, R. (1975) 'Transsexualism and transvestism', in R. Stoller *The Transsexual Experiment*, London: Hogarth Press.

Suggestions for further reading

You will not be surprised that I recommend beginning with Freud, particularly his (1919) paper 'A child is being beaten' *Standard Edition*, vol. 17, pp. 175–202 (London: Hogarth Press); 'Fetishism' (1927) *Standard Edition*, vol. 21, pp. 149–57; and 'Splitting in the ego in the process of defence' (1938), *Standard Edition*, vol. 23, pp. 271–8, which was published posthumously in 1940. More recent work that has extended our thinking about perversion includes: Janine Chasseguet-Smirgel's *Creativity and Perversion* (London: Free Association Books, 1985), and her (1976) paper 'Freud and female sexuality: the consideration of some blind spots in the exploration of the

"Dark Continent" ', *International Journal of Psychoanalysis* 57: 275–86; Mervin Glasser's (1978) paper 'The role of the superego in exhibitionism', *International Journal of Psychoanalytic Psychotherapy* 7: 396–403, and 'Some aspects of the role of aggression in the perversions', in I. Rosen (ed.) *Sexual Deviations*, 2nd edn (Oxford: Oxford University Press, 1979, pp. 278–305); Adam Limentani's (1977) paper 'The differential diagnosis of homosexuality', *British Journal of Medical Psychology* 50: 209–16; 'Homosexuality in women' by Joyce McDougall in J. Chasseguet-Smirgel (ed.) *Female Sexuality* (London: Karnac, 1970, pp. 171–212); and a paper by Robert Stoller entitled 'Transsexualism and transvestism' in *The Transsexual Experiment* (London: Hogarth Press, 1975, pp. 170–81).

Chapter 16

Trauma and the possibility of recovery

Caroline Garland

As well as pleasure, excitement and happiness, vital ingredients in a life, we encounter shock or turmoil or pain – equally, even though unwelcome, part of the experience of being alive. Recovery from upsetting or disturbing states of mind often takes time, but out of the recovery can come added strength, wisdom and resilience. Perhaps this is a part of what is meant by *learning from experience*. This chapter, however, is about why, at some times and for some people, the support of family and friends is not enough, and a traumatic event remains an open wound, deeply preoccupying to the wounded and often very perplexing and taxing for the unwounded. Friends may say to the sufferer, 'put it out of your mind', or 'what you need is a good rest'. And not only friends – in a much publicised rape case in the mid-1990s, the judge seemed to feel that all that was needed for the young lady to recover her equilibrium was a large cheque and a holiday in the sun.

There appear to be two quite separate attitudes to trauma around in society. It is part of common wisdom that horrific events disrupt the personality, and yet somehow that knowledge lives side by side in a disconnected fashion with the equally common belief that people can 'get over' such events quickly, especially if given a rest or monetary compensation. This is not the experience of those who treat survivors of seriously traumatic events, nor is it the experience of many survivors of both large and public or small and private catastrophes. It not only takes time, but also hard internal work before a new internal equilibrium can be established.

This is because a traumatic event is one that causes damage to the functioning of the mental apparatus; damage which can go on to become a chronic deterioration in states of mind and in personal relationships, as well as creating unhelpful alterations in habitual defensive procedures. As well as understanding the impact of certain kinds of event on the mind, we also need to know about individual differences: why some people recover better or more quickly than others, and some do not recover at all. By 'recovery' is not meant achieving a pre-trauma condition once more, but achieving a state of mind in which the event is not felt to be the only or the most significant experience in that individual's life as a whole.

In this chapter I try to show some of the ways in which a psychoanalytic understanding of trauma can throw light on these troubled and troubling aspects of human behaviour, taking into account both the internal world of the individual and the external world of the event. Traumatic events of course can happen at any stage of life. The child's internal world is deeply and irrevocably formed by its early relations with its primary objects (caretakers) and these, in combination with the infant's accompanying phantasies about the nature of its objects, will determine the nature of its engagement with the world. When trauma is severe and prolonged in childhood it can affect adversely the whole of adult development and personality. Sometimes childhood trauma is 'forgotten' – split off from conscious awareness and denied. Sometimes too the significance of events in childhood is not recognised and felt (that is to say truly understood) until many years later, when the child – perhaps by now an adult – finds itself in a setting safe enough to allow such early states of mind to emerge. However, it can also be difficult to distinguish between fact and phantasy when it comes to memories of childhood. The earlier the assaults on the ego, and the more extreme they may have been, the harder it is to sort out what may in reality have happened. The validity of 'recovered memories' has been the subject of painful debates between public and professionals. In psychoanalytic treatment, the emphasis will be on the nature of the derivatives of those early relationships, whatever they may have been, as they emerge in the room between the patient and the analyst. This means that establishing the facts of the past, which anyway may not be possible, is felt to be less crucial than establishing the fact of the patient's reality as it is lived out in the present. This is the area in which therapeutic engagement can be most powerful in effecting change for the better.

The nature of breakdown

Traumatic events can equally often erupt in adult life, making an impact on relatively formed and reasonably well-functioning individuals. After such an event, there are two (often overlapping) states of mind that emerge in the survivor. There is the initial breakdown, a catastrophic disruption of normal mental functioning, which is what happens when there is an event big or sudden or horrible enough to overwhelm the mind's everyday ability to filter, or screen out excessive or painful stimuli. Freud (1920) called this screening capacity 'the protective shield', psychologically accurate if neurologically invisible. The survivor is shocked and confused, perhaps unable to take in what has happened. He or she may become silent and withdrawn, or compulsively talkative and active, but in either case normal functioning is in a state of disintegration. Thinking or behaviour can become incoherent. This is effectively a breakdown: a breakdown of the individual's defences, deployed since the beginnings of life against overwhelming anxiety. This stage can last for hours or days, but when the traumatic event is prolonged and severe it can be seen to be more or less universal, overriding individual differences.

The second stage is slower to make itself visible. To the outside world, the survivor may appear to be functioning once more. He or she may even be back at work, or socialising again. However, internally the picture may be different. This longer term internal situation is the outcome of two powerful factors. First, there is the way in which we have from infancy onwards attached all our experience to some notion of an agent, an object felt to be responsible for this or that perception, sensation or other internal state. Not surprisingly, the kind of relationship associated with a catastrophic event is felt to be intensely persecutory, linking with the earliest and most paranoid of phantasies about the nature of our objects, which is to say the safety of the universe. It is not surprising that survivors can feel overwhelmed with confusion, demoralisation and hopelessness. Second, there is our powerful inbuilt drive to organise and make sense of our own experience, perhaps especially the apparently arbitrary. In the struggle to give meaning or sense to the catastrophic event we link it with what is already familiar, or with whatever resembles it in some important respect. This process, which is linked to what Freud (1920) called 'binding', is partly responsible for the entrenched quality that so often characterises a traumatised response.

A trauma in the present will link up with troubled relationships and disturbing events from the past and give fresh life to old or buried issues which may have been more or less manageable up to that point. This factor makes an important contribution to individual variation in the response to an event. The certain outcome is that whatever the physical damage, the long-term problem will be the repair of the survivor's relations with his social world: both the actual people around him and the representations of those figures, or parts or functions of figures, that he carries inside him for good or ill – his internal objects. Eventually the current external event will cease to feel like a new experience, since it is the external confirmation of ancient fears and phantasies about the unpredictability or untrustworthiness of internal objects, of the world itself. In severe trauma, states of chronic mistrust can develop and are hard to shift. It seems as though in the unconscious no one can believe in chance or in accident: there must be *a reason* why this terrible thing happened, a *somebody* who made it happen, or who failed to prevent its happening. These are the difficult issues that have to be addressed in treatment.

In fact the history of psychoanalysis and the development of Freud's understanding of trauma are closely linked. In his earliest work on mental disorder, Freud (1893) believed that hysteria was the product of the repressed memory of certain very intense or painful experiences. The feelings that accompanied such experiences were, he proposed, preserved in a hidden and 'strangulated' state. These bottled-up feelings then emerged in 'hysterical symptoms' (symptoms for which there was no clear organic cause) but which managed to be symbolic of the repressed memory. At that time, Freud felt that *catharsis cures*: if the original events are brought into consciousness and put into words (the 'talking cure'), especially if they are accompanied by the original intense feeling they provoked, then the symptoms will disappear. Although Freud at first believed that repressed traumatic memories were invariably sexual, he later writes of his frustrated conclusion that although phantasies of sexual seduction by the parents might be universal, actual seductions were not. Yet it was this recognition, however unwelcome at the time, which led to his revelatory understanding of the importance of infantile phantasy.

Once released from his belief that early trauma was the sole basis for neurosis, his interest in the external event as a pathogenic factor diminished and he developed and deepened his revolutionary exploration of the unconscious, along with an increasing respect for the power and force of psychic reality. In 'Mourning and melancholia' (1915b) Freud went on to lay the foundations for modern psychoanalysis through opening up a view of the mind as an *internal world* populated by objects in dynamic relations with each other. This work was developed by others, most powerfully by Melanie Klein through her highly original work with children.

Treating trauma

Treatment of the survivors of traumatic events involves an *application* of these and other aspects of psychoanalytic theory, making use of a psycho-analytic understanding of behaviour in the service of a particular individual's well-being. Treatment, we might say, begins with the sense of being listened to by someone whose intention is to understand. If the therapist can take in something of the magnitude of what has happened to the patient, internally and externally, without being altogether overwhelmed by it, there is the hope once more of re-establishing a world with meaning in it. Traumatic events often obliterate the meaning the world once had – wipe out its original struc-tures, expectations and values – and it becomes necessary to build it anew, taking these deeply troubling events into account.

However, traumatised patients can present therapists with some difficult issues. The damage to the patient is often obvious and painful, stirring up a powerful wish to help in its repair. The temptation for the unwary or untrained therapist is to offer him or herself as a good object and this wish may overwhelm the analytic stance, in which, for instance, the feeling of helplessness experienced by the therapist is used as a means of learning about the patient's state of mind. Freud (1926) pointed out that prolonged help-lessness is the essence of trauma. The horror of this helplessness is often communicated both consciously and unconsciously by the patient to the therapist, who needs to recognise, contain and perhaps interpret this state of affairs, rather than to act it out by being 'helpful'.

Effective treatment is made more difficult by two further factors. Traumatic events inevitably stir up considerable amounts of hostility in the survivor, which tend to be projected straight out of awareness and into the external source of grievance. It is strikingly difficult to help traumatised patients recognise and take back their own hostile and destructive impulses, rather than to continue to attribute all hostility and aggression to the other, the perpetrator (whether state-sanctioned torture, or British Rail, or shoddy builders in earthquake areas). The failure to know about one's own violent impulses inevitably leaves such patients in the position of chronic victim. Sometimes this may amount to no more than a phobic avoidance of places or times that trigger memories of the traumatic event. At first, and up to a point, avoidance may not only work but also have some self-protective function. When an event has been particularly terrible, it cannot be taken in all at once, and the survivor may need to proceed gradually with its processing and with the digestion of its full implications.

However over time it can be maladaptive. Gradually larger and larger areas of the world can seem increasingly able to serve as reminders of the avoided event. I saw a man who was caught in the King's Cross underground fire, by now many years ago. At first he could not continue to travel to work by tube: it stirred up too much anxiety. Gradually, this avoidant behaviour spread to trains in general, and then to travel in cars, and then by any means other than on foot. Later still, he became overcome with anxiety if his children proposed to travel anywhere either. Here, the whole world outside the immediate confines of the home came to seem dangerous, and this man's life became increasingly restricted by his growing agoraphobia. His rage about what had been done to him had been projected outwards into the external world, which came to seem to him increasingly violent and dangerous. Sometimes it is the whole mind that is evacuated, often self-destructively through, for example, alcohol or drugs, which blur or obliterate the memories and associated feelings. Sometimes this evacuation takes place in a dangerous or violent fashion through action – suicide, murder.

The second and most important difficulty in providing treatment is the patient's inability to get his or her experiences into a form in which they can be held in the mind, *thought about* and worked over in symbolic form, rather than being *gotten rid of* in various ways. The resort to action as opposed to thought is common. An adolescent who had been raped, but who had kept this fact secret from her friends, became very disturbed one evening to hear her friends apparently joking about rape. She left the pub in which they had been drinking and climbed 40 feet up some scaffolding nearby, scaring her companions who begged her to come down. From her point of view the fear and disturbance was now located in them rather than in her, and she was able to *look down on them*, and on the fear, from a lofty position.

Although phobic avoidance and the use of drink and drugs is common, *getting rid of* is often achieved through habitual mechanisms of defence (denial, projection, projective and/or introjective identification). Shifts in *identifications* are fundamental to the defences employed by survivors dealing with trauma. I suggest that the renewed clinging to certain kinds of identification are resorted to by the survivor as a retreat by the traumatised ego to a kind of pre-thought position. The unconscious aim is twofold. First, identification is a means of avoiding an unbearable mental pain, suffered when it is feared that the damage to oneself and one's internal objects is beyond repair. A young bomb disposal officer had failed to complete his work in time to avoid being blinded and having his legs blown off. The colleague he was working with was killed outright. He lost his wish and his will to be alive. He turned down the chance of a psychoanalytic therapy, which would have meant facing the pain of his radically altered life, and he retreated to isolation, obscurity and a long death-in-life. His identification was with the dead colleague and with those whom he had failed to rescue in earlier missions, compounded by earlier disturbing phantasies concerning the nature of the relationship between his parents. Second, post-traumatic shifts in identification can be an attempt at recovery of thought – *reculer pour mieux sauter*. Within the protection provided by this retreat away from thought and into an identification, a form of proto-thought, it can be possible from time to time to make small forays out into the world once more, by *thinking about what one is doing before one does it*. Each time, some small ground can be regained in the areas of imagining, remembering, considering, reflecting and deciding – each of these functions of thought, rather than simply of action.

Clinical experience tends to show that the choice of object for identification depends upon the survivor's conception of the original event. When it feels as though something painful and unpleasant has been done to oneself, the movement is towards an identification with the hostile object who is felt to have brought about that state of affairs. This reverses the direction of the traumatic event, provides the sufferer with a sense of agency once more (as opposed to helplessness), and perhaps allows for the gratification of revenge when, as sometimes happens, the done-to now has become the doer. Freud's (1920) description of the little boy's game with the cotton-reel is a beautifully observed and understood instance of this process. Upset by his mother's comings and goings, the child repeatedly threw out of his pram a cotton-reel on a string ('Gone'), and then hauled it in again ('Da!' – *there* it is!) This child did not, as modern children tend to do, aim his act directly at his mother, but instead threw out an inanimate object which we imagine stood for, or symbolised the mother. (In fact, it might also represent her act, what he feels she does to him. Either way, he is employing a sophisticated system of symbolic representation to stand for the original events.)

When on the other hand someone has survived an event in which others have died, the survivor may be left with a considerable burden of guilt. He may feel that his life has been bought at the expense of others' deaths (Freud

1915). Making an identification with the dead or damaged, ceasing to have a life with anything lively or pleasurable in it, can feel like a way of avoiding that guilt (as in the bomb disposal officer), and perhaps also therefore of avoiding anxieties about vengeful ghosts. The ghosts, as Freud points out in this paper, are the representations of those over whom the survivor has triumphed, by remaining alive where they have died. This is particularly so when the survivor has lost others who are felt to be central to his well-being, or feels himself in some way to be responsible for their loss.

Here are some examples from current clinical practice, to illustrate ways in which painful mental events can be evaded, even temporarily obliterated, rather than thought about and worked through, and their consequences dealt with. Although these difficulties in mentalising painful events – thinking about them – have striking features in common, the particular expression of the defence is unique to each patient.

Clinical examples

An identification with a rejecting object

Traumatic events do not have to involve major external disasters. Here is an example from adult life, occurring within a full analysis. The patient, a man in his fifties, felt himself to be at the top of his profession, a 'top lawyer'. He was an only child, one of those war babies who met his father for the first time when he was four and a half years old. Neither parent was ever quite forgiven for their reunion, which exposed the boy to an Oedipal anguish that dominated his adult life both with his family and at work, and his analyst was hard put to modify this state of affairs. In the early hours of a Thursday morning I had become unexpectedly unwell. I telephoned him at home to cancel his Thursday and his Friday sessions, telling him I would certainly be back at work on Monday. All his sessions were at 7 am. On Monday there was no patient and no message. At about 7.20 I went downstairs to the front door of the building to get the newspaper, and I found a note from him dropped into the letterbox. He had had to 'dash into work early for a crucial meeting' and he had just had time to write this note, put it into an envelope and drive out of his way to deliver it on his way to his crucial meeting. On Tuesday he was 20 minutes late for his session, and seemed to have forgotten that he had not attended at all the day before. During the half-hour we had left, some work was done on the significance of the 'crucial' meeting having cropped up when it did, and I thought he understood something about his need to reverse an unpleasant event which he saw as having been done *by* me, not a 'top' person, *to* him. He left the session with many apologetic flourishes. Not surprisingly in retrospect, he missed the Wednesday session too without warning. Two sessions cancelled at very short notice by me had had to be matched by two sessions cancelled without warning by him. My interpretations after the first missed session had not been able to touch the imperative nature of the urge to even the score in an actual, bodily, concrete way.

This episode and Freud's grandson's game with the cotton-reel have certain features in common. In each case, what was experienced as traumatic was one of those painful but necessary developmental steps. A male is left temporarily by a woman, *the mother*, either in actuality or in the transference. In both cases the mother is felt to be a central figure, a good object in spite of her absences and the young child's growing struggle with the knowledge of her relationship with father. In each case there is a *reversal* of the direction of the original action: the one who has been left now becomes the one who leaves, or who rejects. This implies that the agent has ceased in some respects to function only as himself, and has divided himself in two. He now presents himself to himself, and to his mother (or mother in the transference), as in some central respect identified with the mother who went away. In a complementary way, the other, the original leaver, has now been identified as the one who is left. Thus there is both an *introjective* identification and a *projective* identification. The introjected object has clearly already had projected into it some complicated feelings. The lawyer behaved as though the absence had been the kind of casual insult that 'top people' habitually inflict on lesser beings. It may reflect the parents' lack of comprehension of the terrible shock he had endured when his father returned and deprived him quite suddenly of sole possession of his mother. In the cotton-reel game, the object that is identified with is one that goes out worryingly often, even though she also returns. The reasons for mother's absence seem to be puzzling the child. I say this because there is no implicit hypothesis about the *causation* of the absence contained in the nature of the identification with the object that absents herself. Perhaps he is struggling with the idea that mothers are just like that, they go away, and you simply have to put up with it and be 'good' (Freud's word for him) because mothers don't like upset or protest. In both cases, it is clear that what is having to be dealt with is the experience of getting stuck with some anxiety-producing event that cannot properly be located in the mind and thought about – and which therefore has to be enacted, or re-enacted, in a concrete or bodily way, as a way of representing it to the self.

However, there are also important ways in which these two incidents differ. In the first, the 'top lawyer' cannot bear to know he has any feelings at all about my absence. Perhaps that would make him feel small and unimportant, as he did when his big powerful soldier father re-entered the home and took away his mother. Those feelings have to be emptied in their entirety into me, who caused his distress, and this can only be done by enacting the entire procedure in reverse, and, I think, watching carefully the effect on me. Freud's grandson, on the other hand, was to some extent aware that he felt sad when his mother went away and joyful ('Da!') when she returned.

Identification with the lost object; the recovery of mind

My next, more complex example shows how with some patients, there can, over time, be real shifts away from defensively formed total identifications and towards a recovery of mind. A young woman of 23, an only child, presented in a state of shock and breakdown. She was struggling to hold on to her mental functioning after a very affecting traumatic event. Her mother had recently been murdered by her husband, the patient's stepfather, with repeated hammer blows to the head. He had then tried and failed to kill himself, and at the time of her first meeting with me he was still unconscious and in intensive care. In her meetings with me I felt there was a powerful enactment of the acute problems this presented her with. The identification with her murdered mother, refusing to lose her by keeping her alive by means of the identification, meant that she too lost her mind. She lost her capacity to use words at all. At these times she entered a kind of mute, trance-like state which had so frightened her boyfriend that twice he had called an ambulance. Her alternative was to sever meaningful connections with the words she was using and chatter in a manic over-animated way about everything she was managing to sort out for herself since the murder.

In the first meeting, I thought that I could see the way she had begun to find of solving this problem. This was to split her mother in two. There was a secret mother who was still alive and lively, hidden inside her and with whom she could safely be identified in an almost triumphant way. There was also a brutally murdered mother whom she had to get rid of if she was to function at all. She did this by talking about the actual moments of the murder most tellingly, so vividly that I found myself shaken, for a moment almost unable to get my breath.

I managed to describe to her the way in which she got me to feel the horror of the murder, to have as it were the murdered mother inside me, so that she could feel free to keep the live mother all to herself, inside her and away from danger. She seemed to get hold of this notion with both surprise and a kind of relief. At the beginning of the second session she went straight back to it. She had said to her boyfriend after the session that when she had told me something about the way her mother had died, I had winced, and she had told him that she didn't think I'd winced in an 'oh poor you' kind of way. 'Do you know what I mean,' she said to me. 'There wasn't a kind of cow of a psychotherapist who talked and winced at all the appropriate moments, but actually it was genuine, it had made you think, "Oh God!" – and how weird that was, because it happened to me but it was you thinking "Agh".'

I left alone that reference to a 'cow of a psychotherapist' because it seemed to contain a spark of liveliness. Not all her own aggression to her mother had been projected into the stepfather. I thought in particular it enabled her to express some of her hatred of the mother who had been a cow for leaving her effectively orphaned, and of me for leaving her over the weekend. Yet there remained in this young woman a profound pull towards the literality of an identification and away from the 'mentality' of the thoughts about the murder.

For some weeks she was deeply possessed by the need to become pregnant, to keep alive the mother who had had her *in* her in a very literal way. It also meant that she tended to seize on new ideas with tremendous relief, as something to fill and occupy her mind, pushing out the all-too-vivid thoughts of the murder and thus keeping at bay the overwhelming urge to turn to an identification. At times this switched to an identification with the murdering stepfather, whom she was genuinely afraid of killing. A few weeks later, in fact she did perform an act of semi-symbolic murder, which was also a desperate further attempt to rid herself of the sense of being lumbered with the murdered object. She took various bits of her stepfather's clothes and pushed them through the letterbox of the woman with whom he'd been having an affair, together with a violent letter. In this act she carried out not an actual murder but a token, representative version of the murder. Very importantly, it contained both concrete elements (the hacked up clothes) and mentalised elements (the letter), both of which I thought had to be there if the projection of extreme distress was to work. Yet already there has been a shift away from the tendency to exist in a total introjective identification with the murdered mother toward something alive, if dangerous. (Murder, in this sense, can be seen as a defence against suicide.)

Over 18 months later there was a further shift away from an enacted identification and towards a recovery of her capacity to symbolise action through thought, in that she could verbalise a *wish* to do something, allowing the spoken words to stand for the action. She told me she still had in a bag in her attic the bloodstained dressing gown her mother had been wearing when she had been struck down. This stood in a concrete way for the last of her physical mother, and she could not yet relinquish it. She wanted instead to arrange her hair like her mother's, to put on the dressing gown, and to stalk down the ward in the prison hospital towards her imprisoned stepfather, to give him 'the fright of his life'. 'But,' she added, watching me carefully, 'I won't do it.' Here the identifications are complex – that with the murdered mother is clear, becoming her vengeful ghost; but also with the murderer, the man who gave her mother 'the fright of her life'. The element of rage in her has an important defensive function, as it must do in all those survivors who suffer from greatly increased irritability – a frequent post-traumatic symptom – since it has a powerful organising function as well as being a sign of life in its own right. The broken down fragments of the ego can reorganise themselves around a powerful state of rage, and give some semblance of coherence to a very damaged personality. (The violent irritability of borderline personalities is probably clung to for this kind of reason.)

A further 18 months later, this young woman, who was in a good partnership, gave birth to a healthy baby girl. At first her anxiety about the baby's well-being was overwhelming, going as far as midnight dashes to hospitals with a sleepy baby whom she was afraid was dying. Here I think the identification that was most overwhelming was that of being a failed mother, as in a sense her own was. She had longed for her presence during the pregnancy and had expressed anger with her mother's stupidity for not seeing what 'a dead loss' her husband had been, so avoiding being murdered. For her, the baby's crying was also her own, and it felt unbearable. However, after two months when the new family had somewhat settled down, and the baby was breastfeeding satisfactorily, she and her partner decided to try to help the baby move out of their own bed and into a crib. She decided that she would pick up the baby whenever it cried, and then put it down again in its own crib, instead of taking it once again into their bed. Here we can see the struggle to free herself from the overwhelming identification with the crying baby, and to function instead as the good, alive mother who is able to care for the little girl. Then she told me that whenever the baby cried, she would rush to it saying, 'Mummy's coming, Mummy's coming!' This was one of the only times I ever saw visible tears. She said, 'I'm saying it to her, but I'm also saying it to myself, though I know I'll never see *my* mother again.' I felt that for the time being she had been able to move out of the pull of some deeply unhelpful identifications and into a position where she could once again think her thoughts instead of having to enact them. She could in fact begin to mourn her mother, instead of being stuck with identifications that veered towards either melancholia or mania (Klein 1940).

For this young woman, the mourning for her murdered mother is proceeding. Much depends on how her life progresses. Some traumatic events are too great, and some are too sustained to allow for a wholly satisfactory recovery and some degree of dissociation from the physical details of the traumatic event may always remain. This may be a way of dealing with something that is too primitive, too central to the survivor's own identity, to be able to be symbolised, as with the murder of a girl's mother.

Other individuals cannot achieve this kind of move out of an identification and into a capacity for symbolic thought. When symbolic thinking remains impossible in the area of the trauma, the survivor is particularly susceptible to what is called a 'flashback'.

The flashback

A senior fireman had been awarded the highest honours for his work in rescuing a family in a near-fatal fire. However, after more than 20 years of work (and he was only in his early forties) he was now retired on sick pay, his marriage had ended and he lived alone in a state of alcoholic near-breakdown. During his first consultation he talked about how he used to manage after a fire in which things had not gone well. He said that when he'd had a bad day he couldn't go home right away, he'd hang about the station or the pub, having a few drinks with the crew, and waiting for it all to settle down. He'd be relatively calm by the time he went home, a place he regarded as an oasis of domesticity. He never talked about his work at home because he could not bear his wife and children to know what was going on inside his head – 'bodies' he called it, 'bits of bodies all burnt and blackened and twisted'. He told me he liked to do the cooking at home, because he'd learned to cook for the whole mess when he was a new recruit to the fire service and he enjoyed it. But it soon emerged that this was only the excuse. If his wife cooked, she'd sometimes let whatever it was catch on the bottom of the saucepan, and there'd be a whiff of burning, and he'd suddenly explode with rage. It terrified his wife, as well as puzzling her. He described her saying to him, 'But it's only a bit of bacon, look I'll do some more', but it was too late. He was caught in the flashback, terrified and angry, the anger being the attempt to hold himself in one piece by organising himself around the rage.

As I described earlier, the capacity to think about a traumatic event can be severely restricted. Indeed, in one sense that inability to think about something is what we mean when we say someone has been traumatised: we are talking about the existence of chronic damage to the mental apparatus. When the capacity to symbolise has gone, it becomes impossible to tell the difference between something that *stands for* a potential danger (a symbol) and something that *actually is* a potential danger. Thus any stimulus evocative of the original trauma will produce not recollection or thought or working through, but a flashback. Signal anxiety (Freud 1926) in the area of the trauma is invariably replaced by automatic anxiety, or the flashback. The flashback is external evidence of the (usually) discrete area of permanent damage to mental functioning created by severe trauma.

Hanna Segal's (1957) work on symbolisation is central to this way of understanding the long-term outcome of trauma. She makes a crucial distinction between a true *symbol* and a *symbolic equation*. In the second, something that the experiencing individual knows to differ from the thing symbolised is nevertheless felt about and responded to as though it were the thing itself. The fireman knew that the burning bacon was not a burning human being, but he felt about it and responded to it emotionally and physiologically as though it were. In a helpless way, his traumatised ego refused to recognise a distinction between the two, for the purposes of its own survival. Segal (1957) and Bion (1959) concur in their descriptions of how the loss of the internal container (our modern way of describing the psychic consequences of Freud's breach in the protective shield) results in the loss of the space in which mental activity, or symbolisation, can take place. The process of recovery therefore becomes impossible without a fresh reworking of experience within a process of containment. This is the point of a psychoanalytic understanding of the consequences of severe trauma. The containment provided by the analyst/therapist within a safe setting is the basis for the treatment of the traumatised individual, founded upon a repair or restoration of the internal good object, which in turn leads to a (cautious and provisional) renewal of trust in the external world. Interestingly, those traumatised by 'acts of God' (since we attribute even earthquakes and hurricanes to some kind of personal agency) may suffer no less in this respect than those who have suffered a direct personal assault, such as rape or a mugging.

In conclusion, the effect of traumatic events in adulthood can present the survivor with three major obstacles to the normal processes of assimilation, integration and recovery. The first is the process by which events in the present give fresh life to unresolved issues from the past, and become bound to them meaningfully and in an intractable way. The second is the refusal (inability) of the traumatised ego to recognise the existence of symbols in the area of the trauma. This can extend to words themselves – certain words (*burning* or *killed*, for instance) are felt to re-evoke the original events rather than simply to stand for them. 'Working through' – the analytical process that is necessary if traumatic events are going to be understood, thought about, and integrated into conscious functioning, rather than unconsciously sought out and helplessly repeated – is particularly difficult when some of the words one might use in treatment are felt to recreate the event itself. The third is the defensive resort to complex identifications and enactments, some of which are motivated by the need to avoid unbearable guilt, and others to avoid unbearable helplessness.

Psychoanalytic thinking and theory help us to understand the need for these defensive manoeuvres, the particularity of the forms they take, and the intransigent ways in which they operate. Most importantly, this form of treatment, whether in an individual or a group setting, also offers a route towards recovery. It cannot of course bring back the lost or dead, or put back the body parts that have been destroyed. This is the most painful of its limitations. Life for the survivor of a major trauma cannot be the same as the life that existed before the event, whether there has been lasting physical damage or not. There has to be a period of mourning for whatever has been lost, and mourning is always hard and prolonged work, even with a reasonably intact ego. The individual may not feel he or she has the personal resources to engage in this work, especially as some of the mourning must be for the lost aspects of the self – for the lost world of trust, the pre-trauma life and identity. Yet the work of mourning itself is crucial if the individual is to be able to move on from a life-breaking trauma, since mourning is a key process in the development (as it is in the recovery) of symbolic thought. When mourning fails, and thought remains impossible, the individual is stuck with a life conducted in terms of identifications, and their troubling enactments.

However, the treatment in psychoanalytical therapy of a patient who presents following a traumatic event, even many years later, offers the chance of a translation of these identifications and enactments into mental processes, sometimes for the first time. It makes possible a transition from the stage where the survivor is stuck with the trauma as the dominating feature of mental life, to a subsequent stage in which it has become a part of the whole, still present, still painful, but able to be contemplated without a flashback, without being plunged in it once more. When the traumatic event can become part of the survivor's overall emotional functioning, instead of remaining a split-off and avoided area, a 'foreign body' in the mind, then concrete thinking and identifications no longer have to take the place of flexible and creative thinking, feeling and imagining. In other words, there is the possibility of a personal future once more.

References

Bion, W. (1959) 'Attacks on linking' and 'A theory of thinking', in *Second Thoughts: Selected Papers on Psychoanalysis*, London: Maresfield, 1984.

Freud, S. (1893) 'On the psychical mechanism of hysterical phenomena: a lecture', *Standard Edition*, vol. 3, London: Hogarth Press.

——(1915a) 'Thoughts for the times on war and death', *Standard Edition*, vol. 14, pp. 273–302, London: Hogarth Press.

—— (1915b) 'Mourning and melancholia', *Standard Edition*, vol. 14, pp. 237–60, London: Hogarth Press.

—— (1920) 'Beyond the pleasure principle', *Standard Edition*, vol. 18, pp. 1–64, London: Hogarth Press.

—— (1926) 'Inhibitions, symptoms and anxiety', *Standard Edition*, vol. 20, pp. 75–175, London: Hogarth Press.

Klein, M. (1940) 'Mourning and its relation to manic-depressive states', *The Writings of Melanie Klein*, vol. I, London: Hogarth Press, 1975, pp. 344–69.

Segal, H. (1957) 'Notes on symbol formation', in *The Work of Hanna Segal: A Kleinian Approach to Clinical Practice*, New York, London: Jason Aronson, reprinted 1981.

Suggestions for further reading

Fiction

Many of the most interesting and thoughtful writings about trauma and its long-term consequences occur in literature. The greatest of all is Herman Melville's *Moby Dick* (1850, reprinted in Penguin Classics, 1992). This is essential reading. It is the story of (amongst a great deal else) a driven man's 'quenchless feud' against the perpetrator of his trauma, and the fearful impact of that on those who sail with him. Pat Barker's (1991) *Regeneration* (London: Viking, reprinted Penguin, 1992) provides a fascinating account of the traumas of war and their treatment, of great historical interest as well as clinical accuracy. Erich Maria Remarque also deals with the effects of war on young men, in his brilliant account of the effects of World War One on a cohort of young soldiers. *All Quiet on the Western Front* (1929) was originally published in this country by Putnam. As he says: 'This book is to be neither an accusation nor a confession, and least of all an adventure, for death is not an adventure to those who stand face to face with it. It will try simply to tell of a generation of men who, even though they may have escaped its shells, were destroyed by the war.' A more modern account, this time of a young woman's trauma and a unique approach to dealing with an unbearable loss, is provided by Thomas Keneally, in *Woman of the Inner Sea* (1992, reprinted Sceptre Books, 1993). Paul Celan (*Collected Poems*, trans. Michael Hamburger, Anvil Press, 1995) has a remarkable capacity to articulate the impact of trauma and loss on the deepest levels of the mind, where words cannot usually be found.

General

There are many general works that begin to be more academic without being in the least unavailable to the general reader. Here are a few of them. Bruno Bettelheim's chapter 'Trauma and reintegration', in B. Bettelheim (ed.) *Surviving* (New York: Knopf, 1979) is an interesting and informed essay on the consequences of being a survivor of the concentration camps. Arthur Hyatt Williams is a distinguished psychoanalyst and former forensic psychiatrist who has written of his life-long work in this field in his book *Cruelty, Violence and Murder: Understanding the Criminal Mind* (London: Karnac, 1998). Henry Krystal, in H. Krystal (ed.) *Massive Psychic Trauma* (New York: International Universities Press, 1976) provides a scholarly account of what the concentration camps did to man, both individually and in groups. Finally, Ben Shephard has produced a riveting, lively and well-written history of military psychiatry in the twentieth century, including a well-researched critical look at the modern culture of 'trauma', in *War of Nerves* (London: Jonathan Cape, 2000).

Psychoanalytic

These are more technical, but extremely readable, and show the ways in which psychoanalysts of differing eras and schools of thought have attempted to understand the impact of trauma. Freud's (1915) 'Thoughts for the times on war and death' *Standard Edition*, vol. 14, pp. 273 (London: Hogarth Press) is essential reading, highly relevant for society today. It looks not only at the impact of war, but at the contribution of guilt to the difficulty of being a survivor. Freud's (1915b) 'Mourning and melancholia' (*Standard Edition*, 14: 239–58) sets out not only the basis of psychoanalysis today in terms of an understanding of the process of *identification*, but uses this to provide a profound understanding of what can go wrong with normal mourning to produce pathological states of melancholia. Melanie Klein's 'Mourning and its relation to manic-depressive states' (*Collected Works 1921–1945*, London: Hogarth Press, 1935) takes Freud's work further, showing in detail the roots in infancy of the development of various forms of defence against mourning. For an understanding of the processes underlying the inability to symbolise, so often a feature of post-traumatic states, Hanna Segal's (1957) 'Notes on symbol formation', in *The Work of Hanna Segal: A Kleinian Approach to Clinical Practice* (London, Jason Aronson, 1981) is a seminal work. These, as well as other papers, have provided the theoretical basis for the work carried out in the Tavistock Clinic's Trauma Unit, which is written about in

C. Garland (ed.) *Understanding Trauma: A Psychoanalytical Approach* (2nd edn, Karnac, 2002). This book contains a collection of technical but clearly written essays on both theory and clinical work, including a study of the effects of trauma on the

Index

Abraham, K. 65–6, 73, 191
absence, effects of 69–72, 172; *see also* breaks
adaptation to environment 81–94
addiction 4
adolescence 129–40
anal character 21, 25
anxiety 16, 76, 85, 86, 99, 125–6, 137–8, 157, 189, 203–4, 216, 234–45, 250
anxiety, reactive or instinctual 240–1, 255–7
anxiety self-preservative 233–7
anxiety, separation 25, 98, 163, 236, 252–3
attachment theories 6, 9, 76, 217–18
autism 4, 75, 78, 99

Bion, W. 29, 78, 85, 102, 103, 104, 160
body, influence on the psyche of 4, 9, 81–94, 109, 110–11, 115, 117, 123, 125, 130, 133, 136, 139, 140, 143, 145–9, 166, 175, 218, 228
Bowlby, J. 76, 77, 82, 215, 218
breaks, impact of 47–51
British psychoanalysis 5, 6, 77, 82, 83, 183, 211–26

case histories 2–4
character 21–2, 40, 130, 134
Chasseguet-Smirgel, J. 123, 144, 146–52, 237, 244
child analysis 5
clinical examples of: repression 20; id vs. aggression 28; projective identification 30–1, 44–5, 69–71; paranoid-schizoid position 41–2; use of counter-transference 42–4; depressive position 47–51; envy and guilt 67; false self 89–90; concretization 99–100; female body image 150; Oedipus complex 159–64; projective identification 201–5; perversion as defence 238–40; identification with rejecting object 252–3; with lost object 254–6
clinical issues 3–5
container, containment, holding 29, 31, 55, 86, 78, 97, 100, 102–3, 115, 182, 192, 213, 257
'Controversial Discussions' 6, 83, 211, 214–15, 218
core complex 227, 236–7

core gender identity 139
corrective emotional experience 196
counter-transference 35, 43–4, 77, 182, 189–91, 192 et seq., 208, 218, 241–3, 249, 254
creativity 22, 56–7, 62, 64, 68, 75, 78, 87, 120
curiosity 77, 101, 217

death instinct 240–1
defences, defence mechanisms 9, 10–13, 15–38, 41, 145, 156, 182, 188–9, 250–1, 258; Freud on 15–26; *see also* envy
denial of reality 55, 112
depression 55–6
depressive position 12, 47–58, 71
Deutsch, H. 190
dreams 20, 45, 49, 50–1, 77, 78, 96, 99, 105–22, 188
drives 6, 7, 123, 240

ego psychology *see* North American psychoanalysis
environmental failure 83–5, 86, 88, 100–1
envy, defences against 12–13, 43, 59–73, 101; of penis 142–51; as innate 69, 150
Erikson, E. 136, 149

Fairbairn, W.R.D. 10, 28, 84, 90, 112, 215–16, 220, 225
false self, empty personality 31–3, 94–5, 75, 88–90, 183, 241–3
father, role of 84, 92, 124, 132, 178–9
fear of success 61
feeding, problems with 69–70, 85, 97, 174
femininity 143–6, 148–51
feminist view of psychoanalysis 124, 129–35, 142–4, 145, 231
Ferenczi, S. 96, 110, 111, 191, 212, 216–17
flashbacks 256–7
Freud, Anna 5, 18, 27–8, 33–4, 76, 83, 125
Freud, Sigmund (major references only) on psychoanalysis 2–3; on drives vs. objects 138, 197–8; model of mind, repression 9–11, 19–20, 240, 248, 253; on the defences 15 et seq., 21–3, 129, 170, 185–9, 196, 232, 244, 247; on anxiety 170, 249, on mourning 25,